best hikes with **KIDS**

SAN FRANCISCO
BAY AREA

best hikes with **KIDS**

SAN FRANCISCO BAY AREA

WITHDRAWN

Laure Latham

THE MOUNTAINEERS BOOKS

THE MOUNTAINEERS BOOKS
*is the nonprofit publishing arm of The Mountaineers, an organization
founded in 1906 and dedicated to the exploration, preservation, and
enjoyment of outdoor and wilderness areas.*

1001 SW Klickitat Way, Suite 201, Seattle, WA 98134

© 2011 by Laure Latham
All rights reserved

First edition, 2011

Manufactured in the United States of America

Copy Editor: Jane Crosen
Cover and Book Design: The Mountaineers Books
Layout: Emily Brooks Ford
Cartographer: Pease Press Cartography
All photographs by the author unless otherwise noted

Cover photograph: *Watching for seals from the Pigeon Point lighthouse*
Frontispiece: *Taking a climbing break in Sunol Regional Wilderness*

Library of Congress Cataloging-in-Publication Data

Latham, Laure.
  Best hikes with kids San Francisco Bay area / Laure Latham.
     p. cm.
  Includes index.
  ISBN 978-1-59485-496-5 (ppb)
  1. Hiking—California—San Francisco Bay Area—Guidebooks. 2. Family
recreation—California—San Francisco Bay Area—Guidebooks. 3. San
Francisco Bay Area (Calif.)—Guidebooks. I. Title.
  GV199.42.C22S269455 2011
  917.94'6—dc23

                              2011022170

ISBN (paperback): 978-1-59485-496-5
ISBN (e-book):978-1-59485-497-2

CONTENTS

A Quick Guide to the Hikes 10
Acknowledgments 19
Introduction 21

LEGEND

——————	freeway	🚻	restroom
——————	highway	Ⓦ	water
——————	minor paved road	🚗	parking
========	gravel road	🗼 ⌂	lookout tower/ lookout on ground
··············	featured trail	↑	ranger station
················	other trail	■	building/point of interest
80 280	interstate highway	][	bridge
101	U.S. highway	)(	pass
12 128	state highway	|	gate
	body of water	▲	campground
～～	river or stream	⊼	picnic area
～～	waterfall	▲	summit
	marsh	⚒	mine
	park or preserve	🔭	viewpoint
	private land	⊓	bench
🌲	significant tree	----------	boardwalk
Ⓣ	trailhead/start point	⊔⊔⊔⊔	steps

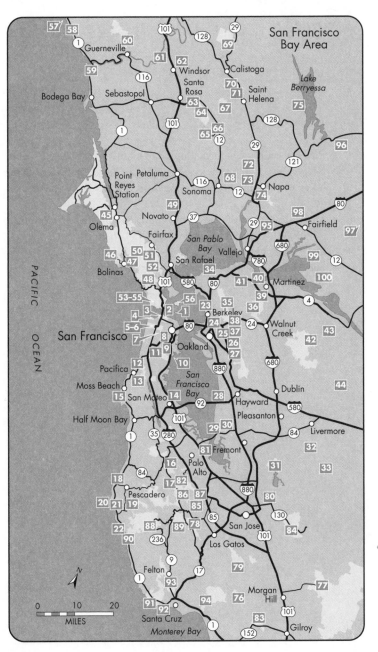

San Francisco Bay Area

57 58
1 Guerneville
60
61
59
62 Windsor
Santa Rosa
116
Bodega Bay   Sebastopol
63
64
65 66
12
Point Reyes Station   Petaluma
49
Novato
45
Olema
Fairfax   San Pablo Bay
46
50
51
47   San Rafael
52   34
48
53-55   56   35
4   3   2   23
5-6   1   Berkeley
7   24   38
8   25 37
11   26
9   Oakland   27
10
12   San Francisco Bay
Pacifica   13
15   San Mateo
Half Moon Bay
1   35   280
84
18
20 21   19   Pescadero
22
90   236
9
Felton
93
91
92   94
Santa Cruz
Monterey Bay

101
128
29
69
Calistoga
70
71   Saint Helena
75   Lake Berryessa
67
128
29   121
72
68   73
Sonoma   12   Napa
116   74
37
29   95
98   Fairfield
Vallejo   97
780   680
99
41   40   Martinez   12
580   80   39   100
36
24   Walnut Creek   4
43
42
680   44
880   Dublin
28   Hayward   580
92   Pleasanton
29   30   84   Livermore
81   Fremont   32
16   Palo Alto   33
17   82   31   80
86   87   880
85   130
78   85   San Jose   84
89   101
88   Los Gatos
79   77
76   Morgan Hill
83   101
1   152   Gilroy

PACIFIC OCEAN

N

0   10   20
MILES

A QUICK GUIDE TO THE HIKES

To quickly select a hike your family will like:

- Pick the county where you intend to hike.
- Narrow down your choices by difficulty level. Note that some hikes include options of varying difficulty. (E= easy; M= moderate; D =difficult)
- Make sure the trail is accessible now. (SP=Spring; SU=Summer; F=Fall; W=Winter; YR=Year round)
- Browse the highlights to get a sense of the hike.
- See the full hike description for distance, elevation gain, seasonal specifics, and other details. Happy trails!

NUMBER AND NAME	DIFFICULTY	SEASON	HIGHLIGHTS
San Francisco County			
1. Alcatraz Island	E	SP, F	Secret gardens and bay views on an iconic prison island
2. Presidio of San Francisco/ Golden Gate Promenade	M	YR	Wave Organ, beach trails, and Golden Gate views of San Francisco Bay
3. Presidio of San Francisco/ Lobos Creek Dunes	E	YR	Elevated boardwalk through restored sand dunes
4. Lands End/ Coastal Trail and Sutro Loop	M	YR	Historic baths, windswept vistas, shipwrecks, and cypress groves
5. Golden Gate Park West/ Lakes Loop	M	YR	Windmills, lakes, and bison in the city
6. Golden Gate Park East	M	YR	Themed gardens, two bridges, and an island
7. Mount Sutro	E–M	YR	San Francisco's only cloud forest
8. Glen Canyon Park	E	YR	Creek paths, willow groves, and great rock formations
9. McLaren Park	M	YR	Lakes, city views, and guerrilla labyrinth
10. Candlestick Point	E	YR	Fishing pier, bay stroll, and musical sculptures in a city park
San Mateo County			
11. San Bruno Mountain State Park	M	YR	Open mountain trails to an overlook of San Francisco Bay
12. Mori Point	M	YR	Seaside trails, bluffs, and protected ponds
13. San Pedro Valley County Park	E	YR	Creek walk at the foot of Montara Mountain

NUMBER AND NAME	DIFFICULTY	SEASON	HIGHLIGHTS
14. Coyote Point	M	YR	Peninsula walk to overlook of bay; finish at a nature museum
15. Fitzgerald Marine Reserve/ Pillar Point Bluff	M	YR	Tidepools, cypress grove, and bluff walk to Pillar Point with ocean vistas
16. Windy Hill Open Space Preserve	E–M	YR	Forest walk to a protected sausal pond on a former ranch
17. Skyline Ridge Open Space Preserve	E	SP, SU, F	Level loop around a pond with a nature museum
18. Pescadero Marsh Natural Preserve	E	YR	Follows the estuary of a creek that flows to the beach
19. Butano State Park	M–D	SP, SU, F	Walk along a creek at the bottom of a redwood canyon
20. Pigeon Point	E	SP, F, W	A lighthouse on ocean bluffs; beach with tidepools
21. Wilbur's Watch	E–M	SP, F, W	View gray whale migration from hills near the ocean
22. Año Nuevo State Reserve	M	SP, W	Largest gathering of elephant seals on the California coast
Alameda County			
23. Albany Bulb	E–M	YR	A reclaimed landfill with guerrilla art installations
24. Lake Temescal Recreation Area	E–M	SP, SU, F	Walk around a lake and splash at the beach
25. Joaquin Miller Park	M–D	YR	Walk to redwood and acacia forests; visit estate remnants
26. Roberts Regional Recreation Area	E	YR	Stroll Oakland's redwood hills

27. Redwood Regional Park	E–M	YR	Redwoods by a creek, oak forests on a ridge, ladybugs in winter
28. Hayward Regional Shoreline	M	YR	Windswept trails along San Francisco Bay; bird-watching
29. Coyote Hills Regional Park	M	YR	Fresh water, salt marshes, and an Ohlone shell mound
30. Ardenwood Historic Farm	E	YR	A working Victorian farm with orchards and animal pens
31. Sunol Regional Wilderness	E	SP, F, W	Walk along a creek and up a nature trail in rolling hills
32. Sycamore Grove Park	M	SP, F, W	Groves of ancient sycamores, historic almond and olive orchards
33. Lake del Valle	E–M	YR	Hike a lakeshore and end with a splash at the beach
Contra Costa County			
34. Point Pinole Regional Shoreline	E–M	YR	The site of an old dynamite factory right on the bay
35. Tilden Regional Park	M–D	SP, SU, F	Open views, Inspiration Point, and a shaded creek finish
36. Briones Regional Park	D	SP, F, W	Hike the ridge line of rolling hills in the East Bay
37. Huckleberry Botanic Regional Preserve	E–M	YR	Follow a nature discovery trail on a botanical preserve in the Oakland hills
38. Sibley Volcanic Regional Preserve	E–M	YR	An ancient volcano hides a labyrinth and a seasonal pond
39. John Muir National Historic Site/Mount Wanda	M–D	SP, F, W	Hike in the hills behind the John Muir National Historic Site and find a nature trail

NUMBER AND NAME	DIFFICULTY	SEASON	HIGHLIGHTS
40. Martinez Regional Shoreline	E	YR	Explore a restored marsh and find the hull of a shipwrecked boat
41. Fernandez Ranch	M	SP, F, W	Hike old ranch trails in rolling hills
42. Mount Diablo State Park/ Mitchell Canyon	E–M	YR	Birds in a canyon, tarantulas in fall, nature center
43. Black Diamond Mines Regional Preserve	M–D	SP, F, W	Walk through stunning hills and visit a sand mine and a pioneer cemetery
44. Morgan Territory Regional Preserve	M–D	SP, F, W	Blue oak-studded hills, a ridge with vistas, a creek and a pond
Marin County			
45. Point Reyes/Kule Loklo Trail	E	YR	Easy stroll to a reconstructed Miwok village in a grassy meadow
46. Point Reyes/Palomarin Nature Trail	E	YR	Discover a fern canyon by a creek, a stone's throw from the ocean
47. Martin Griffin Preserve	E–M	SP, SU	Hike up a canyon to spot protected nesting egrets
48. Muir Woods	M	YR	An iconic ancient redwood grove and an old camp
49. Olompali State Historic Park	E	YR	Check out a reconstructed Miwok site, a Victorian ranch, and a Grateful Dead hangout
50. Mount Tamalpais Watershed/ Cataract Falls	M–D	SP, SU, W	Cataract Creek falls in seven consecutive waterfalls up a steep trail
51. Mount Tamalpais Watershed/ Bon Tempe Lake	M	YR	Hike around a lake, past spillways between lakes
52. Mount Tamalpais State Park/ East Peak	E	SP, F, W	Stunning views on a level trail, gravity car exhibit

53. Marin Headlands/Wolf Ridge	D	YR	Strenuous hike with amazing views
54. Marin Headlands/Rodeo Beach	E–M	YR	Hike along a lagoon and visit the Marine Mammal Center
55. Marin Headlands/Tennessee Valley	M–D	YR	Ridgetop trails with coastal views
56. Angel Island	M	YR	Hike around the island to a Civil War–era garrison
Sonoma County			
57. Salt Point State Park	M–D	YR	Hike through a pygmy forest and see a prairie on the north coast
58. Fort Ross State Historic Park	E–M	YR	Hike on coastal bluffs by a historic Russian fort to the beach
59. Sonoma Coast State Park/Kortum Trail	M–D	YR	Trail along uplifted marine terraces, past mammoth rubbing rocks to a beach
60. Armstrong Redwoods State Natural Reserve	E	YR	Ancient redwood grove near the Russian River
61. Riverfront Regional Park/Lake Benoist	E	SP, SU, F	Former quarries turned into fishing lakes by the Russian River
62. Foothill Regional Park/Three Lakes Loop	M	SP, F, W	Hike through an oak forest and along three lakes
63. Spring Lake Regional Park	E	YR	Loop around a lake, splash in a swimming lagoon
64. Annadel State Park/Lake Ilsanjo	M–D	YR	Obsidian trails through forests and meadows, to a lake
65. Jack London State Historic Park	E	YR	Discover the ranch Jack London built in the Valley of the Moon

NUMBER AND NAME	DIFFICULTY	SEASON	HIGHLIGHTS
66. Sonoma Valley Regional Park	E–M	SP, F, W	Trail through oaks and on old railway tracks
67. Sugarloaf Ridge State Park	M	YR	Follow a nature trail and a Planet Walk in the Sonoma mountains
68. Bartholomew Park Winery	M	YR	Walk in forested hills and ancient vineyards in Sonoma
Napa County			
69. Robert Louis Stevenson State Park	M	SP, F, W	Hike up Mount St. Helena to the silver mine site that inspired scenes of *Treasure Island*
70. Bothe–Napa Valley State Park	M–D	SP, F, W	Canyon with views of the northern Napa Valley and redwoods
71. Bale Grist Mill State Historic Park	E–M	SP, F	Hike up and over an oak and madrone hill from a working grain mill to a pioneer cemetery
72. Alston Park	E–M	SP, F, W	Hike on ancient orchards and up a hill for views of Napa
73. Westwood Hills Regional Park	M–D	SP, F, W	Hike up and down hills to a scenic view of the city of Napa
74. John F. Kennedy Memorial Park	E	YR	Stroll along the Napa River
75. Lake Berryessa Recreation Area/Smittle Creek	E	SP, F, W	Explore the shores of Lake Berryessa and finish with a splash at the beach
Santa Clara County			
76. Uvas Canyon County Park	M–D	YR	Hike along laurel and oak canyons to a creek with winter waterfalls

77. Henry W. Coe State Park	M–D	SP, F, W	Rolling hills, views, and nature trails
78. Sanborn Skyline County Park	E–M	YR	Redwood groves and nature trail along the San Andreas Fault
79. Almaden Quicksilver County Park	M–D	SP, F, W	Hike to an old quicksilver mining camp
80. Alum Rock Park	M–D	SP, F, W	A canyon and a creek where remnants of Victorian spa days linger
81. Palo Alto Baylands Nature Preserve	E–M	YR	Explore a marsh on the bay and an outdoor sculpture park
82. Los Trancos Open Space Preserve/San Andreas Fault	M	YR	Hike trails in the forest of Los Trancos to Lost Creek, and finish with an earthquake interpretive trail
83. Mount Madonna County Park	M–D	YR	Ruins of a 19th-century estate and hike redwoods and open trails on the mountain
84. Joseph D. Grant County Park/ Three Lakes Loop	M–D	SP, F, W	Discover three lakes in a park where the ranch house is haunted
85. Picchetti Ranch Open Space Preserve	E–M	YR	A historic working winery, historic orchards, lake trails, and a seasonal pond
86. Monte Bello Open Space Preserve/Black Mountain	D	YR	Hike from a nature trail by a creek to a summit overlooking the Santa Cruz Mountains
87. Rancho San Antonio County Park/ Deer Hollow Farm	E	YR	Stroll wide trails through meadows to a working farm
Santa Cruz County			
88. Big Basin Redwoods State Park/ Sempervirens Falls	M–D	YR	Hike through ancient redwoods to a waterfall and giant rock slab

NUMBER AND NAME	DIFFICULTY	SEASON	HIGHLIGHTS
89. Castle Rock State Park	E	YR	Discover the greatest climbing rocks in the Bay Area
90. Big Basin Redwoods State Park/ Rancho del Oso	M–D	YR	Hike from the beach to a nature center in redwoods, and up a mountain
91. Wilder Ranch State Park/ Fern Grotto	E	YR	Coastal bluff trails to a fern cave at sea level on the beach
92. Natural Bridges State Beach/ Monarch Butterfly Nature Preserve	E	SP, F, W	Hike through a protected grove of monarch butterflies to a spectacular beach
93. Henry Cowell Redwoods State Park	E	YR	Easy hike with ancient redwoods, river splash spots, and steam trains
94. Forest of Nisene Marks State Park/Maple Falls	D	YR	Follow the footsteps of redwood loggers to a waterfall hidden at the back of a narrow canyon
Solano County			
95. Lynch Canyon Open Space Park	E	SP, SU, F	Stroll along grassland past owl habitat to a reservoir
96. Stebbins Cold Canyon Reserve	M	SP, F, W	Hike up a canyon to find the walls of an old homestead cellar
97. Jepson Prairie Preserve/ Vernal Pool Loop	E	SP, F, W	Explore the only remaining prairie of the Bay Area
98. Rockville Hills Regional Park	M	SP, F, W	An old rock quarry, hidden caves and two lakes
99. Rush Ranch Open Space/ Suisun Marsh	E	YR	Nature trail going through a marsh at a historic ranch
100. Grizzly Island Wildlife Area/ Howard Slough	E–M	SP, F	Elk and waterfowl sightings from flat levee tops

ACKNOWLEDGMENTS

I would like to thank all the friends who accepted invitations to hike with me in all reaches of the Bay Area, as well as the rangers, docents, parks and open spaces employees, and media people who helped me get this book done. Also a great thank-you to the nice folks who let me photograph their families on the trails, even though they didn't know me.

I will probably forget some names, but here goes: Thank you to Inga and Tony Lim, Alexandra and Olivier Rossi, and Rossana and Michael Rossetti for being such frequent hiking companions and having kids the same ages as mine who created welcomed entertainment on the trails. Lots of other friends joined us in our adventures, including Sue Collins, Megan and Tom McVay, Cithlally Castille, Becky Mortimer, Doug Nugent, and Ila and Bharat Popat. The fantastic Golden Gate Mothers Group Magazine team volunteered to hike trails in San Francisco, and my writing friends Deborah Davis and Jeanine Castello guided me on their favorite East Bay hikes. For the wonderful advice and questions on the nitty-gritty of hiking with kids, I thank all the hikers and parents of the Bernal Heights Parents, Works For Me, and Bay Area Hiking groups. For tips on nature stewardship and her support, my friend Christine Sculati was always someone I could rely on, and her husband Martin Lanner provided amazing tech support for this project.

From the parks and open spaces, I want to salute for their tremendous help Sue King, Leigh Ann Maze, Kelli English, Damien Raffa, Robyn Ishimatsu, Ellen Visser, Allison Meador, Gary Nafis, Loretta Farley, George Durgerian, Thomas Martian, Joyce Nichols, Nina Nowak, Rupa Bose, Mike McGraw, Chris Lynch, Martha Nitzberg, Dorothy Mackay-Collins, Jim Brainerd, Ken Poerner, Steve Kraemer, AnnetteColeman, Jack Owicki, Susan Blake, Ken Lande, Peter Ehrlich, Judy Lieberman, Joyce Penell, Rupa Rose, and Marylin and Bill Bauriedel.

Thanks to Ben Pease of Pease Press Cartography for providing accurate and detailed maps of several Bay Area places.

The entire children's books department of the main branch of the San Francisco Public Library (SFPL) got together to suggest book titles that would connect children with nature. Hurray for public libraries for being so supportive! Individual thanks go to SFPL contributors Christy Estrovitz, Carla Kozak, Valerie Reichart, Pat Dimmick, Jennifer Collins, Naima Dean, Catherin Starr, Anne Lane, Nina Pogosyan, Jim Jeske, Pam Owl, Pauline Harris, Joseph Liebman, and Katrin Reimuller.

For guiding me through the book process, I owe eternal gratitude to colleagues from the Bay Area Travel Writers Association, National Writers Union, and Outdoors Travel Writers Association, including Sandy Whelchel, Tom Brosnahan, Edward Hasbrouck, Cassandra Vieten, Barabara Mende, Debbie Abrams Kaplan, Lora Shinn, Alison Lowenstein, and Michele Bigley.

Without the team at The Mountaineers Books, this book wouldn't be here. For their trust, expertise, professionalism, and support, I want to thank Kate Rogers, Margaret Sullivan, Mary Metz, and Janet Kimball. Jane Crosen was an incredible copy-editor who pointed at all the hiccups and improved many an idea.

Finally, thank you to my family for believing in this outdoor adventure. My father joined me on hikes and shared his soil science knowledge. My mother joined me on a hill despite a recent hip surgery, and my brother's family hiked with us with their baby and toddler when visiting from France. Last but not least: my husband, Cedric, and my girls Louise and Iris smiled through all the hikes, week after week, month after month, and were the best hiking companions I could have wished for.

INTRODUCTION

Welcome to the *Best Hikes with Kids San Francisco Bay Area*! Whether you're new to the area or a new parent with a love for the outdoors, this guidebook is here to help you discover parts of the Bay Area that are as varied as their microclimates and food specialties. Covering the ten different counties that surround the city of San Francisco, this book gives you pointers for day trips or simple spur-of-the-moment hikes. Here you will find unique places, activities, farms, nature museums, playgrounds, obscure historical landmarks, and fun things that make a nature outing exciting from a kid's perspective. Use it as a starter guide for day explorations, and roam the Bay Area with an open spirit.

WHY HIKE?

Hiking is generally defined as going on an extended walk for pleasure or exercise. When planning a hike, parents look for ways to get out of the house with a green perspective, to exercise, or to share a picnic with friends in a forest setting. Kids, on the other hand, may have a different agenda. Naps, friends, activities, TV, and homework are many of the factors that get in the way of a stroll in the woods. There are also kids who complain about a 4-minute walk to the park, so anything more ambitious sounds plain impossible.

As a result, hiking as a family presents a few challenges but none that can't be overcome with a positive attitude and little steps. Whether you have reluctant hikers at home or kids afraid of bugs, there's a way to make nature outings fun, and that's the purpose of this book.

Since author Richard Louv started a green revolution with his book *Last Child in the Woods*, parents hear on a daily basis that their kids should get connected with nature and the outdoors. Video games and TV are no substitutes for holding a bug or rubbing fingers on a fragrant sage leaf. Since hiking is basically free, apart from transport and good walking shoes, it's fair to say that you have the basics to get out today. At the end of the day, kids will remember a close deer encounter in the forest more than they will an electronic gizmo at the store. The beauty of nature is that you can't plan it.

Last but not least, hiking nurtures the next generation into becoming stewards of this Earth and respecting the world they live in. If you don't know your own backyard, how can you properly care for it? So hike away and enjoy every moment.

Stay for a picnic or a snack at the end of your hike.

HIKING WITH CHILDREN

From the first time they take a step, children are eager to get moving, even if it's not necessarily in a straight line or where parents would like them to go. If you were an active hiker or jogger pre-baby, it's time to reassess your goals. Hiking implies following a designated trail. To little tots, sticking to the designated route is just outlandish. There's so much to explore—a round rock, a gurgling brook, a tiny frog, a shiny leaf. Why keep walking? That's where you as a parent will help channel these exploring endeavors.

If you want your child to enjoy hiking later in life, getting distracted by the world is fine and a small price to pay to foster a love for nature. If your little boy likes the shape of a banana slug or if your little girl prefers digging in the dirt over moving on, let them enjoy the moment. Hiking is above all a way to express your appreciation for nature and the outdoors. It's not a race or a marathon. Mileage can come into the equation later. It's about being outside and getting in touch with your natural environment.

When you are taking your family outdoors and the little ones are having a ball, the trip is already a success because they'll ask you to come back and do it again. As long as you set realistic goals according to your child's age, nobody will be disappointed and you will all come out of the experience with a smile. Here's how to tailor your first hikes to your children's aptitudes.

Babies

Infants grow at such an amazing rate during the first year of their life that you can find different ways to enjoy the outdoors with them, depending on their developmental and behavioral milestones. From the infant to the pre-toddler stage, see how you can make each outing a fun family adventure.

One to Six Months: Babies are the best hikers—on their parents, that is. Newborns can get out for short hikes starting at age one month. When they are still curled up in slings and keeping warm against you, nothing prevents you from taking a short hike to replenish your nature energy.

I remember taking our second baby hiking in the Yosemite's high country when she was seven weeks old. Our oldest was not yet two years old. My husband carried our oldest on his back; I carried our new baby in a front baby carrier and swaddled her in a blanket. We got stuck in a hailstorm and had to take cover at the entrance of a mine shaft, just inside enough to stay dry. I breastfed my baby and she went right back to sleep. Back at the trailhead, I felt reenergized that I was able to explore the Sierras and the beautiful vistas while my baby slept right through the storm and breathed fresh mountain air.

When babies start holding up their head and can transition to a front (or back) baby carrier, you usually free up two hands and can carry a small pack with your day essentials—diapers, wipes, water bottle, rattles, small blanket, and such. At this stage, babies are more awake and start enjoying your outings more consciously. Opening their eyes wide to discover the places you go, they inhale the understory's earthy smell and listen to the birding sounds in the trees. You may not realize it, but it's a full sensory experience their brain processes as you walk.

How long or short should these hikes be? The first one should definitely err on the conservative side. Think half a mile to a mile, flat terrain, and proximity to a parking lot. Progressively you can experiment with longer stretches, insert a feeding break on a bench, sit at a picnic table and enjoy the day, take a nap by a creek and listen. Until kids outgrow the stroller, you are free to hike as long as you want, and you had better take advantage of it.

In terms of timing, babies are usually at their best early in the day and get tired in the afternoon, so try to plan your outings for after breakfast and before lunchtime. You may get fog in coastal areas, sure, but fog has its own charm. As long as baby is appropriately dressed and well fed, you'll be fine.

Six to Nine Months: Hiking at this age is an early dialogue between you and your child. She now understands the concept of play and loves reproducing facial expressions and sounds. Early toothless smiles probably melt your heart. Time to play! Parents are the best toy ever invented. Once on a winter hike in the Santa Cruz Mountains with our then six-month-old, my husband and I spent an hour playing peekaboo with our baby in her back baby carrier. She thought it was the most hilarious thing and imitated us with her tiny hands, hiding on one side and the other of the backpack. It was a two-hour hike in the redwoods, and she didn't fuss once.

From six to nine months, children are learning to distinguish individual sounds in the stream of speech. Apply that to hiking. On your outings, you can start describing what you see to your child in simple words, combining exercise (for you) and intellectual stimulation (for your child) at the same time.

Nine to Twelve Months: Getting bigger and stronger by the day, these babies associate words with objects and get ready to speak. During your next nature outing, sing "The Itsy Bitsy Spider" and other songs that refer to animals and plants. "Baby Beluga," "Baby Bumblebee," "Five Little Ducks," "The Ants Go Marching In," "Five Little Pumpkins," and all your favorite nature-inspired nursery songs will be a hit on the trail. Your child will slowly come to associate wild open spaces with the idea of fun, and this is a great opportunity to build up your animal lullaby repertoire.

Toddlers and Crawlers

Your baby has morphed into a small person whose personality is slowly emerging. It is an exciting developmental stage when kids need constant

motion and can sit up to grab toys. The corollary of this overflow of energy is an amazing aptitude to defy organized directions. Toddlers and crawlers are unruly hikers! These one- to two-year-old kids are discovering the world, and their hunger for new things will stop at nothing. New textures, new smells, new tastes, new sounds are part of their daily routine. Soon your toddler will resist sitting quietly in a baby carrier. All he wants to do is get up and grab the nearest object (your hat, your hair, your glasses,

Enjoy summer days on Silicon Valley trails.

your ears) to play or chew. That's why strollers were invented. If you are in desperate need of a walk in the woods, a jogging stroller will soon become your best friend. Plan your hikes when your child is still rested—mornings are best—so they can relax at home during an afternoon nap.

When you feel that your child is able to walk a city block in a reasonable amount of time, it is time for a hike! At that age, hikes mean a quarter mile or less and your prior understanding that you'll have to pick them up and carry them at some point. Make the experience fun by choosing a short and level nature trail or a familiar park. Only you know what your child can do, so set your ambitions accordingly. Hiking should come as a natural desire to enjoy nature, not as a chore.

From now on, you can alternate stroller and independent walking, progressively phasing out the use of the stroller unless your child needs a rest. This will convey the message that physical exercise and the outdoors are an activity you enjoy. Realistically, you will still probably be using a stroller or carrier for medium to long hikes until age four.

Preschoolers

Comfortable with motion, balance, and coordination, children two to three years old also follow directions. Now is the time to start building stamina, leaving the stroller at home as much as you can. Getting them to walk is not a rewarding job at that age, and strapping a child in a stroller is more efficient, but down the road you'll be glad you insisted on that extra block. By the time your child is four or five years old, they'll be used to long walks.

You can start increasing your hiking distances to half a mile and, by the end of the year, to a mile. If your child likes to kick a ball or blow bubbles, you may want to choose a wide path and just let junior kick the ball or blow bubbles on the trail. Without realizing it, your child will be hiking. If your preschooler loves pushing a toy stroller, let her bring a doll or toy out for a walk. Jumping and tiptoeing can be other active ways to move along. Organize a scavenger hunt by trying to find a short list of items you know will be on the way: a cloud, a leaf, a rock, a snail, a squirrel, etc.

The idea is to keep the outing engaging so walking becomes second nature and your child can focus on the playful aspect of your day. Stop for a snack, pause to gaze at ripples on a puddle, make up a story about a funny tree shape. In a word, relax and enjoy.

From age three to four years, children learn how to walk in a line, run around obstacles, balance on one leg, and push/pull toys. Now is the time to try more rugged terrain such as rocky trails, a slight elevation gain, or trails with steps. You can also expect your child to walk longer stretches, up to two or three miles, without a problem. Sure, you may have to hold their hand, tell them stories, and stop for snacks, but your family will enjoy these short hikes.

Kindergartners and Grade-School Children

At this point, your weekend schedule may become overloaded with classes and playdates, but do try to set aside regular times for short walks as a family and a monthly date for a more intense hike. This way you can keep exercise on your agenda and make nature part of your ordinary environment.

HOW TO MOTIVATE CHILDREN

What's the key to a child's stamina? That's a question for which all parents would like to have an easy answer. When hiking means exercise outdoors combined with leaving the comfort of a child's surroundings, it can quickly become a chore unless you can spice up the adventure with fun spots, rewards, or games. The following sections include tips to motivate a child who is just getting started on a trail and a child who has reached his or her limit way into the hike but is too big for a parent to comfortably carry home. You will also find tips that—hopefully—will prevent major meltdowns on your big day out.

Hiking with Friends

The best motivation for a reluctant hiker? Your child's best friends. Interaction with kids their age is essential for preschoolers and grade-school children. Believe me. A hike with your child's best friends goes twice as fast as a hike without. Starting around age four years, your kids' friends become their universe for better and worse. If your weekends are filled with classes and playdates, how about turning playdates into hikes?

When with other kids, here's what young kids do. First they may act shy and cling to you like glue sticks. Normal. Gradually they glance at the other child and may exchange a word or two. If by chance you come across an interesting bug or rock, you can bet the kids are going to overcome their initial shyness and become exploring pals right away. When this happens (okay, sometimes it takes a while), you can feel confident about your hiking plans. You may even have to start running after the kids to catch up with them. When in groups, children tend to do what

Offer lots of refueling breaks to keep kids energized.

they do at a playgroup: chase each other, stimulate each other's interest, share stuff. Basically they forget that they're hiking.

You, too, can organize regular hikes to connect with your close friends and catch up on their lives. Away from the distractions and noises of the city, you can relax and be yourself. A monthly hike helps maintain ties with friends who've moved away from the area. A weekly playgroup hike allows you to develop friendly relationships in a peaceful setting. Associating the outdoors with a circle of friends conveys an important message to your child: Being outdoors is fun.

Snacks

The way to a young child's enthusiasm often goes through the stomach. Indeed, for very young children, social interaction often isn't enough of a reason to keep going. For them, snacks can yield miracle results combining fuel, nutrition, distraction, and yumminess. You can suggest "rewards" for so many steps, or for the next trail marker, or bring a snack to enjoy at the top of the ridge along with the views.

If you are going to break out the candy bag, better wait until you're way into the hike. Jelly beans every five steps early on in the trail will give a sugar rush to your child as well as temporary whining relief but won't provide fuel for a sustained effort. Think of candy as the ultimate reward, as in this example:

Antje Kann, mother of two, hiked with her family at Mount Tamalpais from Pantoll Ranger Station down to Stinson Beach and took the public bus back up. "It was the longest hike for us so far, about 4 miles, but it was mostly downhill, and amazing," she says, adding that "during the last mile, we could see the beach ahead of us, which was good because the kids were seriously lagging. Our son, who had just turned four, wouldn't have made it without the help of a steady supply of gummy bears at the end. It really seemed that without the extra sugar he would have fallen down at that point—and they were juicy, which helped on a hot day."

Storytelling

Who doesn't love a good story? Kids will literally forget to eat when they are absorbed in a good story. On the trail, try telling a story to a three- or four-year-old to help them walk an extra mile or half or quarter mile. You can hold hands and slowly make your way as your protagonists fend off dragons or marshmallow attacks.

If you're not feeling inspired, classic storybook tales are great starters, but there are thousands of stories to draw from. Prepared by the specialists at the San Francisco Public Library, here is a list of books set in nature that might inspire young hikers:

■ **Woods/forests.** Christopher Bing's *Little Red Riding Hood*, Sylvia Long's *Thumbelina*, Cynthia Rylant's *Hansel and Gretel*, Nicholas Oldland's *Big Bear Hug*, David McPhail's *Lost!*, Nick Sharratt's *The Foggy, Foggy Forest*, Jean Craighead George's *My Side of the Mountain*.

■ **Coast.** Hans Christian Andersen's *The Little Mermaid* (as retold by Mary Pope Osborne in *Mermaid Tales from Around the World*), Disney's *Finding Nemo*, Jules Verne's *Twenty Thousand Leagues Under the Sea*, Liz Garton Scanlon's *All the World*, and Burton Albert's *Where Does the Trail Lead?*

■ **Redwoods.** This is gnome and fairy land for preschoolers, *Star Wars* territory for older kids. Jason Chin's *Redwoods*, Robert Lieber's *The Tallest Tree* (local interest—based on Muir Woods research), S. Terrell French's *Operation Redwood* (eco-tale based in San Francisco).

■ **Urban/city parks.** Paul B. Janeczko's *Stone Beach in an Empty Park* (haiku poems related to city life, nature), Peter Brown's *The Curious Garden*, Marilyn Singer's *City Lullaby*, Mo Willems's *Knuffle Bunny*, Robert McCloskey's *Make Way for Ducklings*.

■ **Nature.** Barbara Berger's *All the Way to Lhasa* (Tibetan folktale), Sebastien Braun's *On Our Way Home*, Denise Fleming's *In the Small, Small Pond*, Don Freeman's *Beady Bear* (cave), Amy

Hest's *When You Meet a Bear on Broadway*, D. B. Johnson's *Henry Hikes to Fitchburg*, and *Henry Climbs a Mountain* (based on Henry David Thoreau), Tony Johnston's *Bigfoot Cinderrrrella*, Jimmy Kennedy's *Teddy Bears' Picnic*, Jeff Mack's *Hush Little Polar Bear* (variety of landscapes), David Macaulay's *Shortcut*, Robert McCloskey's *Blueberries for Sal*, Michael Rosen's *We're Going on a Bear Hunt* (various terrain), Roslyn Schwartz's *The Complete Adventures of the Mole Sisters* (variety of landscapes), David Ezra Stein's *Leaves*, Martin Waddell's *Sleep Tight, Little Bear* (cave), Ashley Wolff's *Stella and Roy*, and *Stella and Roy Go Camping* (local scenes), Jane Yolen's *Owl Moon*, Jeanette Winter's *Wangari's Trees of Peace: A True Story from Africa*, Deborah Lee Rose's *The People Who Hugged the Trees*, E. B. White's *The Trumpet of the Swan*.

In the digital arena, if your children are passionate about video games or specific hobbies, ask them about their current interests and watch their eyes light up as they do all the talking.

In the end, weaving a conversation about a story or specific interest is sure to grab the attention of a child if only because they have your undivided attention.

Arts and Crafts

Some crafts lend themselves particularly well to outdoor explorations and can be prepped ahead of your hike to build up motivation.

■ Spyglasses made out of empty toilet paper rolls provide multiple occasions to stop and look at plants or bugs. Make binoculars by taping two rolls together and have your child paint them his favorite pattern. Tie a knot on both sides with yarn or ribbon, and have kids wear them around their neck.

■ An empty baby food jar or jam jar, with holes drilled or punched in the lid, is the ideal bug box. Just remove the label and pack it along. Don't forget to handle insects very gently and to release them exactly where you found them. You can also recycle a shoe box and create a viewing window in the lid by taping plastic wrap tightly over an opening.

■ A plastic bottle whose top part has been cut off makes a great observation tank for river critters and fishes. Just punch a hole in each side and create a handle with a strong string so the "bucket" is easy to pull out of the water.

- Make a hiking necklace by using the cord of a whistle and stringing alongside the whistle these essential hiking tools separated by beads: magnifying glass, flashlight, compass.
- Fold and stitch several blank pages in the middle and create a hiking journal. Attach a nice pencil, and you're ready to go.
- Sketchbooks are the best tool to get a creative child to look around and express what they see. Find a quiet spot along the trail, sit down, and get the crayons out. Kids don't even have to draw their surroundings to enjoy the moment. It's all about doing whatever art they please in nature.

Kids lose themselves in time and imaginary play when building forts.

Forts, Fairy Houses, and Nature Art

Building structures that foster play-based activities can be done anywhere on the trail with sticks, rocks, leaves, or pinecones. Any spot is good: a riverbank, a beach, a forest. For inspiring examples of forts and shelters in the woods, see D. C. Beard's 1914 book *Shelters, Shacks, and Shanties: The Classic Guide to Building Wilderness Shelters*, which features lots of illustrations and ideas for boys and girls. For instructions on how to build fairy houses, including materials, see the website www.fairyhouses.com and Barry and Tracy Kane's book *Fairy Houses . . . Everywhere!* When it comes to nature art, the gold standard in stunning ephemeral sculptures is British artist Andy Goldsworthy (you can find several books with his photographed work at your local library), but Bay Area artist Zach Pine is also a great resource and organizes regular events open to the public. For online ideas, the website www.wild-zone.net provides examples of creativity with natural materials.

WHAT TO BRING

In addition to the Ten Essentials (see page 34), you will want to be prepared for all possibilities, from weather to hunger.

Infant/Child Carriers

When choosing child carriers for hiking, look for the following features:

▪ **Lightness.** If you want to go the distance, choose the lightest backpack you can find.

▪ **Canopy/sun protection.** Many backpacks have canopies as accessories, some with mesh sides. They are great for kids who are not used to wearing sun hats.

▪ **Frame.** If your child falls asleep during the hike, a frame allows you to gently remove the backpack and set it down while you take a rest without waking your child. If you don't think you'll need it, get a lightweight child carrier.

▪ **Detachable backpacks.** If you don't have a hiking backpack, a detachable backpack allows you to share the load between two people.

▪ **Side pockets.** Pockets allow easy access to milk, water bottles, or snacks without having to open the backpack.

▪ **Adjustable height.** Some carriers can be adjusted to raise or lower an inside seat, so the backpack grows with your child.

▪ **Padded shoulder straps.** These will add immeasurably to your comfort when you also have to carry day trip essentials. What really matters is your personal comfort. Try the backpack at the store with your child inside. An empty backpack doesn't feel like a full one.

Clothing

Regardless of the season, hiking in the Bay Area usually calls for extra layers and long sleeves for simple reasons. Close to the coast, climates can change within minutes and fog can roll in as fast as a running horse. Inland, unstable weather can result from vast open plains or windy ridges. Hiking in forests cools down any hike, but redwood groves can also be damp and cold even during nice weather. For this reason, layered clothing allows you to strip down or add layers as needed.

Long sleeves and long pants are an absolute necessity in poison oak and tick country (which is pretty much the entire region) and will provide basic sun protection for children at play.

As for any day out, you may want to pack a change of clothes, including underwear and shoes, in case your child trips in a puddle or slides down a muddy section.

Winter is the Bay Area's rainy season. For winter hikes, dress your kids as you would for a playground or outdoor outings, always adding a warm rainproof jacket with hood. Rain boots can work very well as trail shoes. Count on many trails being muddy. Keep an extra pair of shoes in the trunk of the car to change into after your hike.

Springtime can still be rainy, but sunny days bring out the best wildflower color displays at open spaces and parks. This season is, understandably, when hibernating hikers get out of their houses with cameras after months of rainy days. Fog can still roll in most days, but it usually burns off by midday—so again, layered clothing is the best solution to any springtime outing.

Summers are hot and dry inland, chilly and foggy on the coast, so prepare according to the area you'll be exploring. In very hot parts of the Bay Area, make sure children are properly protected from the sun: hats, long sleeves or sunscreen, sunglasses. Sporting goods stores carry UV-protective cotton clothing for children. When exploring swim or shore areas, don't forget swimsuits.

Fall may be the nicest season (after spring) to hike, with long sunny days, turning colors, crisp mornings, and warm days. As late as Halloween, T-shirts and light pants are appropriate clothing, and you may even be able to pack swimsuits for an impromptu splash.

Footwear

When choosing shoes for your child, think about the kind of terrain you are going to tackle and how often you plan to do it. If you are heading out on wide fire roads or level paths along the bay, good walking shoes such as sneakers are enough and you don't need special shoes. If you are planning regular hikes with elevation gain, eroded trails, or rocks, your child will need the same quality shoes as you do. Don't skimp; get hiking boots that provide ankle support as well as breathability and good traction. For hikes on muddy trails, good rain boots may be your safest bet, provided they are comfortable enough for the duration of the hike. Whichever shoes you choose, don't get them too small! Err on the side of slightly too big (but not so big as to result in blisters) rather than too small or just the right size. If in doubt, ask a shoe store clerk. When feet hurt, children stop walking. It's as simple as that.

Healthy Snacks

Nutrition on the trail helps everyone maintain their stamina and keeps the whole family happy so they enjoy the outing. Here are a few ideas to get you started.

Drinks. In winter, pack a thermos of hot water so you can whip up a trailside hot chocolate or apple cider from powdered drinks. For a savory change, broth or miso soup work wonders to warm up anyone when temperatures are low. In the spring, water is the best way to hydrate on the trail. Pack roughly one quart per person per day. In the summer, if it is going to be very hot, double the amount of water you carry, to be on the safe side. Even if most parks have a potable water source, dry conditions can result in water shortages and you are better off filling your own water bottles before getting to the trailhead. In the fall, the days are getting cooler. Use your common sense to decide whether water bottles or hot drinks are most appropriate.

Food. The following are nutritious snacks that will keep your child energized on hikes:

- Granola bars or fruit bars
- Honey or agave sticks
- Dried fruits (apricots, prunes, figs, dates, cranberries, acai berries, apples, pears, peaches, bananas, pineapple), dried nuts (raw unsalted almonds, filberts, pecans, walnuts, macadamias, coconut, pistachios), and dried seeds (pumpkin, sunflower)
- Cheese cubes of your child's favorite cheese; in hot weather, drier cheeses such as aged Monterey Jack, cheddar, gouda, or pecorino will keep better than soft cheeses because of their lower water content
- Fresh fruits; small fruits are best for quick snack breaks—baby bananas, small apples, Asian pears or tangerines, cherries, blueberries, strawberries
- Fresh veggies such as carrots, celery, cucumber, and fennel cut into sticks
- Whole-grain crackers, chips, cereals, or cookies
- Semisweet chocolate chips
- Boiled eggs; try quail eggs for bite-sized boiled eggs
- Tofu in cubes, seasoned as you like it
- Iron-intensive foods such as seaweed squares or kale chips
- Small containers of apple, apricot, pear (or any other fruit) sauce or butter

The Ten Essentials

The Mountaineers recommends ten items that should be taken on every hike, whether a day trip or an overnight trip. When children are involved and you are particularly focused on making the trip as trouble-free as possible, the following Ten Essentials may avert disaster:

1. **Navigation** (map, compass, GPS). Don't assume you'll just "feel" your way to the summit. Teach your children how to read a compass, too. Whistles can help locate someone if they are disoriented.

2. **Sun protection** (sunglasses, sunscreen, and sun hat). Look for sunglasses that screen UV rays and sunscreen with a broad spectrum of UVA and UVB, with a minimum SPF rating of 15 to 30. For sun hats, make sure they cover the neck as well as face of your child. It is important to protect children from the sun even in cooler temperatures, as children get sunburned even in wintertime.

3. **Insulation** (extra clothing). It may shower, the temperature may drop, the fog might roll in, or wading may be too tempting to pass up. Be sure to include waterproof gear, extra shoes and socks (especially a pair of shoes that can be used for wading when bare feet might mean sliced toes), a warm sweater, and hats and mittens.

4. **Illumination** (headlamp or flashlight). With battery-operated lights, check them before the hike. To avoid checking, choose good-quality crank-up or solar-powered lights. Glow sticks can also work to signal your location.

5. **First-aid supplies.** Don't forget to include Tecnu or a similar topical ointment for poison oak, Band-Aids for blisters, baking soda for insect stings, and any special medication your child might need for an allergy to bee stings or other insect bites.

6. **Fire** (firestarter and matches/lighter). If you must build a fire, these are indispensable.

7. **Repair kit and tools** (including knife). You never know when you might need to fix a boot, strap, or other piece of equipment. You'll be sorry if you need to and your duct tape and knife are in a drawer at home.

8. **Nutrition** (extra food). Too much food is better than not enough.

9. **Hydration** (extra water). Always carry sufficient drinking water in reusable bottles, and don't plan on refilling them in creeks or lakes unless you have iodine tablets that neutralize most water contaminants. Bay Area creeks, springs, and ponds are notoriously infected with the parasite *Giardia lamblia*. To avoid "beaver fever," also known as giardiasis, a water filter or purifier is necessary when drinking untreated water.

10. **Emergency shelter** (tent, space blanket, tarp). Chances are you won't need any, but shelter is a necessity if you get stuck on the trail unexpectedly.

WILDLIFE ENCOUNTERS

You may be surprised to get to a trail and see a large coyote or mountain lion warning sign asking adults to supervise small children so they don't go off on their own. Is this really an issue? How seriously should you take those signs? Thanks to incredible habitat diversity and wide-open spaces, wild animals are indeed a reality of hiking trails in the Bay Area. Though chances of wildlife encounter are minimal for big mammals, they exist nonetheless, and you should be prepared.

Should you stumble upon wildlife, please do not, ever, feed wildlife. Not on your hikes, not in your backyard, not in your dreams, not out of good intentions. By feeding wildlife, you are creating problems, disturbing natural balances, and running risks. First, you may get bitten or attacked by a startled animal you are trying to feed. Second, fed animals lose their fear of humans and can become aggressive to other humans. If too aggressive, they may have to be destroyed. Last, feeding wildlife can result in animal numbers beyond what the ecosystem can support. As a reminder, wildlife includes ducks, squirrels, geese, gophers, and chipmunks. Cute is not an excluding factor.

For great advice on Bay Area wildlife and tips to help with hurt animals, check Wild Care Bay Area's programs in animal aid, advocacy, and education (www.wildcarebayarea.org).

Mountain Lions

About half of California is prime mountain lion habitat, and this habitat is shrinking as our cities expand. This explains why you will see so many mountain lion warnings on trailheads, sometimes even in San

Francisco. Also called cougars, mountain lions are powerful animals, and any encounter could prove fatal. Sand colored, they have black-tipped ears and tail and measure 7 to 8 feet when adult, with weights varying between 65 and 150 pounds. The good news is, mountain lions are elusive animals and your odds of meeting one on the trail are actually very low. Some rangers have never even seen them in their parks, yet they are probably somewhere hiding.

Nocturnal predators, mountain lions hunt their prey (deer, elk, other mammals) between dawn and dusk. You can reduce the odds of encountering them by hiking during the day, if possible as a group.

On the trail, always keep children in sight and within arm's reach, especially if the trail has bends and vegetation that could conceal a mountain lion from your sight. Mountain lions seem to be drawn to children because of their small size.

In the case of an encounter, follow this advice published by the California State Parks:

■ **Do not attempt to approach a mountain lion.** Most mountain lions will avoid confrontation. Give them a way to escape.

■ **Stay calm and face the lion.** Do not run, because this may trigger the lion's instinct to attack. Try to appear larger by raising your arms and opening your jacket. Pick up small children so they don't panic and run. Avoid bending over or crouching.

■ **Discourage an attack.** If the lion approaches or acts aggressively, shout and throw branches or whatever can be obtained without turning your back or bending over.

■ **Fight back if attacked.** A good walking stick can be useful in warding off a lion. Because a mountain lion usually tries to bite the head or neck, try to remain standing and face the attacking animal.

Reptiles

Snakes are common animals on the trails, particularly in warm weather. Most likely you will hear a rustling noise in the grasses or bushes and see a slithery shape disappear out of sight under rocks before you've had time to react.

For kids, snakes are easy wildlife to spot because they are on the ground. Any snake sighting adds excitement to a hike! As exciting as it may be, teach your kids to keep a safe distance and not touch the snakes. Some Bay Area snakes are venomous and bites are more severe on children than adults.

To prevent your child from touching a snake and potentially getting bitten, tell them to always look where they are going to put their hands if they are climbing rocks or trees. The best rule is "If you can't see your hands, don't go there." Along the same lines, remind them not to walk through tall grass where they can't see their feet. If you cross paths with a snake, simply watch from a safe distance and enjoy.

To learn from a snake sighting, try to photograph the snake or to remember its characteristics (head shape, scale pattern, color, size). Based on your observations you and your child will be able to later identify the animal at home and learn about its behaviors.

Among the reptiles you may see are gopher snakes, garter snakes, king snakes, whip snakes, rattlesnakes, ring snakes, racers, and boas. There are many more, and some park districts publish brochures specific to the snakes of their parks. The East Bay Regional Park District (ebparks.org/activities/naturalists) has a great brochure series on local flora and fauna that includes snakes.

Ready to learn more about Bay Area snakes? Check out California Herps (www.californiaherps.com), a website dedicated to reptiles and amphibians in California. You can find photographs, videos, detailed information on the snakes' habitats and habits, and even browse range maps per animal.

Note that snakes in our parks are protected and sometimes endangered. It's best to just leave them alone to go on with their day.

Snakes are masters at camouflage; stay alert to see them!

Coyotes, Foxes, and Bobcats

Smaller mammals than the mountain lion, coyotes, foxes, and bobcats are also more abundant in the wild and even in our backyards. While coyotes and foxes are part of the canine family, bobcats belong to the wildcat family. According to the Humane Society of the United States (www.hsus.org), red foxes and gray foxes—the most commonly seen foxes—are not dangerous to humans unless rabid, a rare occurrence. Coyotes, which look like medium-sized German shepherds, are afraid of humans and not interested in confrontations. Bobcats, roughly twice the size of a household cat, have a dark spotted coat and usually run away from humans.

In case of an encounter with any of these mammals, do not try to feed them, and keep children close to you. They will likely run away, and you'll have a story to tell at your child's next playdate.

Skunks, Raccoons, and Rabies

Raccoons and striped skunks are common animals in the Bay Area and, like most wildlife, best left alone. However, whereas most animals are harmless, raccoons and skunks are potentially dangerous and should be avoided for safety reasons.

Skunks, as all kids have seen in cartoons, have a white stripe on their back and a black body. When threatened, they spray a stinky scent on their opponent. Since they can spray as far as 20 feet and up to 10 feet high, getting sprayed is a high risk if you get close. While it may be tempting to follow Curious George's example and "wash" sprayed items in a tomato juice bath, the following home remedy has been reported to be more effective to reduce the smell: 1 quart hydrogen peroxide, ¼ cup baking soda, 2 tablespoons liquid soap. You can also find commercial neutralizers or odor-maskers, but before using any remedy on hair and skin, particularly on children, ask your doctor's advice first.

Beyond the spraying issue, skunks can be dangerous to humans because of rabies. The rabies disease affects the nervous system and is fatal, both to animals and humans. Though rabies symptoms in skunks are many, abnormal behavior is the most obvious tip-off. Fear the worst if you see a skunk during daytime—they are usually shy nocturnal animals. "Mad dog" syndrome (foam around mouth, dilated pupils, aggressivity) is another tip-off. In any case, if a rabid skunk bites a member of your party or your pet, treat it as an emergency and rush to the hospital for treatment.

Raccoons, easily recognizable by their "masked" face and ringed tail, are so common in urban areas and so fearless that they can be a big problem for humans. Distant cousins of the bear family, they can become aggressive when confronted, and bite. Unfortunately their boldness makes them easy for children to approach. Because of the risk of rabies, bites, distemper, and the deadly ringworm parasite *Baylisascaris procyonis*, always keep a safe distance from raccoons.

LEAVE NO TRACE

The Leave No Trace commandments of outdoors ethics can be summarized as follows:

■ **Plan ahead and prepare.** Know the conditions and regulations where you are going to hike.

■ **Travel and camp on durable surfaces.** Hike on trails to minimize foot impact on the local environment and when in doubt, prefer rocks to dirt areas.

■ **Dispose of waste properly.** Pack it in, pack it out! Picnic leftovers, wrappers, snack containers, and the like need to be packed out and disposed of properly after your hike. To encourage kids, pack an empty trash bag and reward them for filling it with waste along the trail. Many parks reward such good behavior with actual badges, stickers, and books.

■ **Leave what you find.** Take only photos, and don't take anything you find along the trail. That goes for rocks, animals, and seashells as well as plants.

■ **Respect wildlife.** Don't disturb wild creatures, or bribe them with food. Just watch and enjoy.

■ **Be considerate of other visitors.** Be quiet on the trail, yield to faster hikers on the trail, and picnic at a distance from other hikers.

To find out more, check out the website of the Leave No Trace Center for Outdoor Ethics at www.lnt.org.

PLANT SAFETY

Most preschoolers can identify a few commercial logos but how many plants can they name on the trail? By learning about their environment, children strengthen their bond with the Earth and acquire useful wilderness skills.

Poison Oak

"Leaves of three, let them be. If it's hairy, it's a berry. If it's shiny, watch your heinie." This rhyme should be the first rhyme your kids learn on the trail, together with the idea that they should always hike in the middle of the trail and avoid touching plants. A constant feature of most Bay Area trails, poison oak is a deciduous plant that grows as ground cover, bush, or vines from along the coast to 5000 feet up in the mountains. Skin exposure to poison oak can cause terrible rashes and makes this plant a major danger for kids who are very tactile. Before heading out on the trails, learn how to identify poison oak and be prepared for an emergency.

The University of California–Davis describes poison oak as a woody shrub or vine that loses its leaves in winter. In open areas under full sunlight, it forms a dense, leafy shrub usually 1 to 6 feet high. In shaded areas, such as in coastal redwood forests and oak woodlands, it grows as a climbing vine, supporting itself on other vegetation or upright objects using its aerial roots. The leaves come in triplets with a shiny appearance, and turn red in the fall before falling off in the winter. The infamous poison oak rash is the body's reaction to urushiol oil (the same irritant found in poison ivy). Once on your skin, it spreads just like an oil would, with your body heat, and the allergic reaction comes from your body's autoimmune system.

To prevent a poison oak rash, you can use one of several commercial topical products, such as Tecnu cleanser, before the hike. After contact,

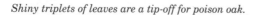

Shiny triplets of leaves are a tip-off for poison oak.

you can apply these products to keep from spreading the oil. Hand sanitizer or rubbing alcohol will also work; some people swear by dish soap. The main thing to remember is that when you wash it off, you should only use cold water; warm water will spread the oil. If the itchiness and symptoms persist, consult a doctor.

Poison Hemlock

As common as poison oak on the trails, poison hemlock is highly toxic and lethal when ingested. Socrates was fed poison hemlock tea as his death sentence in 399 BC. An herbaceous plant looking much like parsley, poison hemlock has a smooth, purple stem and triangular, finely divided leaves. Its seeds resemble those of fennel, and its root resembles a parsnip. With a hiking pole or stick, push the leaves aside and show the stem with purplish red dots to your kids. The stains are called "the blood of Socrates." In no case should you let your children touch poison hemlock.

Edible and Useful Local Plants

If your kids like to taste every single plant that looks yummy to them and if you want to try your hand at cooking with native plants, *The Flavors of Home: A Guide to Wild Edible Plants of the San Francisco Bay Area*, by Margit Roos-Collins, is a precious trail companion, as well as Charlotte Bringle Clarke's *Edible and Useful Plants of California*. Look for ranger programs on edible native plants in the park closest to your home, or contact your local foraging society to learn about foraging walks on which you learn which plants in your larger backyard are edible.

To learn about local mushrooms, find the nearest mycological society and sign up for beginner classes to learn to identify them. The North American Mycological Association (www.namyco.org) lists all active clubs by geographical origin. In the Bay Area, you will find clubs in San Francisco, San Leandro, Santa Rosa, and Santa Cruz. Mushroom expeditions with kids can be lots of fun!

The experts in local edible foods are obviously Native Californians. To learn about how they cook, their associated traditions, and edible native plants and wildlife, read *Seaweed, Salmon, and Manzanita Cider: A California Indian Feast*, by Margaret Dubin and Sara-Larus Tolley or *The Ohlone Way* by Malcolm Margolin. You'll never look at acorns quite the same way.

GETTING AROUND THE SAN FRANCISCO BAY AREA

Usually getting to trailheads involves driving private cars from your home to the park, but in some cases, you can use public transit to minimize the carbon footprint of your trip.

Buses, Trams, and Shuttles

In **San Francisco**, public transit is operated by the **San Francisco Municipal Transit Agency** (www.sfmta.com), **Muni** for short, which runs buses, trams, and cable cars.

In **San Mateo County**, **SamTrans** (www.samtrans.com) provides bus service between cities and to and from BART stations.

In **Santa Clara County**, the **Santa Clara Valley Transportation Authority** (www.vta.org) provides bus and rail service in the Santa Clara Valley.

In **Marin County**, bus services are operated by **Marin Transit** (www .marintransit.org) and **Golden Gate Transit** (www.goldengate.org).

In **Sonoma County**, **Sonoma County Transit** (www.sctransit .com) offers a comprehensive bus service that connects with local transit agencies such as **Santa Rosa Transit** (www.ci.santa-rosa.ca.us /department/transit), **Petaluma Transit** (www.cityofpetaluma.net /pubworks/transit-sub), and **Healdsburg In-City Transit** (www .ci.healdsburg.ca.us).

In **Napa County**, **Napa County Transportation & Planning Agency** (www.nctpa.net) runs the **VINE**, a fixed-route bus system from Santa Rosa to Vallejo.

In **Solano County**, transit agencies include **Vallejo Transit** (www .vallejotransit.com), **Benicia Transit** (www.ci.benicia.ca.us/transit), **Fairfield and Suisun Transit** (www.fasttransit.org), and **Rio Vista Delta Breeze** (www.rio-vista-ca.com/transit).

In **Santa Cruz County**, **Santa Cruz METRO** (www.scmtd.com) offers a local bus service.

In **Contra Costa County**, **County Connection** (www.cccta.org) provides fixed-route bus service and paratransit.

In **Alameda County**, **Alameda-Contra Costa Transit** (www .actransit.org) connects Alameda and Contra Costa counties by bus.

Trains

Bay Area Rapid Transit, better known as **BART** (www.bart.gov), offers train service that connects the San Francisco Peninsula with Oakland,

Berkeley, Fremont, Walnut Creek, Dublin/Pleasanton, and other cities in the East Bay.

Caltrain (www.caltrain.com) provides commuter train service along the San Francisco Peninsula, through the South Bay to San Jose and Gilroy.

Amtrak (www.amtrak.com) connects cities in California and features a few stops in the Bay Area.

General Commuter Info

A single portal incorporates information from all agencies and can help you route a trip in a few clicks. The statewide transit website (www.511 .org) is the answer to all your public transit questions and includes useful info on commuting (including bicycles, trains, and carpools) as well as trip planners. If you want to do the reverse search, Transit & Trails (www.transitandtrails.org) lets you find public transit information for a specific trailhead.

RESOURCES

Viewed from the stratosphere of the outdoor enthusiast, the Bay Area is a colorful puzzle of green spaces managed, groomed, and designed by lots of entities with varying geographic scopes or missions. At the outdoor-recreation Thanksgiving table, they should all receive heartfelt thanks from hikers for maintaining miles of trails in great hiking condition, often with dedicated volunteers. They also organize hundreds of family events and ranger or docent-led walks for children every year, so check out their websites to learn more about them.

Governing agencies:

California Department of Fish and Game, www.dfg.ca.gov
California State Coastal Conservancy, www.scc.ca.gov
California State Parks, www.parks.ca.gov
Don Edwards San Francisco Bay National Wildlife Refuge, www.fws .gov/desfbay
East Bay Regional Park District, www.ebparks.org
Golden Gate National Parks Conservancy, www.parksconservancy.org
Land Trust of Napa County, www.napalandtrust.org
Marin Agricultural Land Trust, www.malt.org
Marin Municipal Water District, www.marinwater.org
Marin Open Space Trust, www.marinopenspacetrust.org

Midpeninsula Regional Open Space District, www.openspace.org
National Park Service, www.nps.gov
Peninsula Open Space Trust, www.openspacetrust.org
San Francisco Parks and Open Spaces, http://sfrecpark.org/Parks.aspx
Santa Clara County Parks, www.parkhere.org
Solano Land Trust, www.solanolandtrust.org
Sonoma Agricultural Preservation and Open Space District, www.so
nomaopenspace.org
United States Geological Survey, www.usgs.gov

Regional trail projects:
Bay Area Ridge Trail, www.ridgetrail.org
California Coastal Trail, www.californiacoastaltrail.info
San Francisco Bay Trail, www.baytrail.org
Transit and Trails, www.transitandtrails.org

Organizations with a recreational, educational, or interpretive focus:
Crissy Field Center, www.crissyfield.org
National Audubon Society, www.audubon.org
Nature in the City, www.natureinthecity.org
Sierra Club, www.sierraclub.org

Organizations with a focus on wheelchair- or stroller-accessible trails:
Bay Area Hiker, www.bahiker.com/extras/allaccess.html
California State Parks, http://access.parks.ca.gov
San Francisco Bay Area Wheelchair Accessible Trails, www.wheel
chairtrails.net
Stroller Hikes, www.strollerhikes.com
Trail Center, www.trailcenter.org/guides/disabilities/disabilities.htm

Resources for kids:
Several websites are great resources for online learning or to connect kids to trails in playful ways that might spice up your usual hike.

Best Hikes for Children in the Bay Area, www.facebook.com /BestHikes. A Facebook page listing nature outings, trail tips, and family events throughout the Bay Area.

Children and Nature Network, www.childrenandnature.org. A network created to encourage and support the people and organizations working nationally and internationally to reconnect children with nature.

Geocaching, www.geocaching.com. Geocaching is a high-tech treasure hunting game played throughout the world by adventure seekers equipped with GPS devices. The basic idea is to locate hidden containers, called geocaches, outdoors and then share your experiences online. Download a geocaching adventure on your phone, and ask your kids to find it!

Kids in Parks, http://kids.parks.ca.gov. California State Parks programs for kids.

KQED Quest, www.kqed.org/quest/. A KQED multimedia series exploring Northern California science, environment, and nature.

Let's Go Chipper! www.letsgochipper.com. Award-winning educational apps, books, movies, and music that connect children with nature and the great outdoors.

Letterboxing Kids! www.letterboxing.org/kids. Discover a fun outdoor activity that combines treasure hunting with rubber stamping.

URBIA, www.urbikids.com. An ongoing series of seasonal passports for families and school groups to self-guided adventures in special natural places around San Francisco.

Wild Care Bay Area, www.wildcarebayarea.org. Programs in animal aid, advocacy, and education.

USING THIS GUIDE

Before choosing a hike, read the description at home. It will help you get an idea of what to expect: the type of terrain, the trail and route, options to cut the hike short or not (some hike descriptions provide a shorter or longer alternative to fit different needs). Based on the description, figure out how long it will take you to reach the trailhead from your home, and how long to allow for the hike plus stops along the way, so you can plan your day accordingly. Each hike includes driving directions and public transit options when they exist.

Name. This is the name of the park, open space, or preserve as it will appear on most road maps.

Number. Use the hike number to locate the route on the overview map.

Maps. The name of the topographic map published by the United States Geological Survey (USGS—www.usgs.gov) is included for your reference. Many outdoor recreation and sports stores, as well as big public libraries, stock USGS maps. Topos are a good supplement to the maps in this guide because the contour lines indicate elevations and terrain features, but many are outdated and do not feature hiking trails. For up-to-date and complete maps of your hiking trails, contact the park rangers, visitor and nature centers, or local governing agencies. Online, you can find and share maps with friends at Find Recreation (http://findrecreation.parks.ca.gov/), an online portal of the California State Parks covering most green spaces in California. This site offers options to show campgrounds and hiking trails on 3-D maps and regular maps.

Information. This provides the name and phone number of the agency that manages the land or maintains the trails for that area. You can call the agency's number if you have questions before you go, or check current conditions on the website directly.

Fees. In some cases, a fee is charged for entry or parking. These fees are minimal ($5 to $10) and some do not apply to people with yearly park passes. Be aware that fees increase and some places only charge on weekends or during the summer season. It's best to come prepared with some cash ($1 bills are very useful) as most parks provide envelopes to self-register with cash. If you are going to use some trails very regularly, membership makes financial sense and helps fund park services such as trail maintenance. If you see donation boxes, be generous, as most of these agencies can use all the help you can provide—whether in money or volunteer hours.

Type. *Day hike* means that this hike can easily be completed in a day or part of a day for most families. There is no campground or shelter along the route. *Day hike or overnight* indicates trails along which you will find campgrounds to stay overnight and these campgrounds are shown on the trail map. Though usually longer than others, these hikes can also be completed in a day.

Difficulty. Hikes are rated for children as easy, moderate, or difficult. Ratings are approximate and take into consideration various factors: distance, elevation gain, creek crossings, steep steps, or trail conditions. *Easy* hikes are relatively short, smooth, gentle trails suitable for toddlers and early walkers; usually 2 miles and under or completely level. *Moderate* hikes are generally 2 to 4 miles long and feature more than 500 feet of elevation gain. The trail may be rough and uneven. *Difficult* hikes are between 4 and 8 miles long and can feature between 500 and 2000 feet of elevation gain. The trail may be rough and uneven but is more likely to offer a variety of landscapes as well as viewpoints. Expect children's pace to be slower on steep or eroded terrain. On both *moderate* and *difficult* trails, hikers should wear sturdy hiking boots and carry the Ten Essentials. It's best to gain experience as a family on the easiest trails first. Don't reject a hike based on a difficulty rating, however, before noting the turnaround point or an optional shortcut.

Season. The seasons listed are when the trails are hikable. Almost all hikes listed are open year round, with a few exceptions in Solano County. Before going, check that the trails are open when you are planning to visit. For full-flow waterfalls and creeks, choose winter and spring.

Distance. This is the loop or round-trip (out-and-back) hiking distance. If a side trip to a waterfall or view is included in the text and on the map, it is included in the total distance. An alternate route described within the text is not factored into the total.

Hiking time. Again, this is an estimate based on length of hike, elevation gain, and trail conditions, but it will very much depend on your family's conditions that day. Some days your child will walk like a trooper and be fully immersed in the outdoors; another day you'll have to take it slower and shorter. It's hard to predict. Short rest stops are factored in, but not longer rests for meals on the trail.

High point/elevation gain. The number given reflects the height above sea level of the highest point on the trail. Elevation gain indicates the total number of vertical feet gained during the course of the hike. When analyzing a hike, this notation will be more significant than the high point in determining the difficulty. In cases where the notation is for "elevation loss," you'll start the hike on a downhill. Just remember to save your energy for the return trip!

Getting there. These directions will tell you how to get to the trailhead from the closest major freeways. You may still need road maps or a GPS to get to the start of the directions.

On the trail. For loop hikes (the majority of the hikes), the entire route is described. For out-and-back hikes, the route is described for your hike in; any potential difficulties you may encounter on the return trip are addressed at the end of each entry. The symbols within the text, in the margins, and on the maps indicate turnaround points, views, campsites, picnic spots, and caution spots (see the map legend and Key to Symbols below).

Happy hiking!

Key to Symbols

At the beginning of each hike, you'll also find symbols highlighting additional fun or important features of the trail or the area. Use these in conjunction with the Quick Guide to the Hikes at the front of the book to choose the outing that is just right for your family.

Accessibility. These hikes include paved trails accessible to wheels (strollers, wheelchairs). Inquire about actual conditions before hiking.

Bike paths. These hikes are at parks and open spaces that have gentle biking trails, either as multi-use trails or as separate bike paths. Some are level and easy, others are steep. Inquire about specifics before hiking.

Campgrounds. These hikes are in parks or open spaces that have campgrounds where families can go car-camping or have campsites along the trail.

Dog-friendly. These hikes are at parks and open spaces that welcome dogs. Some are off-leash, some are on-leash, some restrict dog access to specific areas. Inquire about specifics before hiking.

Drinking water. On these hikes you can find water at drinking fountains at the trailhead. Note that some drinking fountains are seasonal, so to be on the safe side, fill up before the hike.

Fog. On foggy days, the visibility on these hikes decreases significantly, temperatures feel colder, and trails take on an eerie atmosphere. Be prepared (with warm clothing) or avoid these routes during summer months and other heavy-fog days.

Fun extras. These hikes are in parks that feature kid-friendly highlights such as playgrounds, nature centers, farms, sculptures, seasonal events, or performances.

Restrooms. On these hikes you can find restrooms at the trailhead, sometimes on the trail. Some are flush toilets, others Porta-Potties.

 Splash zone. These hikes include a spot where children can get their feet wet, wade, or swim.

A NOTE ABOUT SAFETY

Safety is an important concern in all outdoor activities. No guidebook can alert you to every hazard or anticipate the limitations of every reader. Therefore, the descriptions of roads, trails, routes, and natural features in this book are not representations that a particular place or excursion will be safe for your party. When you follow any of the routes described in this book, you assume responsibility for your own safety. Under normal conditions, such excursions require the usual attention to traffic, road and trail conditions, weather, terrain, the capabilities of your party, and other factors. Keeping informed on current conditions and exercising common sense are the keys to a safe, enjoyable outing.

—*The Mountaineers Books*

SAN FRANCISCO
COUNTY

ALCATRAZ ISLAND

BEFORE YOU GO
Maps: USGS San Francisco North. Free map at ferry pier.
Information: Ranger station (415) 561-4900.
www.nps.gov/alcatraz

ABOUT THE HIKE
Day hike; Easy; Spring, Fall
2 miles, round-trip
Hiking time: 1–2 hours
High point/elevation gain: 140 feet/130 feet

GETTING THERE

■ From San Francisco, take a ferry at Pier 33 at Embarcadero and Bay streets for Alcatraz Island (www.alcatrazcruises.com). Reservations recommended, especially around holidays and school breaks.

■ There is no public transit.

ON THE TRAIL

Best known for the twenty-nine years when the island served as a federal penitentiary for the worst criminals from 1934 through 1963, Alcatraz Island is not your everyday Hollywood hike. Accessible only by a 10-minute ferry ride from San Francisco's shore, Alcatraz Island was a bird island, a Civil War–era fort, a penitentiary, and finally was occupied by American Indians before becoming a national park. Escaping from the rock? Overdone. Try escaping *to* the rock to see the green side of Alcatraz. On this solitary rock sticking out of San Francisco Bay grow lush gardens that once represented the only mental escape of the island's residents.

Reading the middle-grade novel *Al Capone Does My Shirts*, by Gennifer Choldenko, is highly recommended for all middle-graders coming to visit the island. They will be thrilled to recognize places mentioned in the book.

From the dock landing, proceed up the paved ramp that leads to the cellhouse. At 0.2 mile, the road turns in a hairpin and continues to ascend the rocky island. Look for an exposed rock wall showing you what the island looked like before it was planted. All the dirt that supports the living plants of Alcatraz was brought in buckets from Angel Island.

Opposite: Hiking the cloud forest trails

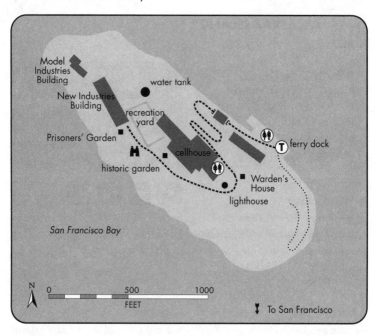

At the third hairpin around 0.4 mile, turn left up the ramp, away from the water tank. These walls were lined with cannons in the Civil War era. By the sign OFFICERS' ROW, look over the parapet to see the restored Officers' Row gardens. Here, medicinal and herbal plants grew next to three homes with terraces looking out on the city.

Continue up the ramp to the ruins of the Warden's House, a Mission Revival building across from the lighthouse. Turn around the lighthouse and at 0.5 mile, go down West Road toward the gardens. Facing the Golden Gate and its westerly winds, this side of the island can be fiercely windy and cold. Going down the road, look for a bird rookery at 0.6 mile and go under a big New Zealand Christmas tree, a tree that produces a brilliant display of red flowers in season. The little building farther along on your left was a tool shed.

At 0.7 mile, you arrive at the terraces planted by the inmates of the cellhouse, most fervently by Elliott Michener, a convicted counterfeiter who spent days terracing, planting, and plotting the garden (as well as dreams of an escape, which he never pursued). A pioneer sustainable gardener, Michener also built the little birdbath that stands next to the fig tree. In line with the island's dry climate (there is no water source), the gardens are tended in a sustainable manner: plants on the west side are mostly succulents that need little or no water; rainfall is stored in water tanks for the garden's usage; removed invasive plants end up in a compost pile.

Past the garden is a closed area of great interest. Prisoners on good behavior were allowed to go down from the recreation yard to the industry buildings at the far end of the island. Laundry was one of the activities done there. To earn this privilege, prisoners had to go through a metal detector. And at the end of their workday, they were allowed to pick a flower in the garden and bring it back to their cell.

The Alcatraz cutting gardens were planted during the Civil War.

From this point, you can either retrace your steps to the dock or walk up the stairs to the cellhouse's recreation yard and visit the cellhouse.

WHO KNEW THERE WERE CHILDREN AT ALCATRAZ?

The best-kept secret of Alcatraz is that children of the lighthouse keeper, army officers, prison guards, and Native American leaders lived here too. What was life like for a kid who grew up in a maximum-security prison? Children played football with white balls that could be seen in the fog. They sang carols at the Warden's House and to the prisoners at Christmastime. They organized dances, too. The book *Children of Alcatraz: Growing Up on the Rock,* by Claire Rudolf Murphy, has all the secrets—from the Gold Rush era to the 1970s. Can your kids find something fun to do on Alcatraz?

PRESIDIO OF SAN FRANCISCO/ GOLDEN GATE PROMENADE

BEFORE YOU GO
Maps: USGS San Francisco North. AAA San Francisco map.
Information: Golden Gate National Parks Conservancy (415) 561-3000.
www.parksconservancy.org

ABOUT THE HIKE
Day hike; Moderate; Year round
3.2 miles, round-trip
Hiking time: 1–2 hours
High point/elevation gain: 0 feet/0 feet

GETTING THERE

■ From San Francisco's Fort Mason, drive west 1.3 miles on Marina Boulevard.

■ Stay straight on Mason Street as Doyle Drive directs left-lane traffic onto the Golden Gate Bridge. The Crissy Field East Beach parking lot is directly on your right.

■ Crissy Field is easily accessible via Muni bus.

ON THE TRAIL

The Golden Gate Promenade along the western end of San Francisco Bay connects many historical landmarks from Aquatic Park to Fort Point, passing every family's sweetheart place for kids, Crissy Field. This shorter version starts at one of the weirdest lesser-known San Francisco landmarks and stops at the Warming Hut, where an organic café and nature-oriented bookstore attract thousands each year. Stop for a warm drink, stay for the views, come back for a picnic on the lawns. This place has come to represent a slice of San Francisco life, and local crowds know it. Expect heavy traffic on sunny days.

From the East Beach parking lot, get on the dirt-and-gravel pathway, heading east to the St. Francis Yacht Club. Continue past the yacht club to the jetty on a path that seems to lead nowhere but passes a stone tower. Beyond the stone tower, keep going to some stairs. Lo and behold, at the end of the jetty at 0.2 mile, looking out on Alcatraz and the Golden Gate Bridge, lies an acoustic sculpture made by Exploratorium artist-in-residence Peter Richards in 1986. This creation of PVC tubes and cement pipes produces musical sounds thanks to the crashing

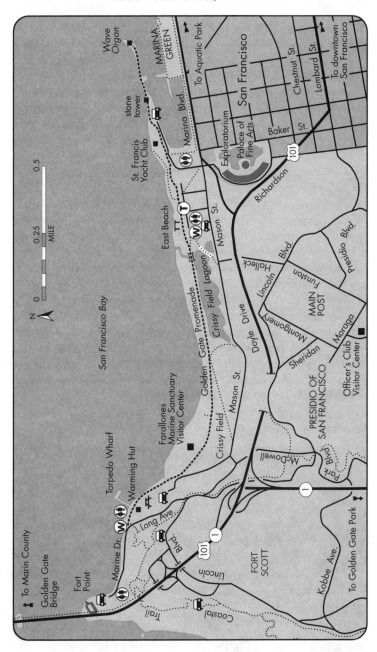

waves coming to wash ashore. For best results, visit the *Wave Organ* at high tide. Even if no sounds come out of the tubes, the whole place is still plain surrealistic, and the rocks supporting the jetty are home to dozens of small red crabs that scurry about. Kids love it.

Come back on the jetty and to the East Beach parking lot, heading toward the Golden Gate Bridge this time. At 0.5 mile the path passes a sand lagoon whose brackish waters have delighted generations of young beachgoers. Even on foggy days, there are always families around the lagoon.

Between the lagoon and the Farallones Marine Sanctuary Visitor Center at 1.4 miles, the path follows a tidal marsh that was restored after being used by the army as training grounds for tanks and an airfield. Today, planted dunes and seabirds show nothing of the trauma the place suffered from the 1920s to the 1970s. If you have time, stop by the marine sanctuary's visitor center. This small facility (www.farallones .org) contains educational hands-on activities for the preschool-to-sixth-grade set and visitors.

Keep going on the promenade until you reach Torpedo Wharf, a popular spot for fishing and crabbing, across from the Warming Hut building at 1.6 miles. The café is a nice spot for hot chocolate and sandwiches, and is well-stocked in local books and gifts for children and adults. If you want to reach Fort Point at the foot of the Golden Gate Bridge, continue another 0.3 mile on the promenade. When ready, retrace your steps to the East Beach parking lot.

Children of all ages enjoy the Golden Gate Promenade.

PRESIDIO OF SAN FRANCISCO/ LOBOS CREEK DUNES

BEFORE YOU GO
Maps: USGS North San Francisco. Free map at visitor center at the Presidio's main post.
Information: Presidio Visitor Center (415) 561-4323.
www.presidio.gov

ABOUT THE HIKE
Day hike; Easy; Year round
0.8 mile, loop
Hiking time: 1 hour or less
High point/elevation loss: 100 feet/negligible

GETTING THERE

- From San Francisco downtown, drive west to Lake Street until you reach 25th Avenue.
- Turn right (north) on 25th Avenue and right again at El Camino del Mar onto Lincoln Boulevard. The parking lot for the Lobos Creek Dunes is across from Bowley Street.
- Muni buses 29 and 1 stop nearby.

ON THE TRAIL

A boardwalk undulating through San Francisco's dunes? This is not a dream, it's a reality in the Presidio where Lobos Creek flows toward the Pacific Ocean. Close to Mountain Lake Playground and Baker Beach, this trail is the perfect toddler outing on any day of the year. Even when it rains or when the fog seems too thick to consider going out, you needn't worry that your kids' shoes will get muddy, as the boardwalk is elevated.

Since the trail is short, pack a few homemade telescopes or looking glasses to examine the vegetation (and winged creatures) along the path. More than sixty native Californian species grow here, and the area is a hot spot for birding because of the freshwater source. To enjoy the peak wildflower season, come in the late spring. You will find self-guided brochures for the interpretive trail in boxes at the end of the boardwalk and at the visitor center at the Presidio's main post.

From the parking lot, get on the boardwalk by the kiosk and start your day exploration. Whether your child is the explorer or the runner type, the boardwalk is a playful way to zigzag between the dunes. It's kid-friendly in more ways than one, since it was made out of 280,000 recycled plastic milk bottles!

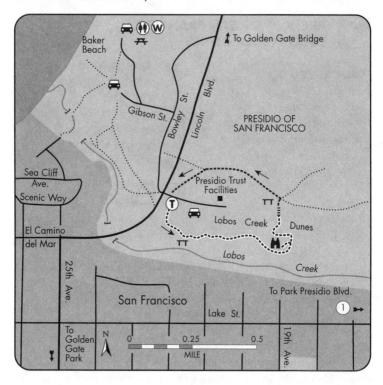

The boardwalk curves left to follow the course of Lobos Creek, the last free-flowing creek in San Francisco and the Presidio's only water source. Though you can't see the creek well from the trail, it's down there, a protected habitat bordered by a green carpet of watercress. Up to the late 1800s, the city's active watersheds featured creeks, springs, marshes, and even lakes. Most are buried under our feet now, and the cityscape has completely altered what this area looked like before urban planning culverted creeks, filled marshes, and paved sand dunes. As a result, this trail is a unique opportunity to enjoy a restored San Francisco habitat as if unspoiled by human hands.

Continue on the level boardwalk as it gently winds through the dunes. At 0.4 mile, an offshoot on your left takes you to a platform overlooking the dunes. Keep going until the end of the boardwalk at 0.5 mile. From there, you can either retrace your steps on the boardwalk, or step toward a row of sandy stairs leading to a grove of cypress trees. If your child loves to sift through sand or build forts out of sticks, the

Even in the fog the Lobos Creek boardwalk attracts young nature admirers.

cypress grove is the place to let loose! Plus, you might see banana slugs on damp days.

From the cypress grove, turn left (west) on the sand-and-dirt trail to get back to the parking lot at 0.8 mile. If you want to see Lobos Creek flowing into the ocean, you can find it at Baker Beach.

BANANA SLUGS

Usually bright yellow, banana slugs are very common in Northern California, particularly in redwood forests. Though most are yellow, their bodies can also be white, brown, or green with spots. Their body color depends on what they eat and how moist their habitat is. That's why the best time of the year to look for banana slugs is the rainy season—fall and winter. Banana slugs love it when it's wet! When it's too dry or too hot, banana slugs do their summer thing: bury themselves under leaves, cover themselves in mucus, and wait until the dry season is over. This is called *estivation,* the summer equivalent to hibernation.

When you see a banana slug, get at slug level and watch the tentacles. One pair is larger and senses light; another is smaller and senses smell. Yes, tentacles instead of a nose. Banana slugs are really cool animals.

4 LANDS END/COASTAL TRAIL AND SUTRO LOOP

BEFORE YOU GO
Maps: USGS San Francisco South. Map posted at trailhead.
Information: Presidio Visitor Center (415) 561-4323.
www.nps.gov/goga

ABOUT THE HIKE
Day hike; Moderate; Year round
2.8 miles, round-trip;
Sutro landmarks extension, 1 mile, loop
Hiking time: 2 hours
High point/elevation gain: 150 feet/minimal

GETTING THERE

- From San Francisco downtown, drive west on Geary Boulevard 5 miles and stay right as it splits into Point Lobos Avenue at 40th Avenue. Park at the Lands End parking lot on the right after El Camino del Mar.
- Muni bus 38's terminal is located at Point Lobos Avenue and 48th Avenue, 200 yards from the Lands End trailhead.

ON THE TRAIL

With knockout views of the Golden Gate Bridge, dog-friendly trails, and wind-sculpted Monterey cypresses, the cliff-top paths of Lands End are a dream urban escape. Combine this hike with a visit to the Cliff House and the Sutro landmarks to discover the incredible Victorian world of Adolph Sutro, one of San Francisco's most famous characters. Philanthropist and millionaire, Sutro built huge public baths and museums, a railroad, classical gardens, and an extravagant Gothic Revival house at the edge of a continent. This is where your hike starts.

Because of sheer drops and many stairs, the Coastal Trail is best for parents with babies in carriers or with children used to walking. With a stroller the Coastal Trail is difficult to navigate without help, but the Sutro legacy section is entirely stroller-friendly.

From the Lands End parking lot, find the sign for the Coastal Trail heading north to Eagles Point. This paved trail winds up a small hill to merge at 0.1 mile with another trail that comes from El Camino del Mar. Turn left on a wide path that uses the old bed of the Ferries & Cliff House Railroad, a steam train line that ran along Lands End. For five cents, passengers could hop onto open cars and enjoy a ride from

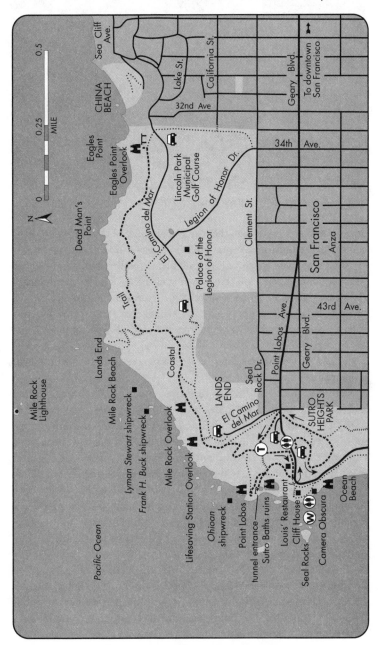

Spectacular views of the Golden Gate from the Coastal Trail near Lands End

downtown San Francisco to the windswept dunes of the continent's edge where Sutro's fantastic recreational facilities awaited them.

At 0.3 mile you reach an overlook above the lifesaving station. The white column at sea is all that remains of the Mile Rock Lighthouse, a three-story 1906 structure that strong currents made exceedingly difficult to build and to approach. The keeper was transported by boat, snagged a Jacob's ladder hanging from the catwalk, and climbed 30 feet above raging waters to reach the base of the lighthouse. Several shipwrecks line these shores, and some mossy boat skeletons can still be seen at the bottom of the sea.

Continue on the trail which turns into a sand path with a few steep and eroded portions. After it levels out at 0.7 mile, a separate trail leads to the Legion of Honor. Turn left and keep to the Coastal Trail. At 0.8 mile, stairs on the left lead to Mile Rock Beach a guerrilla rock labyrinth on the bluffs. Continue until you reach a stairway at 0.9 mile. After roughly 100 steps, a higher bluff provides a well-deserved rest before going down (more steps) to a level stretch along the Lincoln Park Municipal Golf Course. At 1.4 miles, Eagles Point platform marks the end of the hike and a nice picnic spot with splendid views of the Golden Gate, the strait that connects the Pacific Ocean and San Francisco Bay. Retrace your steps back to the parking lot.

To explore the Sutro landmarks from the Lands End parking lot, find the paved path west of Louis' Restaurant off Point Lobos Avenue. Go down to the Sutro Baths ruins, formerly the world's largest public baths. Built in 1896, the huge steel-and-glass structure contained six swimming pools of varying temperatures filled with ocean water.

Walk back up the path and cross Point Lobos Avenue to get to the lot for Sutro Heights Park. A paved ramp at the eastern end of the lot leads you to quiet lawns and a white Victorian kiosk, remains of Sutro's house, and landscaped gardens. Turn right to loop around the parapet and foundations of the house. At the edge of the lawns, bear left on a wide alley to return to Point Lobos Avenue. Cross at El Camino del Mar to come back to the parking lot via a pedestrian ramp.

To learn more about the fascinating history of the Sutro landmarks, visit the Cliff House to see before and after photos—and drink a cup of hot chocolate if the winds are chilly.

GOLDEN GATE PARK WEST/LAKES LOOP

BEFORE YOU GO
Maps: USGS Point Bonita and San Francisco North.
Information: San Francisco Recreation & Parks (415) 831-2700. http://sfrecpark.org

ABOUT THE HIKE
Day hike; Moderate; Year round
3.1 miles, loop
Hiking time: 2–3 hours
High point/elevation gain: 50 feet/50 feet

GETTING THERE

- From Great Highway between John F. Kennedy Drive and Martin Luther King Jr. Drive, turn east into the parking lot for the Beach Chalet Visitor Center.
- Muni bus 5 stops at La Playa Street and Fulton Street.

ON THE TRAIL
Entirely planted by landscape architects on sand dunes that shifted with the western winds, Golden Gate Park is an iconic green space loved by San Franciscans as their extended backyard. Birthday parties, concerts, nature hunts, athletic events, African drum sessions—the park is used for every imaginable recreational activity, including hiking.

Closer to the ocean, the western part of the park remains largely quieter than the eastern part, despite beautiful sights. This hike is a great opportunity to discover a more secluded face of Golden Gate Park as well as fun local trivia.

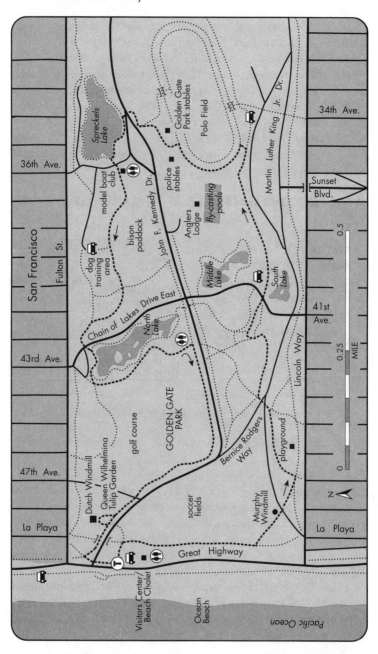

From the parking lot, walk north to a red monolith. It is a monument to Captain Roald Amundsen, the famous Norwegian explorer who was the first to navigate the Northwest Passage from the Atlantic to the Pacific. Walk around the Beach Chalet and turn right on a wide gravel path. Protected from the ocean's gusts of wind by a thick tree line, the path runs parallel to the beach. At an unsigned fork at 0.35 mile, turn left to reach the base of Murphy Windmill.

Cross with caution to find a narrow dirt path with a cut tree stump across from the corner of Martin Luther King Jr. Drive east of the mill. This path connects with a wider multipurpose trail. Turn left, and left again on the paved trail that starts at Lincoln Way and 47th Avenue. At 0.6 mile, you pass a playground with a blue boat structure in a meadow under Monterey pines. Continue on the paved trail, staying left at the fork. Cross to the yellow post left of the sign for Bernice Rodgers Way, and at 0.65 mile turn right on a paved trail lined on both sides with tall trees.

As you reach the Golden Gate Park's gardeners' sheds, turn right and go between yellow posts to follow the path with a pedestrian marking on the ground. At the next street crossing, you are on Chain of Lakes Drive East. Though there is no street sign, look for the street name carved into the pavement. After the 1906 earthquake, city planners decided to mark street names in pavement so that it would be easier to reconstruct the city should the buildings fall. Cross and keep going straight.

At 0.9 mile, walk by South Lake, one of three lakes forming the Chain of Lakes. Created from freshwater swamps, these lakes were landscaped with artificial islands, a gazebo, and footbridges. Proceed straight past a yellow post. This flat section of the trail feels very removed and offers perfect stroller terrain.

At 1.2 miles, a short uphill section lands in front of the Polo Field, formerly known as the Golden Gate

The Dutch windmill at the western end of the park is a delight to children.

Stadium. Built in 1904, it was envisioned to be the biggest amphitheater in the world but remained unfinished, and the current track is only half of the originally planned circumference. Turn left on the wide path that borders the polo field under a line of eucalyptus trees. Through the trees, you soon discern the eerie fly-casting pools of the Anglers Lodge. Children will love the sight of colored floating rings in blue pools to practice casting accuracy when fishing.

At 1.45 miles, you reach the Frederick C. Egan Memorial Police Stables where you might see some horses outside. Past the last building, turn left and down to a paved road leading to Spreckels Lake. Turn left and cross John F. Kennedy Drive to get to Spreckels Lake, famous for its model boats. Turn left to follow the lake and look for a turtle-shaped water sculpture. Kids may find real turtles on it. Turn left on the ramp that goes down the hill and across the road toward the restrooms.

At 1.65 miles, turn right to get on the trail that runs behind the bison paddock, past a dog park to North Lake. At 2 miles, turn right before the path goes down and curve slight left to reach the northern end of North Lake. Cross Chain of Lakes Drive East and continue westward on the trail around this pretty lake. At 2.4 miles, turn right on a trail that runs parallel to John F. Kennedy Drive, passing the Golden Gate Park Golf Course. At 2.9 miles, take time to explore the Dutch Windmill and admire the flower displays on the large lawn. In the spring, the Queen Wilhelmina Tulip Garden blooms with 10,000 tulips planted the previous fall.

At 3 miles, cross John F. Kennedy Drive at Great Highway and get on the short dirt path back to the parking lot.

GOLDEN GATE PARK EAST

BEFORE YOU GO
Map: USGS San Francisco North.
Information: San Francisco Recreation & Parks (415) 831-2700. http://sfrecpark.org

ABOUT THE HIKE
Day hike; Moderate; Year round
2.4 miles, loop
Hiking time: 1–2 hours
High point/elevation gain: 425 feet/425 feet

GETTING THERE

- From San Francisco downtown, drive west on Fell Street.
- At the entrance of Golden Gate Park, turn right on John F. Kennedy Drive and park around 10th Avenue.
- Walk to the Music Concourse (between the De Young Museum and the California Academy of Sciences), where this hike begins.
- Muni bus 44 stops at the Music Concourse, bus 5 stops at Fulton Street and 8th Avenue, and N-Judah Muni streetcar stops at 9th Avenue and Irving Street.

ON THE TRAIL

Closer to San Francisco's vibrant neighborhoods, the eastern part of Golden Gate Park reveals some exceptional natural beauty.

From the big fountain on the Music Concourse, head southeast to the California Academy of Sciences (www.calacademy.org) housing a rain forest, a planetarium, and an aquarium. Walk along the building and turn left (south) at the bicycle parking. Take a right on a dirt path to get to the Shakespeare Garden where plants refer to Shakespeare's writings. Arching crabapple trees and an antique sundial make it a wonderful place to rest.

Exit the garden and turn left (west) to Martin Luther King Jr. Drive. Cross at the south corner and at 0.2 mile, walk inside the San Francisco Botanical Garden (www.sfbotanicalgarden.org, closed major holidays, fee for non–San Francisco residents). Grab a map of the garden and proceed to the Friend Gate, passing through the Garden of Fragrance, the Rhododendron Garden (with its medieval stones), and the waterfowl pond (good for turtle-spotting).

If the garden is closed, simply follow Martin Luther King Jr. Drive north to the Friend Gate. Cross Martin Luther King Jr. Drive and at 0.5 mile, bear left on a paved path with a bamboo forest to the right. Turn left at the fork 50 yards farther and climb steps to reach Stow Lake, a popular family spot with its paddleboats, waterfall, and Chinese pavilion. Cross the road and circle the lake going left (west) on the paved path until you reach the aptly named Rustic Bridge, arching over the water.

Cross Rustic Bridge and turn right to a path on the left that goes uphill. Turn left again to reach a reservoir and left along the reservoir to reach the top of Strawberry Hill, with breathtaking views of the city at 1.2 miles. This 425-foot promontory was named after the

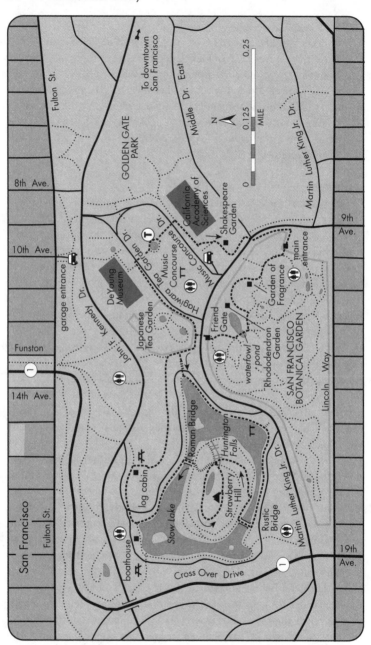

wild strawberries that once covered its slopes, but they are long gone. The rock wall is all that remains of Sweeny Observatory, a castle-like amphitheater so big that horse carriages could circle inside the courtyard. It crumbled in the 1906 earthquake, and today the ruins offer an irresistible climbing wall for kids.

Come down Strawberry Hill, passing left of the 110-foot waterfall down staircases that curve left and then right to take you on the Roman Bridge. This flat bridge is where carriages went to ride to Strawberry Hill. Turn left (west) and walk toward the boathouse. At the northwestern edge of the lake, a dirt path connects the Stow Lake path with the road below. Turn right on that path. Can you find a hand-hewn chair made from a stump?

Climbing on top of Strawberry Hill

Cross the road and go left 20 feet to a wide paved path. Turn right and go down between tall trees, staying parallel to the access road until you see the picture-book-perfect Pioneer Log Cabin. Turn right after the cabin and walk to the picnic area south of the meadow. Turn left on a level path that meanders through the next two meadows and a forest. It will curve right and rise to meet a paved path.

At 1.8 miles, turn right to reach the outer walls of the Japanese Tea Garden (http://japaneseteagardensf.com, open every day, admission). Turn left along Martin Luther King Jr. Drive, and left again on Hagiwara Tea Garden Drive. The oldest public Japanese garden in the United States features a teahouse (with child-friendly food and drink options), a moon bridge, a koi pond, stepping stones, and pagodas. Return to the Music Concourse by following Hagiwara Tea Garden Drive toward the De Young Museum.

MOUNT SUTRO

BEFORE YOU GO
Maps: USGS San Francisco North. Free map online at sutrostewards.org
Information: Save Mount Sutro Forest, www.sutroforest.com

ABOUT THE HIKE
Day hike; Easy/Moderate; Year round
1.5 miles, loop
Hiking time: 1 hour
High point/elevation gain: 908 feet/300 feet

GETTING THERE

■ From San Francisco downtown, get on Market Street northbound and turn right on 17th Street.

■ Turn left on Clayton Street and bear right on Twin Peaks Boulevard. Continue straight as Twin Peaks Boulevard becomes Clarendon Avenue.

■ Turn right onto Christopher Drive, which becomes Crestmont. Park on the street. The hike starts at the West Ridge trailhead across from 365 Crestmont.

■ There are many public transit options to reach this hike, although most include a solid flight of steps to reach the trailhead. If you take Muni to Lawton and 7th Avenue, you'll go up Warren Drive and climb the long Oakhurst steps.

ON THE TRAIL

Best seen in heavy fog and wrapped around Mount Sutro in bushy green and muddy paths, you will find San Francisco's cloud forest, a place where eucalyptus trees reach 200 feet and sway in the wind far from city noises. This forest was planted over a century ago by Adolph Sutro, one of the most colorful characters of the city's history (see Hike 4). The current 80 acres are survivors from a 1100-acre eucalyptus forest that covered much of San Francisco's western neighborhoods. Today Mount Sutro is surrounded by residential streets, but its trails give the feeling of a remote lost-world kind of place.

Older children will enjoy the ethereal look of the forest with its tall trees, while new parents will find much peace on the serene trails and

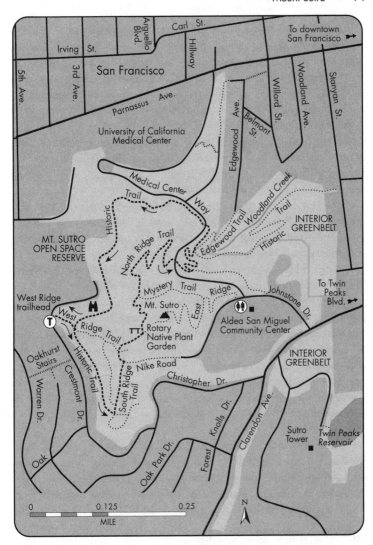

green slopes. Note that because of steep drops next to the trail, strollers and young hikers are not advised. Also, gear up with waterproof footwear and rain clothes. Even on summer days, trails are muddy and fog drips down from the trees. Now you can enjoy a unique city escape, before refueling at the many cafés and eateries down in Cole Valley.

From 365 Crestmont, the West Ridge Trail starts as an unmarked trail across the street, a simple flight of stairs ascending the mountain. Start here and get ready for a rough and rugged beginning on a steep trail busy with roots and bushes. Less than 0.1 mile later, the path widens and levels out while ferns appear left and right. At 0.1 mile, turn right on the Historic Trail. Mossy trunks and craggy chert outcrops line the path.

At 0.14 mile, turn left on the South Ridge Trail toward the summit. Going up slightly, the wide path traverses thick stands of tall eucalyptus trees that dwarf everything around them. When fog infiltrates the forest and gives it that surreal feel, gnomes and fairies could be hiding behind ferns, and you wouldn't be surprised.

Turn left toward the summit on Nike Road, a paved road that evokes the Cold War past of Mount Sutro. In the 1950s and 1960s, a radar site stood on top of the mountain, ready to control Nike missiles stationed at the Presidio army base.

This road leads you to a native plant garden (funded by the Rotary Club to commemorate the founding of the United Nations in San Francisco) and to a short trail that leads to the summit, a large clearing framed by eucalyptus trees. This is a good snack stop. If you visit the summit, return to Nike Road and turn right. At 0.2 mile, turn left on the narrow North Ridge Trail that crosses the native garden and zigzags down the mountain through a damp mixed forest that feels like a rainforest. Keep straight to stay on the North Ridge Trail. Right before you reach a paved road, show a moon-shaped cave to your child. Cross very carefully (cars don't expect pedestrians) and resume your hike on the other side.

Almost right away around 0.6 mile, make a hard left onto the Edgewood and Historic trails. At the next (unmarked) fork, bear left to go up the Historic Trail and cross the paved road again. The University of California–San Francisco (UCSF) Medical Center stands beneath you.

The Historic Trail traverses a steep hillside. This is the most beau-

tiful part of the hike, with open views of the forest whose trees stand tall wrapped in ivy. Because of precipitous drops, keep children on the trail, away from the edge. Ascend gradually until you reach a gap in the forest with a view

Exploring caves on the trail

right (north) across Golden Gate Park and the Marin Headlands. In a few steps you come to the sign for the West Ridge Trail; turn right and retrace your steps to the trailhead on Crestmont Drive.

THE RANDALL MUSEUM

A few blocks east of the Sutro Forest, the Randall Museum (www.randallmuseum.org) is the go-to museum for San Francisco families with its live animals' room, educational programs, and crafts activities. Run by the San Francisco Recreation and Parks Department, the Randall Museum is next to a playground, a dog run, and a rocky open-space hill. The museum's popular annual events include Bug Day, Halloween Fest, and Holiday Crafts Day. When you go there, look for the resident rabbits, the tiny owls, the buzzing beehive, and have your child play on the earthquake-simulation construction game.

 GLEN CANYON PARK

BEFORE YOU GO
Map: USGS San Francisco South.
Information: San Francisco Recreation & Parks
(415) 831-2700.
www.sfrecpark.org

ABOUT THE HIKE
Day hike; Easy; Year round
0.7 mile, round-trip
Hiking time: 1 hour
High point/elevation gain: 140 feet/140 feet

GETTING THERE

■ From I-280 southbound in San Francisco, exit at Monterey Street and head north on Bosworth Street.

■ From I-280 northbound coming from south San Francisco, exit at San Jose Avenue and make a tight right onto Bosworth Street on Rousseau Street.

■ Turn right on Bosworth Street and drive 0.5 mile to Elk Street.

■ Turn right onto Elk Street and park near Chenery Street.

■ Glen Canyon Park is easily accessible by public transit. It is a few blocks from the BART Glen Park Station or accessible via Muni bus 44; stop at Bosworth and Elk.

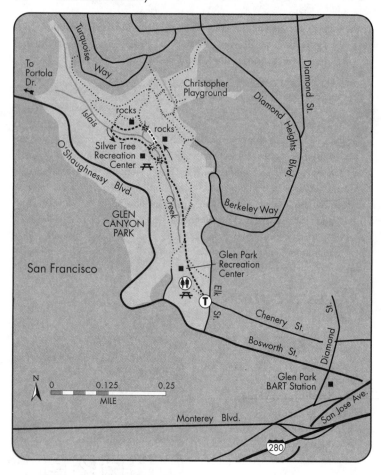

ON THE TRAIL

One of San Francisco's village-type neighborhoods, Glen Park has a lot to offer to families within a few blocks: a public library, a recreation center, a BART station, family-friendly restaurants, and even an LA-style deep canyon where local kids play in the creek when days are nice. In Victorian days, an amusement park thrived here with animals, balloon ascents, and a tightrope walk across the canyon by Jimmy "Scarface" Williams. On its steep flanks, Glen Canyon boasts some impressive rock outcrops where local climbers like to boulder in the sun. At the bottom of the canyon, Islais Creek flows in the shade of a jungle jangle of willow trees. Whether you decide to go up high or stay at creek level, Glen Canyon is a short and sweet family hike for all levels. Note that trails can be narrow, and only umbrella strollers would be able to navigate most portions, some with a little acrobatics.

From the junction of Chenery and Elk streets, look for the metal gate above the paved way that leads to the Glen Park Recreation Center. The gate marks the entrance to the canyon, and the paved trail curves under blue gum eucalyptus trees that were planted by Adolph Sutro in 1886. Several interpretive signs tell you about the canyon's rock outcrops, coastal scrub community, or grassland community. Continue on the large road past two bridges and turn right onto a trail marked by four wooden posts at 0.1 mile.

The willow thicket you enter is just the beginning of a dense willow forest covering all the length of the canyon. At 0.15 mile, an elevated boardwalk crosses a delicate area around the creek. Back under willow trees, you cross a bridge and have the option to explore the aerial views of Glen Canyon as a set of stairs shoots up the hill at 0.2 mile. If you want a fun adventure on the rocks, walk up the stairs and see the big boulders before coming down at the next set of stairs.

If you stay on the unmarked creek-level trail, continue until you reach the second set of wooden steps. There, around 0.35 mile, turn left (west), or go straight if you came down the stairs. This seemingly obscure trail turns left immediately to bring you back on a parallel trail across the creek running all the way under the willows. Expect a green tunnel, twisted trees, and countless dinosaur-train opportunities on branches closer to the ground. For little climbers, this area is a natural playground.

Walk past a native plant garden beyond a wooden fence and come out of the willows south of the main dirt road at 0.6 mile. Turn left on the bridge and rejoin the main dirt road. Across the creek on the slopes, picnic tables and the Silver Tree Parks and Recreation building welcome children year round for recreational activities, including evening campfires in the summer months. Retrace your steps on the main road.

Trees serve as jungle gyms at Glen Canyon Park.

MCLAREN PARK

BEFORE YOU GO
Map: USGS San Francisco South.
Information: San Francisco Recreation and Parks, http://sfrecpark.org and McLaren Park, www.jennalex.com/projects/fomp/homepage/index.html

ABOUT THE HIKE
Day hike; Moderate; Year round
2 miles, loop
Hiking time: 1–2 hours
High point/elevation gain: 495 feet/300 feet

GETTING THERE

■ From US 101 in San Francisco, take the Paul Avenue exit and head west on Mansell Street.

■ Park next to the Louis Sutter Playground, accessible from University Street between Dwight and Wayland.

■ The park is accessible by Muni; buses 29, 52, and 54 stop at the playground or within blocks.

ON THE TRAIL

Sandwiched between Visitacion Valley, Excelsior, Crocker-Amazon, and Portola, McLaren Park (named after John McLaren, the superintendent of Golden Gate Park from 1887 to 1943) is a community park with surprisingly large green spaces. Besides two playgrounds, a big dog area (off-leash and on-leash), an amphitheater, and two lakes, the park also includes 7 miles of hiking trails that will give anybody a good workout since the terrain is an incline. As a pleasant bonus, McLaren Park features a seasonal marsh around the resurgence of Yosemite Creek, one of San Francisco's original creeks.

From the Louis Sutter Playground, head south on a short trail that goes up the hill. It intersects with a paved trail. Turn right (west) to a thick stand of willows announcing the creek. At 0.1 mile, you get to a boardwalk with wooden seating areas overlooking Lake McNab. You are standing over Yosemite Creek, which feeds the lake before traveling underground to San Francisco Bay. Continue to another boardwalk and walk up in a pine grove to a road junction at 0.2 mile. Cross Shelley

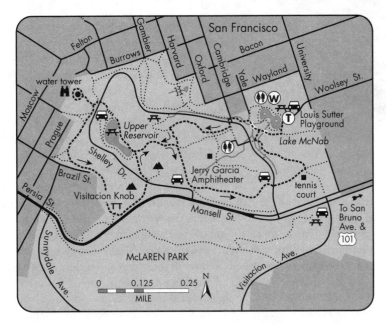

Drive with caution and walk briefly on a paved trail before turning right uphill on a dirt path.

Bypassing the Jerry Garcia Amphitheater (named after the leader of the Grateful Dead, a native son of the Excelsior district), walk up the hill and reach a wider trail at 0.4 mile under tall cypress trees. Turn right on the main stretch to follow a grassy slope and get to the Upper Reservoir. At 0.7 mile, turn right to circle the lake counterclockwise. Three animal species thrive in the lake: ducks, turtles, and swimming dogs on their daily walk.

At the end of the lake, walk up a flight of stairs toward the 80-foot-tall blue water tower and cross Shelley Drive to walk up the paved service road to the tank. There, sweeping vistas of the city await you with Bernal Hill north of you. Come down the paved access road and at 1 mile, turn right before the road on a paved trail that descends to a pine grove.

Skirting the hillside, the path loops to the other side and enters planted groves of alders. This shady portion rises gently around Visitacion Knob, the highest point in the park, without actually seeing it. For a fun side trip, explore Visitacion Knob to find a rock labyrinth surrounded by eucalyptus and cypress trees on the ridgeline. On the trail at 1.2 miles, turn left at a bench on another paved path that ascends

Playing in Yosemite Creek at McLaren Park

through eucalyptus trees. Over the hill you reach Shelley Drive. Cross with caution and find a paved trail on the other side. The path curves left down the hill to the Upper Reservoir.

Turn right at 1.4 miles and follow the trail after it levels out to the edge of a parking area. At the edge of the parking lot, a narrow steep dirt trail goes down on the left (east) and cuts through the slope to enter a cypress grove. Go down this trail with caution and walk into the woods. This trail leads to the parking lot for the amphitheater. Cross Shelley Drive with caution and continue on the other side on a paved trail. From dark forests you transition to open meadows and city vistas. After the tennis court, turn left on a paved trail going down the hill (northwest) to another wooded area.

At the bridge, look for a pipe where water comes out clean and cold. This is Yosemite Creek, and if you follow the water downstream (turn right on the paved path that goes downhill heading northeast), you will find watercress growing in abundance. Turn right to a small boardwalk and follow it back to the beginning. Retrace your steps to the parking lot at 2 miles.

10 CANDLESTICK POINT

BEFORE YOU GO
Map: USGS Hunters Point.
Information: Park office (415) 671-0145. California State Parks, www.parks.ca.gov

ABOUT THE HIKE
Day hike; Easy; Year round
1.2 miles, loop
Hiking time: 1 hour
High point/elevation gain: 0 feet/0 feet

GETTING THERE

■ From US 101 southbound, exit at Cow Palace/3rd Avenue and go left over US 101 onto 3rd Street. Turn left on Gilman Avenue and continue onto Hunters Point Expressway.

■ From US 101 northbound, exit at Candlestick Park and turn right on Harney Way. Turn right on Jamestown Avenue and continue onto Hunters Point Expressway.

■ The park entrance is off Hunters Point Expressway to the east. Drive up to the last restroom close to the bay (east).

ON THE TRAIL

Entirely man-made in the early 1940s by the United States Navy, Candlestick Point looks out on southern San Francisco Bay, the East Bay hills, and the San Bruno Mountains. These tidelands were filled to create a naval shipyard, but you wouldn't know it from walking on this portion of the Bay Trail, where oak trees line trails planted with coyote brush and wild fennel, and where colonies of ground squirrels frolic.

Urban in spirit, Candlestick Point is a major family park on weekends when picnic tables and lawns are abuzz with life. Thanks to flat and mostly paved trails, strollers, tricycles, and bicycles are choice modes of transportation for the junior set. The flatness of the land

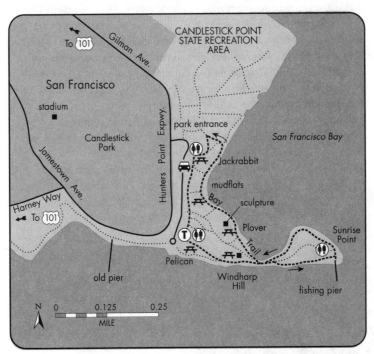

also means that the area gets so windy that it's a dedicated spot for windsurfers.

One word of caution: Time your visit to avoid days when there's a game at Candlestick Park (home to the Forty Niners), when the state recreation area becomes a giant parking lot for fans and tailgaters.

From the parking lot, go through the yellow gate and left on the paved trail that passes the Pelican group picnic area. After 0.1 mile, the trail runs parallel to the bay just a few feet away and curves gently to the left with a meadow on the other side. Advancing toward scenic Sunrise Point, you walk past several picnic areas encased behind wind shelters. At 0.4 mile you reach the point and a fishing pier that juts out 150 feet into the bay. Walk to the end and see if you can spot what local anglers look for: jacksmelt, perch, flounder, even bat rays. Shorebirds flying low fishing are a fun sight for toddlers, as is the sink for washing fish.

Come back on the trail and keep circling the rocky point on a dirt-and-gravel path partially shaded by reclining pines. When the trail forks at 0.6 mile, veer right to follow the bay. Continue 50 feet and look for a metal sculpture to your left next to picnic tables. This sculpture, named *Orchestra for Natives of the Future*, is a metal percussion set that kids will love to bang on. The tiny pinhead drums sound like higher-pitched bells, whereas the column-type ones have deeper resounding tones. Try the awesome slanted drum on the ground, it's way cool.

Continue on the bayside trail past a cove where school groups come to study mudflat birds. The trail bends right and enters a dry marsh with wild mustard and wild fennel on all sides. At 0.9 mile at the concrete wind gate, turn sharp left heading toward iconic Candlestick Park on a paved trail. Turn left at 1.1 miles and right to come back to the parking lot.

On your way out of Candlestick Point, drive north to Yosemite Slough. This is the exit point of Yosemite Creek, one of San Francisco's springs, into the bay.

Opposite: *Fielding rows of cow parsnips on San Bruno Mountain*

Looking out at the bay from the fishing pier

SAN BRUNO MOUNTAIN STATE PARK

BEFORE YOU GO
Maps: USGS San Francisco South. Free map at the trailhead.
Information: Park office (650) 363-4020 or (650) 363-4021. California State Parks, www.parks.ca.gov

ABOUT THE HIKE
Day hike; Moderate; Year round
3.1 miles, loop
Hiking time: 2–3 hours
High point/elevation gain: 1314 feet/650 feet

GETTING THERE

■ From I-280 southbound, take the Mission Street exit and drive north on Mission Street to Market Street. Turn right and proceed northeast on Market Street, which becomes Guadalupe Canyon Parkway.

■ From I-280 northbound, exit at Eastmoor Avenue. Turn left (north) on Junipero Serra Boulevard and right on San Pedro Road. At the junction with Mission Street, bear right onto Market Street, which becomes Guadalupe Canyon Parkway.

■ Continue up the mountain eastbound and look for the park entrance on your left at the pass. Park at the trailhead parking, on the south side of Guadalupe Canyon Parkway.

■ From US 101, take the Bayshore Boulevard/Brisbane exit. Continue north on Bayshore Boulevard to Guadalupe Canyon Parkway. Turn west on Guadalupe Canyon Parkway toward San Bruno Mountain State Park. The park entrance will be on your right at the pass.

■ There is no public transit.

ON THE TRAIL

Hailed as the park with the best views of San Francisco and the bay, San Bruno Mountain State Park is also the largest open space near the city. Covering more than 3000 acres, the park is also a typical coastal ridgetop where the climate changes abruptly and fog rolls in at a chilling pace. Just layer up, and you will be able to enjoy the quiet trails that lead to these spectacular views.

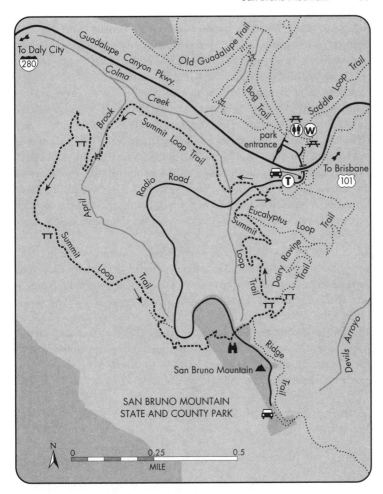

Children with a passion for butterflies should keep an eye out for the mission blue butterfly, an endangered inch-wide butterfly whose wings sport nuances of blues ranging from ice blue on the tip of the wings to deep blue in the center. This butterfly feeds exclusively on lupine bushes, which you'll see lots of on the slopes of San Bruno Mountain.

From the parking lot, follow a dirt path heading right (west) through the native plant garden, and at 0.1 mile turn right on the Summit Loop Trail. This trail goes downhill before crossing Radio Road (there are radio antennas at the summit) and resuming on the other side, close to Colma Creek. Watch for poison oak on these brushy trails. Inside a eucalyptus tree grove, cross a wooden bridge and continue down, following the brook. In the spring, fiddleheads—tender green curled-up ends of native ferns before they unfold—line the trailsides.

Progressing through thick chaparral, the trail goes down until it reaches April Brook, a gurgling seasonal brook; horsetail and cow parsnip thrive along its banks. At 0.6 mile, follow the path as it curves left and starts a steady climb up the mountainside. From this side of the canyon, you get a good idea of what the Bay Area hills would have looked like hundreds of years ago. At 0.8 mile, cross the brook over a bridge and make your way on a drier side that's more eroded, so watch for rocks. A wooden bench allows a small rest stop around 1.5 miles. The path levels out, but you haven't yet reached the summit. Save some energy for the last stretch.

At 1.7 miles, the trail crosses Radio Road again and continues to the summit where a forest of radio antennas awaits you on bare rocks. The good news is, the views are in front of you and don't include the antennas. If the day isn't too windy, it's a fine place to sit down for a picnic lunch. Otherwise, keep going until the trail forks at 2.1 miles and keep straight to stay on the Summit Loop Trail. Follow a series of switchbacks, some steep, down the mountain and end at the junction with the Eucalyptus Loop Trail. Go straight until you find the native plant garden. The parking lot is 0.1 mile to the east.

Enjoy an unbeatable view of downtown San Francisco from San Bruno Mountain.

MORI POINT

GETTING THERE

■ From CA-1 northbound from Pacifica, exit at Sharp Park Road. Turn left on Lundy Way and left again on Sharp Park Road, crossing over CA-1. Turn left (south) on Francisco Boulevard, which becomes Bradford Way as you pass the Sharp Park Municipal Golf Course.

■ Park on Bradford Way next to the Mori Point gate, before Bradford Way curves east back to CA-1.

■ SamTrans buses 110 and 112 stop 0.1 mile away from the trailhead on Bradford Way, and bus 110 connects with Daly City BART station.

ON THE TRAIL

Famous for its surfing spots, Pacifica features small gems like Mori Point and San Pedro Valley County Park, and historical landmarks such as Sweeney Ridge, the Sanchez Adobe, and Milagra Ridge. One of the newest additions to the Golden Gate National Recreation Area, Mori Point protects 110 acres of coastal prairie and riparian habitat above Pacifica's Sharp Park Beach. This is a gorgeous hike on a brisk winter or spring day, followed by hot chocolate to recover from the wind.

This short hike can stop at the beach (1 mile, round-trip) if you want to stay level and enjoy the wondrous sound of waves crashing on this notoriously windy coast. This level stretch is very conducive to a stroller outing, and you can even go up the bluff if you can push the stroller up

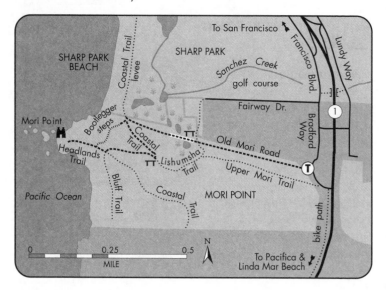

a challenging steep incline. Parking is also available north of Mori Point at the entrance of the golf course.

This walk connects with a popular bike path that goes down the coast to Linda Mar Beach, the most popular surfing spot and a safe beach for kids (Sharp Park Beach is not a safe swimming beach for anyone; people drown there each year). At Linda Mar, kids can also hang out around the Pacifica Skate Park off Crespi Drive and watch acrobatics of skateboarders, young and old.

From Bradford Way, find the gate with a sign indicating Old Mori Road and start your hike past residential houses and eucalyptus trees. Removed from the coastal winds, this section is remarkably quiet except for the noise of traffic driving by and dogs barking. After 0.3 mile, you reach a restoration area near Sanchez Creek with a boardwalk and interpretive signs. Entire hillsides are covered with newly planted native plants, in an effort to restore the original habitat of the native California red-legged frog. Continuing toward the ocean, you walk by several seasonal ponds and notice both wind and wave sound increasing at each step. North of the trail is the Sharp Park Municipal Golf Course.

At 0.5 mile you crest a small bluff and get an outstanding view of Sharp Park Beach. Signs recommend that you stop and listen for the croaking of the red-legged frog. See if you can hear the low-pitched *ribbit-ribbit* of this amphibian.

Make a left on the Coastal Trail and, at the next junction shortly after, a hard right toward Mori Point. At 0.9 mile, you reach the flat top where grassy prairies stretch as far as the cliff's edges. A bench allows you to catch your breath in front of dramatic vistas of Sharp Park Beach. In the spring, carpets of vibrant wildflowers color the bluffs and can be seen as far as

Kids enjoy examining wildflowers on the ocean bluffs at Mori Point.

Point Reyes. To the south stands Mussel Rock and to the north Point Reyes. This point does feel like the edge of a continent, wild and rugged.

From the point, you can retrace your steps the same way or walk down to Sharp Park Beach via the Bootlegger steps, named after the Mori Point Inn that functioned as a speakeasy during Prohibition and for which alcohol arrived by boat directly at the beach. Retrace your steps on Old Mori Road.

13 SAN PEDRO VALLEY COUNTY PARK

BEFORE YOU GO
Maps: USGS Montara. Free brochure with trail map at trailhead.
Information: Park office (650) 363-4020. County of San Mateo, www.co.sanmat eo.ca.us

ABOUT THE HIKE
Day hike; Easy; Year round
0.8 mile, loop
Hiking time: 1–2 hours
High point/elevation gain: 350 feet/100 feet

GETTING THERE
- From I-280, exit at CA-1/Half Moon Bay.
- In Pacifica, turn left (east) onto Linda Mar Boulevard toward the hills.
- When Linda Mar dead-ends into Oddstad Boulevard, turn right and then immediately left into the San Pedro Valley County Park entrance. Park by the nature center.

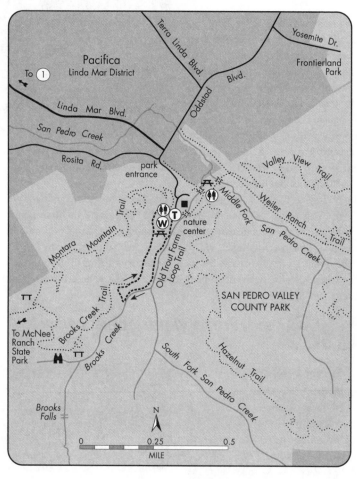

■ SamTrans bus 16 stops at Linda Mar Boulevard and Oddstad.

ON THE TRAIL

San Pedro Valley County Park is one of the nicest surprises on the San Mateo coast, for several reasons. First, tucked at the back of a valley, the park is mostly sunny—a rarity in Pacifica's famously foggy weather. Second, it's just steps away from one of the nicest playgrounds in the Peninsula, Frontierland Park. Families from all over the Peninsula and San Francisco come to enjoy the playground's fort, water features, and open fields. If you need a third reason to visit the San Pedro Valley, en route you pass Sanchez Adobe, the oldest building in San Mateo County and a historic landmark. Add to that the nature center (open on weekends with family programs), great hills for hiking, picnic areas by the creek, and large meadows where deer graze, and you have all the ingredients for a fantastic day out with the kids.

Meandering through lush woods

From the nature center, head south on the Old Trout Farm Loop Trail. Running parallel to the creek, the trail is wide and level, a relaxing amble along the babbling waters of Brooks Creek. Shortly after the trailhead, look for some old tanks on your right. This is where John Gay ran a steelhead trout farm until 1962 when floods washed away his fish farming operation. In the spring, get close to the creek and spot brightly colored adult steelhead trout migrating upstream to spawn. Unlike salmon, these fish can return to the ocean and come back to spawn several years in a row. Brooks Creek merges with the middle fork of Sanchez Creek inside San Pedro Valley County Park and flows down the valley, passing Sanchez Adobe 1 mile downstream.

Willows, horsetail, and blackberry line the sides of the trail. The San Pedro watershed features a lot of native species despite its history of human use. One of the first valleys in the Bay Area to be farmed, San Pedro provided food to the Mission Dolores in San Francisco from the late eighteenth century onward.

At 0.4 mile, the trail passes a gated side road and enters a lush canyon where an old domestic garden used to be. Very quickly the trail bends right to complete a U-turn and traverses Brooks Creek on a bridge. At 0.5 mile, you meet the junction for the trail to Brooks Falls. Though somewhat overgrown with vegetation, the falls trail offers a completely different hike through coastal chaparral with views of the back of the valley. If you still have energy to burn, go for it. The falls will be roughly 0.4 mile up, across from a memorial bench.

Otherwise, simply continue straight on the Brooks Creek Trail and return to the parking area via dense forest of eucalyptus trees.

COYOTE POINT

BEFORE YOU GO
Maps: USGS San Mateo.
Free map at entrance kiosk.
Information: Coyote Point
Recreation Area (650) 573-
2592. County of San Mateo,
www.co.sanmateo.ca.us

ABOUT THE HIKE
Day hike; Moderate; Year round
2.3 miles, loop
Hiking time: 1 hour
**High point/elevation
gain:** 100 feet/100 feet

GETTING THERE

■ From US 101 northbound, exit at Dore Avenue and take an immediate left on North Bayshore Boulevard. Head north toward the Coyote Point Recreation Area park entrance on Coyote Point Drive.

■ From US 101 southbound, exit at Poplar Avenue and turn right onto Humboldt Street. Turn right again onto Peninsula Avenue. Go over the freeway, and then circle around and into the park at Coyote Point Drive.

■ Follow signs east to the parking lot for the Coyote Point Marina.

■ SamTrans provides daily bus service in San Mateo County.

ON THE TRAIL

Once an island separated from the mainland by a salt marsh, Coyote Point was connected to the shore when the marsh was filled for dairy farming in the 1800s. After a short stint as "the Coney Island of the West" in the 1920s, Coyote Point became a merchant marine cadet school, and then a college. Now a 960-acre park, Coyote Point holds CuriOdyssey, the only environmental science education museum on the Peninsula, a hot spot for families who love the aviary and live animal displays. Battered by constant winds, the point is also a locals' favorite for windsurfing, and the proximity to the airport's runways makes it a choice location for plane-spotting. The Bay Trail and the Promenade and Bluff trails add easy and level paths to circumnavigate the park.

From the parking lot next to the Coyote Point Marina/Yacht Club, walk west to get on the Bay Trail. The Poplar Creek Golf Course is on your left. The multi-use paved trail passes eucalyptus groves that give

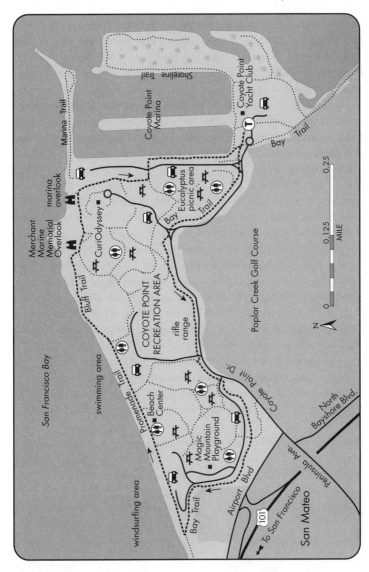

their name to the adjacent picnic area. Farther along on your right, don't be alarmed if you hear gunfire. This is the firing range of the Coyote Point Rifle & Pistol Club. Cross the road and continue on the perimeter of the park.

At 0.5 mile by the double gate right before the entrance kiosk, cross and turn right to remain on the Bay Trail, now lined with recently planted coast live oaks. Across the road stands the Magic Mountain Playground with multi-level slides and buried dragons next to large meadows where wild geese parade.

At 0.9 mile after the Bay Trail skirts the parking lot by the surfing area, make a sharp right on the Promenade Trail and walk toward the rocky outcrop that marks the point. Look at the pilings in the water. Where they stand today, a 468-foot-long pier jutted out into the bay with a 3200-foot boardwalk lining the shore with Ferris wheels, carousels, rides, and restaurants. This was Pacific City, a developers' attempt at rivaling the Santa Cruz Beach Boardwalk—only in San Mateo in 1922. Cold winds and a poor sewage system got the better of the park, which closed in 1923. A lone palm tree is all that remains from Pacific City, remembered on a bronze marker after the Beach Center by a bench.

At 1.3 miles at the end of the beach, continue on the Bluff Trail. Overlooking rocky coves, you climb through eucalyptus trees and mixed chaparral. Pay attention to poison oak, growing abundantly along the trail. Near the top at 1.7 miles, the Merchant Marine Memorial Overlook is a perfect place to sit and relax above the bay. Ask your children to find the eagle and anchor insignia of the merchant marine. The Bluff Trail continues straight toward CuriOdyssey and the marina overlook. This platform is a great spot for watching migratory birds in the spring.

At 2 miles, the trail angles right to come down to marina level on a gently graded path, still lined with tall eucalyptus trees. The white

Pickleweed and mudflats from the Shoreline Trail

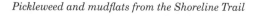

tower in the marina is all that remains from a training building used by the merchant marine to simulate loading and unloading of ships. By the water's edge, peek into the depths. If you are lucky in the spring and early summer, you will see bat sting rays flapping their wings along the water of the harbor. They feed on crustaceans and crabs.

The parking lot is straight ahead. For a short side excursion, turn left on the Shoreline Trail at the end of the parking lot to explore what remains of the original salt marsh.

CuriOdyssey

This multi-level nature and science museum is known throughout the Bay Area for the quality of its environmental education programs and exhibits. From the natural science exhibits to the wildlife habitats or the outdoor netted aviary, CuriOdyssey (curiodyssey.org) is a place where you can spend many hours without realizing it. Check its daily animal programs and special events.

 FITZGERALD MARINE RESERVE/PILLAR POINT BLUFF

BEFORE YOU GO
Maps: USGS Montara Mountain and Half Moon Bay. Trail map of Pillar Point Bluff posted at trailhead.
Information: James V. Fitzgerald Marine Reserve (650) 728-3584. County of San Mateo, www.co.sanmat eo.ca.us. Peninsula Open, Space Trust. www.openspace trust.org

ABOUT THE HIKE
Day hike; Moderate; Year round
3.5 miles, round-trip
Hiking time: 2–3 hours
High point/elevation gain: 140 feet/140 feet

GETTING THERE
■ From CA-1 in Moss Beach, head west on California Avenue. The James V. Fitzgerald Marine Reserve parking lot is at the end of the road by the ocean.
■ The reserve can be reached via a combination of Caltrain (Hillsdale station is the closest) and SamTrans buses (bus 294 runs down the coast from San Francisco).

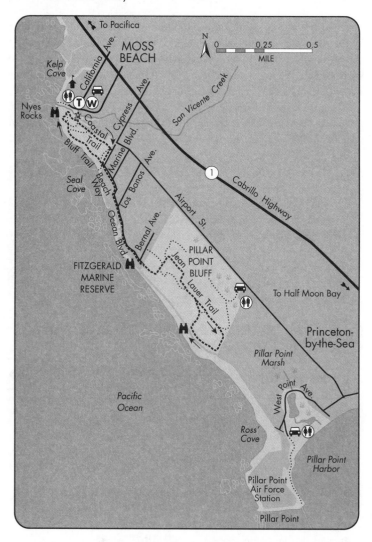

ON THE TRAIL

Windswept Pillar Point Bluff overlooks Pillar Point Harbor and the world-famous reefs where the Mavericks surfing competition takes place. A few miles up the coast, kids from all over the Bay Area come to the James V. Fitzgerald Marine Reserve to observe marine wildlife at the tidepools. Looking for sunflower starfish, green anemones, or purple sea urchins, children lose track of time when searching for the next cool intertidal creature on the reefs. Plan your hike around low tides so you enjoy the best of the tidepools as well as spectacular ocean vistas.

Allow at least an hour for tidepool exploration. The James V. Fitzgerald Marine Reserve Ranger Station carries activity books and field guides for all ages.

Tidepooling at the James Fitzgerald Marine Reserve

From the marine reserve parking lot, find the trail that starts behind the restroom across North Lake Street. A metal bridge crosses lush San Vicente Creek over to a Monterey cypress grove. Lined with horsetail and blackberry bushes, the sand-and-dirt trail dips before turning left. Make another left at the junction to follow the edge of the grove on a level dirt path. This trail is scheduled to become part of the Coastal Trail. At 0.7 mile, turn right onto Cypress Avenue, heading toward the ocean. At the base of Cypress Avenue, the Seal Cove stairs lead to a sandy beach. The road curves left and becomes Beach Way.

Following Beach Way as it becomes Marine Boulevard, you reach the parking lot for the Moss Beach Distillery. Cross the lot and continue on Ocean Boulevard, a partially collapsed road closed to cars after the 1989 earthquake. Now impassable to cars, it's totally safe for pedestrians and the cracked pavement surface is fun for kids. Continue along the Ocean Boulevard oceanside, past local homes, some decorated with a special coastal touch. At 1.4 miles at the junction with Bernal Avenue, the trail for Pillar Point Bluff begins.

Turn left toward the Santa Cruz Mountains and right (south) at the next junction, heading south. This trail merges with a wide dirt service road called the Jean Lauer Trail, a portion of the California Coastal Trail dedicated to Jean Lauer, former manager of the Peninsula Open Space Trust. From the top of the bluff, you can see Pillar Point Harbor to the south, a thriving fishing harbor where you can get fresh fish off the boats every day. A mile out in the ocean is the daredevil spot where the famous Mavericks surf contest takes place on big-wave winter days (www.maverickssurf.com).

At 1.9 miles, the path bends right and turns around to come back on the bluff closer to the ocean's edge. Expect breathtaking views, and maybe a few quail, snakes, and cottontail rabbits. Follow the path uphill to come back to the Jean Lauer Trail and retrace your steps along the same route. At the junction of Beach and Cypress, hike along the Bluff Trail to approach the beach from above.

For other local explorations, the Pillar Point Marsh is located at the northwestern edge of Pillar Point Harbor off West Point Avenue and is a great spot for bird-watching.

WINDY HILL OPEN SPACE PRESERVE

BEFORE YOU GO
Maps: USGS Mindego Hill. Free map at the trailhead.
Information: Midpeninsula Regional Open Space District (650) 691-1200. www.open space.org

ABOUT THE HIKE
Day hike; Easy/Moderate; Year round
1.4 miles, round-trip
Hiking time: 1 hour
High point/elevation gain: 730 feet/130 feet

GETTING THERE

■ From I-280 in Palo Alto, take the Alpine Road exit. Go southwest on Alpine Road for 3 miles.

■ Turn right on Portola Road and go straight for 1 mile. The Windy Hill Open Space Preserve east entrance is on the left.

■ SamTrans public transit stops 0.2 mile from this trailhead at Portola and Grove.

ON THE TRAIL

Covering 1335 acres on the east side of the Santa Cruz Mountains, from the ridge to the Silicon Valley, Windy Hill is named after the breezy bald hilltops along Skyline Boulevard. In fact, they may be the best place to fly a kite on any given day. However, on very windy days you can still enjoy Windy Hill by venturing to the eastern access point of the park down in Portola Valley.

Indeed, the lower reaches of this preserve provide a sharp contrast to the windy top, offering sheltered wooded slopes and a pond. Though bordering a retirement community and close to residential areas, this part of the preserve is surprisingly quiet. You might still hear the distant roar

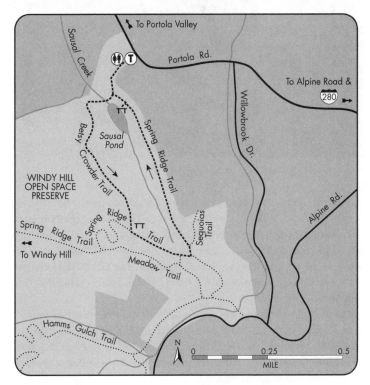

of civilization, but you will not see a single man-made structure—apart from when you walk along the retirement community. On hot days, the trails are sufficiently shaded that you won't get too hot. But the real beauty of this hike is how gentle the slopes are. This factor makes the route perfect for a stroller hike and a moderate workout, or for a beginner junior hiker.

From the parking lot, go straight up the paved path and turn right at 0.1 mile on the Betsy Crowder Trail. Past a gate, a flat path meanders between oak and bay trees. Still under generous tree cover, the trail starts ascending at a moderate pace up the hill. At any moment you may encounter small rodents, deer, or even coyote. Just stay still and make no noise; they will eventually walk away. This trail is also open to equestrian access, so be ready to share the path. Springtime displays wonderful wildflowers, while summers are dark green and white with flowering buckeye trees, and autumn and winter cover the trails with fallen leaves that crunch underfoot.

Shady trails and meadows at Windy Hill

After the trail breaks out on a large meadow, you reach the memorial bench dedicated to Betsy Crowder, the board director of the Midpeninsula Regional Open Space District. Past the next gate at 0.7 mile, turn left on the Spring Ridge Trail, a wide service road. At 0.9 mile, turn left toward Sausal Pond. This wide trail is bordered by tall thistles and coyote bush. Going down, the path follows wooden fences, remnants from former ranching days.

As the road levels out and you walk along the retirement community, keep an eye out on the left for the first glimpse of Sausal Pond through tule reeds. The thick blanket on the pond is azolla, a native fern that turns from green to red to brown. Rich in protein, it's a favorite food of the visiting waterfowl. You can access the pond's shore at the northern end through a small dirt trail and look at the small overlapping scales of azolla.

When you get at the next intersection, turn right and retrace your steps to the parking lot.

SAUSAL POND AND SAUSAL CREEK

Sausal Pond is fed by the waters of Sausal Creek; both get their name from the Spanish word for willow grove. Along its open course, Sausal Creek is sporadically lined with willow trees. The name "sausal" has been used throughout the Bay Area town of Sausalito where willow groves grew around its springs. Sausal Creek is one of twenty-four tributaries of the San Francisquito watershed, but as frequently happens when towns get built, the creek was buried and now runs mostly underground. In a controversial community effort, the creek is to be partially daylighted (brought back to the surface) in downtown Portola Valley.

SKYLINE RIDGE OPEN SPACE PRESERVE

BEFORE YOU GO
Maps: USGS Mindego Hill.
Free map at trailhead.
Information: Midpeninsula
Regional Open Space District
(650) 691-1200. www.open
space.org

ABOUT THE HIKE
Day hike; Easy; Spring,
Summer, Fall
0.5 mile, loop
Hiking time: 30 minutes–1
hour
**High point/elevation
gain:** 1000 feet/50 feet

GETTING THERE

- From the intersection of Skyline Boulevard (CA-35) and Page Mill/Alpine Road south of Palo Alto, take Alpine Road straight across Skyline and after 100 yards, park at the large lot designated for the Russian Ridge Open Space Preserve and the Skyline Ridge Open Space Preserve.

- There is no public transit.

ON THE TRAIL

One of the best-kept secrets of the Santa Cruz Mountains, this wheelchair- and stroller-accessible trail loops around a lovely pond that harbors hundreds of underwater plants and animals. When it is open (from spring through autumn), the fantastic David C. Daniels Nature Center is a place for kids to experiment with imaginative exhibits on the local environment. This hike is definitely an opportunity to see local wildlife and get a sense of pond creatures.

From the parking lot, descend to the Ipiwa Trail, a gently graded dirt trail, and a wooden sign for the David C. Daniels Nature Center. Proceed to a tunnel that goes underneath Alpine Road where voices resonate particularly well. On the other side of the tunnel, you emerge into the Skyline Ridge Open Space Preserve and the views open up on wooded hillsides with coyote brush and live oak. To find out what kind of wildlife you are likely to encounter, stop at the WILDLIFE YOU MAY SEE sign and point out to your children the various fish, mammals, birds, and crustaceans.

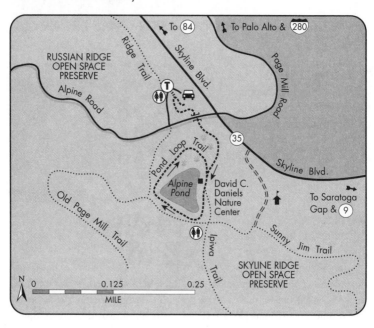

At 0.1 mile, reach Alpine Pond, a bean-shaped reflection of the skies above surrounded by cattail, tule reeds, and willows. Picnic tables grace meadows next to the nature center. The best place to start your exploration is the floating observation platform to the right of the entrance. Look for bluegills swishing in the middle of the mossy clusters swaying underwater. Closer to moisture-loving plants you might spot different species of dragonflies. Have your children see if they can tell the patterns of the bodies and wings apart. Some are spotted, some are not. Some have red bodies, others have blue wings. On the water surface, you might see cormorants gliding. Nature observation doesn't get more hands-on.

Follow the Pond Loop Trail on the left side of the nature center to walk around the pond clockwise. Wide and level, this loop is a pure delight and will lead to many a bug or bird encounter. After the restrooms at 0.2 mile, follow the trail to a wooden gate and find another wooden platform facing the one you were on from the other side of the pond. See if you can scan pond life beyond the tules and willows.

At 0.3 mile after the gate, cross a wooden bridge above the stream that feeds the pond, and keep going straight on the wide trail. After

you find a bench on your right, go down the small path to an opening to watch little pockets of pond life through tule reeds up close. Look for tadpoles and diving beetles.

At 0.4 mile, you are back at the nature center. Retrace your steps back to the parking lot.

Hopping on the boardwalk at Alpine Pond

DAVID C. DANIELS NATURE CENTER

The nature center is open to the public on the weekends seasonally, April through mid-November. Check www.openspace.org for hours. Offering environmental education exhibits for preschool to school-age children, the center features a giant wall puzzle entitled "Build a Pond Community" where children can move shapes around on a giant pond backdrop. Other highlights include pond life mobiles and skulls and skins to touch, plus a special vivarium with a resident gopher snake.

 PESCADERO MARSH NATURAL PRESERVE

BEFORE YOU GO
Map: USGS San Gregorio.
Information: Ranger office (650) 879-2170. California State Parks, www.parks.ca.gov

ABOUT THE HIKE
Day hike; Easy; Year round
2.4 miles, round-trip
Hiking time: 1–2 hours
High point/elevation gain: 50 feet/50 feet

GETTING THERE

■ From CA-1 southbound after Half Moon Bay or northbound after Davenport, turn west on CA-1 at the first parking lot for Pescadero State Beach and Marsh, just after the bridge over Pescadero Creek.

■ From CA-1 northbound, the parking lot is not the one right across from Pescadero Road but the one just after it on the left, before the bridge.

■ Pescadero Marsh is accessible by SamTrans coastal bus 17. Check BART connections with SamTrans buses at San Mateo stations.

ON THE TRAIL

Sprawling from the Pacific Ocean up the estuary of the Butano and Pescadero creeks, the Pescadero Marsh Natural Preserve encompasses 235 acres of protected wetland that provide an important wintering ground for waterfowl on the Pacific flyway. On any given visit you could see great blue herons, snowy egrets, gadwalls, and up to sixty different varieties of birds. The proximity of the wild San Mateo coast beaches and the quaint farming town of Pescadero make this hike part of a full and fun family day trip on the coast. Bring binoculars to better observe the birds, and layer up to withstand coastal winds. Spring is nesting season for great blue herons in eucalyptus trees and winter sees ducks and waterfowl overwintering in the marsh. Two other trails explore the

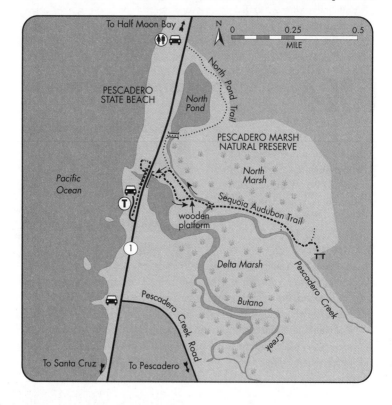

northern and southern ends of the marsh but this one leads you directly to the heart of the marsh along a nature trail and provides safe splashing opportunities by the lagoon.

From the parking area, walk south to find wooden stairs at the sign for guided walks and turn north on CA-1 to cross the bridge. After the bridge at 0.2 mile, turn left to walk down a few steps to the beach. Follow the TRAIL sign pointing left to cross the beach and go under the bridge— an area where you might have to carve your way through driftwood (fort building opportunity!). The brutal pounding of the ocean waves gives way to a quiet sandy lagoon where kids like to run barefooted. This area is a play zone for harbor seals so keep your eyes peeled for shiny black heads sticking out of the water.

Find a sandy path on the left and follow it to a trail sign leading you through the sand dunes. At 0.35 mile, turn right at the first interpretive panel to get onto the Sequoia Audubon Trail. This portion hugs the sandy lagoon closely before trailing off to the left at a fork at 0.45 mile toward a wooden platform. As you reach the platform leading to North Pond at 0.5 mile, continue on the Sequoia Audubon Trail to the right. This open trail through low coastal plants uses elevated levee tops that separate North Pond and North Marsh from most tidal influences of the lagoon. However as you reach a wide culvert (big drain) at 0.6 mile, notice how Pescadero Creek is connected to the North Marsh so sediment moves along down the lagoon. Thanks to exchange mechanisms like this one, the Pescadero Marsh has been restored from dirt filled agricultural land in the 1980s to a healthy wetland.

Scan the North Marsh for egrets and herons and the creek for ducks. As you go further inland along the creek, interpretive signs explain the flora and fauna of this habitat. Eucalyptus

The lagoon is a popular place to spot harbor seals.

trees start lining the trail. At 0.7 mile, a huge eucalyptus tree spreads its branches sideways off the trail and its lower levels provide an exciting opportunity for tree climbing—or a picnic in a tree.

Keep going and notice how the vegetation is morphing into coastal chaparral with the appearance of mugwort, poison hemlock, stinging nettles, and soon, poison oak. After the sign on garter snakes around 0.9 mile, look for a discreet side trail on the right. It goes down the levee to a cove on the creek with benches to observe western pond turtles.

Back on the trail, continue eastward. The trail is now a green corridor completely sheltered from the wind and bordered by willows and blackberry brambles. Look out for poison oak, growing more densely toward the end of the trail. At 1.1 miles, the trail goes up the hill to a bench where you can sit and enjoy the views. Retrace your steps on the same trail. For a diversion at the end, cross the platform toward the North Pond at 1.9 miles and follow the channel along ice plant edges (good for tumbling). At 2.1 miles, turn left toward the bridge on CA-1 and retrace your steps to the parking lot.

19 BUTANO STATE PARK

BEFORE YOU GO
Maps: USGS Franklin Point. Free map at the park entrance.
Information: Park office (650) 879-2040. California State Parks, www.parks.ca.gov

ABOUT THE HIKE
Day hike; Moderate/Difficult; Spring, Summer, Fall
4.5 miles, loop
Hiking time: 3–4 hours
High point/elevation gain: 680 feet/400 feet

GETTING THERE

▪ From CA-1 near Pescadero, turn east on Pescadero Creek Road and drive 2.5 miles to Cloverdale Road.

▪ Turn right (south) on Cloverdale Road and drive 4.5 miles to the Butano State Park entrance. Continue past the entrance kiosk and park at the picnic area parking lot on your right.

▪ There is no public transit.

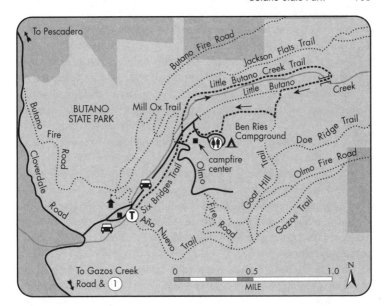

ON THE TRAIL

This cool green canyon lined with lush ferns and redwoods is one of the beautiful landscapes of Butano State Park, a 3500-acre park that spreads from a coastal creek to dry uplands with sweeping vistas featuring an abandoned airfield next to the trail camp. Expect newts and banana slugs (see sidebar in Hike 3) along the trail, as well as a few challenging climbs well rewarded once you reach the creek. If you want to make this a weekend adventure, the campground among the redwoods is very popular with families. Closely following Butano Creek, the trail may be inaccessible due to winter rains, so check the trail status before the hike.

From the parking lot, look left (east) for the Six Bridges Trail, a narrow dirt path that dips between rows of bushes and crosses the first bridge almost right away. The path rises to trace the edges of the canyon before coming down and crossing a second bridge. As you reach maintenance cabins, cross the road and find the trail opposite, rising again steeply. After a fairly level stroll, you come back down the hill with cathedral-type views of the redwood canyon, reaching Olmo Fire Road.

Turn left (west) on Olmo Fire Road and right (east) on the main road, crossing to the north side where your next trail starts. After the Mill Ox Trail at 1 mile, a sign indicates the Little Butano Creek Trail on the left.

Turn left on this level trail that follows the creek upstream for the next 1.5 miles, crossing from side to side.

At 1.1 miles at the first bridge, notice the redwood shoots at the base of existing trees. Redwoods grow all around the creek, enjoying the area's moisture and deep rich soil. Here they can spread their shallow root systems and catch underground water easily. At 1.3 miles, two redwood trees fell across the trail and were cut to provide access. Can you tell where their roots are? You will pass several hollowed-out stumps, each of them a fun treehouse for children.

Several bridges cross the creek, keeping you in close proximity to the creek bed. At 2 miles the trail leaves the creek to climb up to the drier reaches of the canyon. Several hundred feet above the creek, you should watch your children, as the trail is very close to a steep drop. At 2.3 miles, the trail descends to the creek level and ends next to a water pumping station.

Cross Little Butano Creek on a wide bridge and start a long uphill climb on a maintenance road. After a water tank at 2.8 miles, turn left on the Goat Hill Trail, a narrow dirt path that cuts across the canyon sides. At 2.9 miles, turn right at the junction signed To Campground. A wooden fence and steps lead you into the park's Ben Ries Campground, a local family favorite. Turn right on the paved road to exit the campground and left at the gate for the campfire center.

Walk past the campfire center on the Six Bridges Trail, a level path that meanders gently on needle-covered ground, passes the Ed Pollak

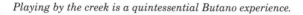

Playing by the creek is a quintessential Butano experience.

Family Grove, and descends the hill on wooden steps overlooking Olmo Fire Road. Cross the bridge and turn left on Olmo Fire Road at 3.8 miles to find the Six Bridges Trail. Turn right and retrace your steps to the parking lot.

WHAT'S NEWTS?

An aquatic salamander, newts are one of the highlights at Butano State Park during rainy months. Orange bellied and 5 to 8 inches long, newts are cute—but refrain from picking them up, as they can secrete a deadly toxin that keeps them safe from most predators. During winter, their breeding season, newts come down from Butano's hills to find a mate in slow-moving pools around Little Butano Creek—by way of the road, if it comes to that. This romantic migration explains the signs posted throughout the park about slowing for newt crossings.

 PIGEON POINT

BEFORE YOU GO
Maps: USGS Pigeon Point to Franklin Point. Free map at the park.
Information: Visitor center (650) 879-2120. California State Parks www.parks.ca.gov

ABOUT THE HIKE
Day hike; Easy; Spring, Fall, Winter
0.5 mile, round-trip
Hiking time: 30 minutes
High point/elevation gain: 50 feet/minimal

GETTING THERE
- From CA-1 southbound in Half Moon Bay, drive 20 miles to Pigeon Point Light Station State Historic Park.
- From CA-1 northbound in Santa Cruz, drive 27 miles to Pigeon Point Light Station State Historic Park.
- Turn west on Pigeon Point Road and park by the lighthouse entrance.
- There is no public transit.

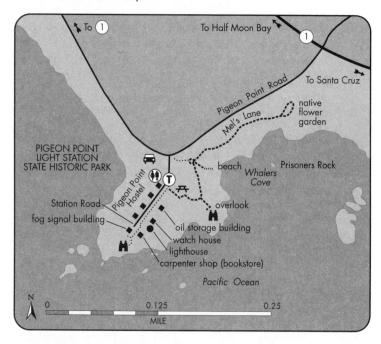

ON THE TRAIL

The Pigeon Point lighthouse is one of the landmarks you can't miss when driving up and down this stretch of coast, and this short hike will get you acquainted with the maritime history of this area. Built in 1872 to guide mariners through treacherous seas, the lighthouse is now a historical park, and the buildings host a youth hostel popular with travelers and families. The Fresnel lens is lighted once a year during an annual celebration held on the Saturday closest to November 15.

Before you start this short hike, walk past the lighthouse and the fog signal building and take your children to a viewing platform over the ocean. Look out closely, and if binoculars are hanging on the fence, use them to see if you can spot a colony of harbor seals lounging around on the rocks or playing in the water. Right above the platform lies the skeleton of a blue whale's head—always fun to watch—and the fog signal building features video presentations on the lighthouse.

To start the hike, walk on the public walkway (Station Road) 200 yards and find a trail heading southeast to a platform overlook. At 400 yards, the overlook embraces panoramic views of the light station complex. Walk north around the cove to go through the white picket fence at the information board. Mel's Lane is an easy sand path that follows the coastline above dramatic Prisoners Rock—named for the fishermen who got trapped by rising tides and took refuge on this rocky island—anchored in the middle of Whalers Cove.

Whalers Cove provides a fun cove to play in after the hike.

The trail follows a fence overlooking Whalers Cove, a sheltered beach that almost became the site of a two-story motel. After 0.25 mile, the trail circles around a small native flower garden. Retrace your steps toward the light station.

The hike wouldn't be complete without a visit to the beach, the very reason why Mel's Lane was created on land purchased to protect this stretch of coast. Go down the log steps. From the beach below, the view of the lighthouse takes on another dimension. South of the beach is a big split rock where tunneling waters create a perfect play lagoon for kids. North of the beach, children will find tidepools and their favorite tidepool animals—mussels, crabs, and sea anemones, just to name a few.

 WILBUR'S WATCH

BEFORE YOU GO
Maps: USGS Pigeon Point to Franklin Point. Trail map posted at trailhead.
Information: Peninsula Open Space Trust, www.openspacetrust.org

ABOUT THE HIKE
Day hike; Easy/Moderate; Spring, Fall, Winter
2 miles, round-trip
Hiking time: 1 hour
High point/elevation gain: 360 feet/260 feet

GETTING THERE

■ From CA-1 southbound in Half Moon Bay, drive 20 miles to Pigeon Point Light Station State Historic Park, 5 miles south of Pescadero. Immediately across from the lighthouse, turn left onto

Pigeon Point Road and follow as it curves around to the right. You'll see the ramp to the parking area on your left 0.8 mile from the CA-1 junction.

■ From CA-1 northbound in Santa Cruz, drive 27 miles to Pigeon Point Road, 0.5 mile before Pigeon Point Light Station State Historic Park. Turn right on Pigeon Point Road and park at the ramp to the parking area, 0.2 mile from the CA-1 junction.

■ There is no public transit.

ON THE TRAIL

For unbeatable views, a mild effort, and with a telescope for whale-watching on clear winter and spring days, Wilbur's Watch is a winner. Don't forget to bring a snack to share on the benches at the top. The views will make you want to stay a while, and kids just can't resist the telescope. Wilbur's Watch was named after Colburn Wilbur, who served as the executive director of the Packard Foundation for almost twenty-five years, helping to protect thousands of acres of land from the California coast to the Sierra Nevada.

From the parking lot, the trail begins as a grassy path heading south above CA-1 before it bends sharply and starts to rise. Coastal chaparral surrounds you with low bushes of coyote brush, coffeeberry, sticky monkey flowers, and poison oak.

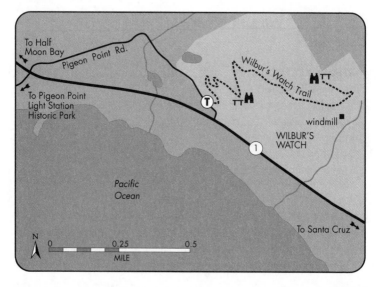

Enjoying the views from the top of Wilbur's Watch

After 0.1 mile, you look down on a pond that's part of the Cloverdale Coastal Ranches. Though it looks entirely natural today, the livestock pond was choked by vegetation that created unhealthy conditions for the California red-legged frog and the San Francisco garter snake. After restoration efforts, it is now a healthy wildlife home again.

Continue your steady ascent. Just before 0.2 mile, the trail brings you to a bench from which you can enjoy views of the coastline and a taste of the local winds.

From here the trail, though sometimes overgrown with grasses, continues uphill, bending left (north) as a wide service road. At 0.3 mile, the trail turns right (east) on a moderate-grade slope. Gaining elevation on the hill, you are now crossing a coastal prairie, away from the traffic noise.

The trail goes over several stone culverts channeling winter rains downhill, and if your kids pay attention, they will probably find scat and tracks (the latter, after rains) of the animals roaming these lands.

After a long, straight stretch, the trail curves left at 0.8 mile in sight of a windmill and finally reaches the overlook at 1 mile. A semicircular arrangement of benches, interpretive signs, and binoculars invite a well-deserved rest. Check the signs to identify the various natural landmarks of the coast, from the Año Nuevo State Reserve to Pigeon Point Light Station State Historic Park. Get children in front of the big binoculars to scan the seas for migrating whales spouting along their coastal route.

Retrace your steps to the parking lot.

AÑO NUEVO STATE RESERVE

BEFORE YOU GO
Maps: USGS Año Nuevo.
Free map at the visitor center.
Information: Año Nuevo
State Reserve (650) 879-
2025. www.anonuevo.org

ABOUT THE HIKE
Day hike; Moderate; Spring,
Winter
3 miles, round-trip
Hiking time: 2–3 hours
**High point/elevation
gain:** 50 feet/50 feet

GETTING THERE

- On CA-1 southbound from Half Moon Bay, drive roughly 30 miles to the Año Nuevo State Reserve park entrance, on the right.
- On CA-1 northbound from Santa Cruz, drive roughly 19 miles to the Año Nuevo State Reserve park entrance, on the left.
- Turn west into the park, and park by the visitor center.
- There is no public transit.

ON THE TRAIL

Año Nuevo State Reserve is synonymous with elephant seals, the largest seals anywhere on the California coast—the best swimmers, too. Thousands of these massive mammals congregate at Año Nuevo in the winter to breed their young, coming all the way from Hawaii and the Aleutian Islands. The point was named New Year's Point on January 3, 1603, by the diarist of the expedition of Spanish explorer Sebastián Vizcaíno. It is one of the oldest place-names in California.

This hike is best done between December 15 and April 1 when mating occurs and pups are born. During that season, you will need to reserve guided walks to see the animals (www.reserveamerica.com). The views and explanations are well worth the two-and-a-half-hour tour, and children emerge from the reserve amazed. From April 1 to December 1, you can visit at your own pace after obtaining a free permit at the visitor center to witness the molting of elephant seals and their fall haulout. The park is closed from December 1 through 15, to allow pregnant females and males to arrive on the beach and form harems. Note that for safety reasons, nobody is allowed to stand closer than 25 feet to elephant seals.

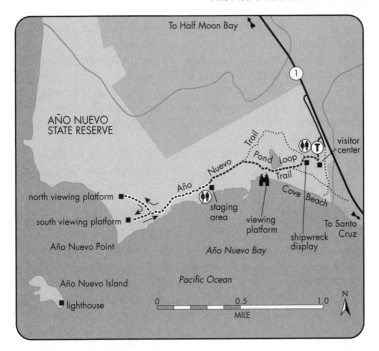

From the visitor center, take a right on the Año Nuevo Trail, a level dirt trail that bends left after 100 yards. At 0.05 mile, the shipwrecked *Point Arena* schooner display is a powerful silent testimony to the dangerous waters around the point. At 0.15 mile, bear left to continue on the Pond Loop Trail and stop at the viewing platform in front of the pond. It's a great spot for bird-watching, and you will see various gull varieties and brown pelicans. At 0.4 mile, your trail merges with the Año Nuevo Trail, turns to sand, and goes straight to a grove of Monterey pines and the staging area for all guided walks at 0.75 mile. Restrooms are on your left. If you are visiting during the season for guided walks and you don't have a reservation, this is your turn-around point.

During permit season, proceed on the Año Nuevo Trail, now heading decidedly for the sea by way of tall sand dunes. Note the sign WILD ELEPHANT SEALS—STAY BACK 25 FEET. If you are lucky to see elephant seals on your visit, do not underestimate their speed or how dangerous they can be. Especially at mating season, males are battle-ready and battle-sized—think 5000 to 6000 pounds with one thing on their minds:

reaching the object of their desire. Keep children close to you and save that wild animal photo op for a more sedate setting.

At 1.2 miles, walk past a bench and cross a boardwalk before entering dune territory. Keep going straight, and at 1.4 miles bear right (follow the fence posts) to reach the north viewing platform above the beach. Look for Año Nuevo Island, once a peninsula, now isolated and home to seals and birds. The ruins you see are remains of the lighthouse that saved lives until 1948.

Turn around and walk back on the trail to the next junction at 1.6 miles on your right, to reach the south viewing platform. Retrace your steps to the trailhead.

ELEPHANT SEALS

How about some fun facts about the elephant seals? These animals live 90 percent of their lives underwater. Females can dive to a mile deep during 30 minutes. During the pup feeding period (28 days), moms lose one-third of their weight. Males only eat 180 days a year. Females live 20 years, males up to 14. Elephant seal pups weigh 60 pounds.

Opposite: *Kids explore rocky boulders along the creek in the Little Yosemite area of Sunol Wilderness.*

Looking down at elephant seals on the beach

ALBANY BULB

BEFORE YOU GO
Map: USGS Richmond.
Information: City of Albany
Parks & Recreation (510) 524-
9283. www.albanyca.org

ABOUT THE HIKE
Day hike; Easy/Moderate;
Year round
1.3 miles, round-trip
Hiking time: 1 hour or less
**High point/elevation
gain:** 50 feet/50 feet

GETTING THERE

- From I-80 northbound in Berkeley or southbound from Richmond, exit at Buchanan Street and go west toward the waterfront.
- From I-580 east, exit at Albany and turn right onto Buchanan Street toward the waterfront.
- Park at the lot for the Bay Trail, across from an entrance to Eastshore State Park.
- The closest BART stations are El Cerrito and North Berkeley. AC Transit bus 25 stops at Buchanan and Pierce, 0.5 mile from the trailhead.

ON THE TRAIL

On an artificial waterfront peninsula jutting out in the bay lies the most unexpected guerrilla art adventure. In a "Mad Max meets Bay Nature" style, the Albany Bulb offers an unorganized outdoor art display that will rock your socks off. The phenomenon started in 1998 when an urban art collective called Sniff started painting large, imaginative murals and erecting driftwood sculptures on the northwest end of the Bulb. In quintessential Bay Area fashion, materials used were repurposed industrial debris or trash. The unique carnivalesque or absurd result is striking, and kids love the craziness of it all.

Haphazardly, the art structures populated the lonely shore. Some were destroyed by natural elements, others removed by vandals, but it seems that the Bulb's art organically regenerates thanks to local art students and local vagabonds. Yes, the Bulb is also home to roughly fifty transients whose tents you might see in the bushes.

Because of the potentially unsafe nature of the materials used in the sculptures, you'll want to watch little hands when you bring young

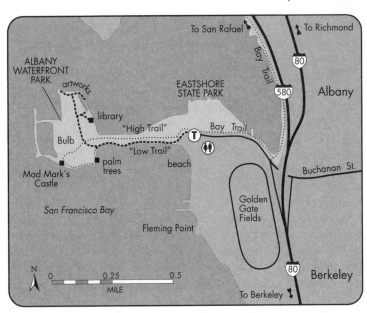

children to the area. Older kids may bring along a sketchbook and come back home with inspiration for their own creation. To extend the experience, drive down a couple of miles to the Berkeley Marina and sign up your children for a few hours at the Adventure Playground (www .ci.berkeley.ca.us) where kids are encouraged to build and paint their own play equipment.

From the parking lot, get on the paved path right of the herons sculpture, heading toward the beach. This is a good spot to watch kite-surfers on windy days. At 0.1 mile, the path angles right, by a half-buried horseshoe-shaped wall, and reaches a circular plaza with benches and signs indicating bay landmarks. Continue on the

Weird art sprouts as artists come by at the Albany Bulb.

trail and turn left to follow the bay on a level dirt road. On the hillsides amid acacias and wild fennel you start seeing paintings on random concrete blocks.

The straight stretch along the bay takes you up a planted dune at 0.4 mile, with palm trees and reeds gracing the shores. Go over the hill and turn right at 0.5 mile, then left and right again down toward the shore on a gentle slope. Out of the blue, a metal female figure appears at the end of the path. With her hands stretched out, she's been compared to a female messiah. At 0.65 mile, this is it! This is where the art happens. To your left (west) are a dragon and a knight, two smoking samurais, and little creatures near the shore. Find the big seesaw for some playground fun next to the dragon.

If you explore the other corner, you'll find big murals, ephemeral sculptures, and mudflats green with pickleweed. Retrace your steps on the same path and look for a LIBRARY sign on the left. It leads you to a collection of used books in a treehouse, in front of other art installations and a Hammond organ. Feel free to contribute to the book collection.

Retrace your steps to the parking lot.

 LAKE TEMESCAL RECREATION AREA

BEFORE YOU GO	ABOUT THE HIKE
Maps: USGS Oakland East. Free map at trailhead. **Information:** East Bay Regional Park District (888) 327-2757, option 3, extension 4555. www.ebparks.com	Day hike; Easy/Moderate; Spring, Summer, Fall **1 mile, loop** **Hiking time:** 1 hour or less **High point/elevation gain:** 300 feet/200 feet

GETTING THERE

- From CA-24 eastbound in Oakland, take the Broadway Terrace exit toward CA-13. Turn right into the parking lot for Lake Temescal Recreation Area.

- The park can be reached with a combination of BART and buses.

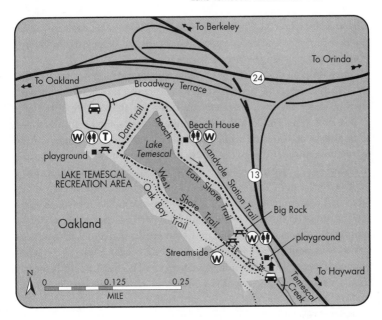

ON THE TRAIL

One of the most popular swimming destinations in the Bay Area, Lake Temescal Recreation Area boasts a sandy beach, two renovated playgrounds, and large meadows for family gatherings. Primarily a hot spot for the preschool set, Lake Temescal benefits from the East Bay's summer sun when San Francisco is all fogged in.

Created when Temescal Creek was dammed in 1870, the 13-acre lake is stocked with fish, and locals come here to cast a line along the tranquil shores. Surprisingly for an urban park bordered by a freeway, Lake Temescal is an oasis of green and relatively quiet.

From the parking lot, get on the dirt path that runs along the lawn area and merges with the paved Dam Trail, aptly named after the thick dam you are walking on. Herds of wild mustangs were used to compact the tons of dirt that were brought in to create the dam in 1868. The dam is 600 feet long, 16 feet wide, and rises 105 feet above the creek.

At the northern edge of the lake at 0.1 mile, the trail turns right (east). Above you are the tracks of the Sacramento Northern Railroad, now the Landvale Station Trail. This 1910s interurban railway connected Sacramento to Chico with Bay Area extensions. It even ran on the Bay Bridge to end in downtown San Francisco, competing with ferry lines to carry passengers across the bay.

Turn right on the East Shore Trail, a wide paved path heading toward the Beach House. This historic stone structure of Craftsman design, with three arching doorways, perfectly captures the spirited life of the pre-WWII Bay Area. Think about the streetcars transporting crowds to set up blankets on the sand while swimmers waded in body-hugging wool jersey tank suits. If you go today, the Beach House has changing booths and showers at beach level and reception rooms with fireplaces upstairs.

The East Shore Trail continues along the lake, bordered by valley oaks, willows, and reeds. Platform and picnic tables provide serene resting stops on the trail. At 0.4 mile, the path reaches large meadows planted with trees. Stop in front of the ranger station and look for cracks in the pavement. You should find parallel lines over a few yards. Without realizing it, you've been hiking along the Hayward Fault. Interpretive signs tell you more about this fault and earthquake activity.

Continue east and cross Temescal Creek on one of the two bridges to start your return route. From here, there are three choices. If you have a stroller, you may want to retrace your steps on the East Shore Trail, as it is paved and level. If you are looking for a workout, the Oak Bay Trail rises on a ridge above the lake (parallel with the west shore) and provides full views of the area.

Squeezed in a heavily urban area, Lake Temescal is remarkably quiet.

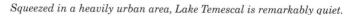

Junior explorers will prefer the West Shore Trail, which hugs the shore and whose platforms are great vantage points to scout the waters for rainbow trout, catfish, bluegill, or largemouth bass. While the other trails connect with the parking on level ground, the West Shore Trail remains at a lower level and requires a set of steps to come back up to the parking lot.

 JOAQUIN MILLER PARK

BEFORE YOU GO
Maps: USGS Oakland East. Free map at trailhead.
Information: East Bay Regional Park District (888) 327-2757, option 3, extension 4555. City of Oakland, www.oaklandnet.com/joaquin millerpark

ABOUT THE HIKE
Day hike; Moderate/Difficult; Year round
3.6 miles, loop
Hiking time: 1 hour or less
High point/elevation gain: 1400 feet/600 feet

GETTING THERE

■ From CA-24 eastbound in Oakland, take CA-13 southbound and exit at Joaquin Miller Road/Lincoln Avenue. Bear left on Monterey Boulevard and cross the freeway to turn left onto Joaquin Miller Road.

■ From I-580 northbound toward Oakland, merge into CA-13 northbound toward Berkeley. Exit at Joaquin Miller Road toward Lincoln Avenue and turn right onto Joaquin Miller Road.

■ Drive 0.8 mile to the park entrance on Sanborn Road (look for the sign WOODMINSTER). Turn left and park by the ranger station.

■ The park can be reached with a combination of BART and buses.

ON THE TRAIL

San Francisco has Adolph Sutro; Oakland has Joaquin Miller. These two colorful characters left a park legacy to their beloved cities, but Miller swallowed goldfish for fun while Sutro collected art. A trip to Joaquin Miller Park will get you acquainted with the man who called his gingerbread house "The Abbey" (no less), accidentally became a Pony

Express rider, a historian, a miner, and a lawyer, but mostly wanted to be a writer, poet, playwright, and journalist. Fellow writer and friend of Mark Twain, Jack London, Ambrose Bierce, and Brett Harte, he is remembered for an undercurrent of fun and humor, and a sympathy for the ostracized and the underdog.

Joaquin Miller Park is perhaps the best spot to entertain children from toddlerhood to high school. While little ones love climbing the mid-twentieth-century stone stairs in the huge landscaped garden with water features (reflection pools and waterfalls) and a playground (Tot Lot), young athletes use the upper trails for racetrack practice at the end of school days. In the middle sits an open-air amphitheater that hosts family-friendly musicals in the summer.

This hike could read like a storybook, except it's the commando version: after the scenic and lulling Sunset Trail, you get a solid workout on the steep Cinderella Trail (a hardworking princess indeed), ending up in the land of giant redwoods where forest spirits dwell.

From the ranger station parking lot, walk on Sanborn Road back toward the entrance. At the yellow gate (roughly 200 feet) turn left on the Sunset Trail, a gravel road that descends to a large meadow and picnic areas. At 0.1 mile, turn left on the Sunset Trail, gradually descending, then leveling up. Ignore the Sunset Loop Trail at 0.4 mile and follow the Sunset Trail under a

Joaquin Miller's upper trails expose fantastic forests.

shaded forest. The trail rises slowly along the sides of a ravine where Palo Seco Creek flows below. Majestic redwood trees rise from the ravine's flanks.

At 0.8 mile you reach a junction with the Chaparral Trail. Bear left to stay on the Sunset Trail until a large bend leads you to Cinderella Creek. The Cinderella Trail starts here, a half-mile relentless climb to the park's higher hills. If you prefer steps, the Chaparral Trail is a better choice. Eroded and steep, the Cinderella Trail is not for the faint hearted, but the trail at the top is worth it, so be patient.

Right before a fork that leads to a picnic area at 1.4 miles, turn right on an unmarked trail that can be easy to miss, almost across from a marker for the Cinderella Trail. Turn right at the next junction and right at the paved trail junction. From this point until almost the end, the trail is relaxingly level with few hiccups.

At the fork with the Chaparral Trail, veer left to contour the hill on the Sequoia–Bayview Trail. A grove of Monterey cypress gives way later to acacia trees, which from afar resemble a bamboo forest. This section is simply lovely. At 1.9 miles keep right on the Sequoia–Bayview Trail, arriving in coast redwood territory, an area that can be damp even in the summer when fog drips to create puddles on the trail.

Continue on the Sequoia–Bayview Trail until you pass a sharp bend with wooden fences. After the bend at 2.9 miles, turn right on the Sunset Trail. Initially steep, the Sunset Trail becomes a pleasant path that widens and leads you back to the meadow.

Retrace your steps to the parking lot.

ROBERTS REGIONAL RECREATION AREA

BEFORE YOU GO
Maps: USGS Oakland East. Free map at trailhead.
Information: East Bay Regional Park District (888) 327-2757, option 3, extension 4555. www.ebparks.com

ABOUT THE HIKE
Day hike; Easy; Year round
1.3 miles, loop
Hiking time: 1 hour or less
High point/elevation gain: 0 feet/0 feet

GETTING THERE

■ From CA-13 northbound in Oakland, exit at Redwood Road. The ramp becomes Mountain Boulevard. Bear right onto Redwood Road. Turn left on Skyline Boulevard. At the next light, turn right to stay on Skyline Boulevard.

■ From CA-13 southbound in Oakland, exit at Joaquin Miller Road/Lincoln Avenue. Turn left onto Monterey Boulevard. Turn left onto Joaquin Miller Road and up the hill, left again onto Skyline Boulevard.

■ Roberts Regional Recreation Area is 1 mile up Skyline Boulevard on the right. Park next to the swimming pool, right after the entrance kiosk.

■ The park can be reached with a combination of BART and buses.

ON THE TRAIL

This popular 82-acre park is covered in redwoods and includes some of the best picnic areas under the trees, just across from a meadow with a "Barrier Free" wheelchair-accessible playground (www.barrierfreeplay ground.org) and an open-air heated swimming pool open from April to October. Great for little kids, this park is also where the two biggest redwood trees of the Bay Area were supposed to be, and their location is marked by a historic plaque near the Madrone picnic area. Towering over 300 feet tall, they were so tall that sea captains used them as navigation landmarks from 16 miles at sea.

For a day out, combine this hike with a visit to the adjacent Chabot Space & Science Center (www.chabotspace.org), a hands-on science museum where kids of all ages can learn about the universe and our planet.

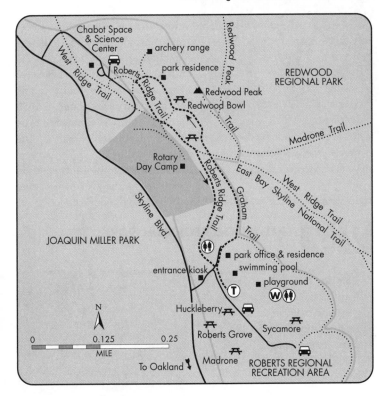

From the parking lot, walk toward the swimming pool and find a paved path that heads up the hill to a park office. Behind the park office, turn right to the connector trail to the Graham Trail. This short dirt road is steep and can be slippery when dry, so be cautious. At 0.1 mile you reach the Graham Trail, a wide service road. Turn left and go up on a moderate grade with views of a ridge with tall eucalyptus trees.

At 0.3 mile, you reach Redwood Bowl, a large meadow with picnic tables around the edges. Bear right onto a dirt trail that skirts the northern edge of the meadow and becomes a stately alley with towering redwood trees at the end of the meadow. Keep going past the picnic tables, restrooms, and a park residence until you reach the archery range at 0.6 mile. Turn left to go uphill, arriving by a big parking lot in front of a domed building. This is the Chabot Space & Science Center. At 0.8 mile, make a sharp left into a smaller parking lot with a telephone, and find the Roberts Ridge Trail. This narrow path meanders

A stately alley extends the Redwood Bowl to the archery range.

nicely through the redwood forest and continues past the four-way junction up in the forest. At 1.1 miles, bear right toward Roberts Park, passing the rustic cabins of the Rotary Day Camp, a 1959 project built to commemorate the club's fiftieth anniversary in the city of Oakland.

The Roberts Ridge Trail leads you back to the area overlooking the swimming complex. Follow the path back to the parking lot.

REDWOOD REGIONAL PARK

BEFORE YOU GO
Maps: USGS Oakland East. Free map at trailhead.
Information: East Bay Regional Park District (510) 562-PARK. www.ebparks.com

ABOUT THE HIKE
Day hike; Easy/Moderate; Year round
2.3 miles, round-trip on the Stream Trail; 3.7 miles looping back along the French Trail
Hiking time: 1.5 hours; 2.5 hours
High point/elevation gain: minimal/400 feet; 500/900 feet

GETTING THERE
- From CA-13 in Oakland, turn left onto Redwood Road and drive 2 miles past Skyline Boulevard to the park entrance.
- Turn left and park at the

Canyon Meadow Staging Area at the end of the road.
- AC Transit from Oakland BART stations services Skyline Boulevard and Redwood Road.

ON THE TRAIL
Redwood Regional Park is Oakland's equivalent of Muir Woods minus the crowds. Before the Gold Rush, the Oakland hills were covered in lush coast redwood forests.

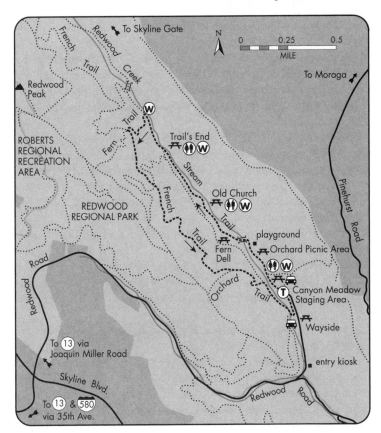

The park still counts four mill sites, memories of fierce logging days. The current trees are second- or third-generation coast redwoods planted after 1906. Rising tall on the Oakland hills, Redwood Regional Park is a gem to discover year round, but especially on hot days when the temperature under the redwoods is 10 degrees cooler than on the ridges.

From the parking lot, get on the Stream Trail, a wide paved trail winding through Orchard Picnic Area. Wheelchair-accessible for its first mile, it is a safe path for toddlers or preschoolers to practice for longer hikes. The meadows are sunny and flat and are peppered with picnic tables, restrooms, and drinking fountains—all good backup spots for an after-hike treat. Signs provide information on the protected habitat of the native rainbow trout and the California newts. After a small play structure, cross the creek and bear right at 0.3 mile toward Old Church/Trail's End.

At 0.4 mile, you enter the majestic world of coast redwoods towering 150 feet above your head. At the Aurelia Henry Reinhardt Redwood Grove, search around your feet and pick up one of the redwood twigs. They are flat and the needles alternate along the stem, making them look like small ferns.

Keep going on the trail along the creek. The trout fingerlings in Redwood Creek migrate downstream into San Leandro Reservoir. That's 2 miles of adventure for tiny little fish that, during the long dry season, need to spawn in ever-shrinking pools. Look for different varieties of mosses on the left side of the trail, as well as sword fern, blackberry bushes, and forget-me-nots.

At 0.5 mile you reach Old Church, a nice picnic area with grills next to an amphitheater. Refill your water bottle at the drinking fountain if needed. Keep going until Trail's End at 0.9 mile, the end of the paved section of the Stream Trail. Can you see the redwood with three trunks shooting up from a single stump? At 1.15 miles you reach the intersection with the Fern Trail.

For a level hike, you can retrace your steps back to the parking lot along the Stream Trail.

For a change of scenery and hills, veer left on the Fern Trail, a tiny dirt trail that winds up the hill. A series of switchbacks gets you to the top of the moderate ascent. At 1.45 miles, turn left on the French Trail. A forest of California oak trees covers the slopes while the undergrowth includes ferns and miner's lettuce. Can you smell the minty-herbal California laurel leaves around you?

Snaking along canyons and ridges, the French Trail loosely follows the course of the creek with rapidly changing vistas on the way. When the drop is steep, hold younger children's hands to avoid slipping.

At 1.85 miles, keep left to stay on the French Trail. Still going up, you may encounter banana slugs (see the sidebar in Hike 3) or bright red mushrooms in the spring. As pretty as they are,

The park's French Trail is lined with mushrooms and ferns in the rainy season.

these mushrooms might be amanitas or fading scarlet waxy caps, both unsafe for human consumption.

At 2.85 miles you reach a junction with the Orchard Trail. Turn left and get ready for a steep descent. Gravel and clay make the trail slippery. At 3.2 miles, turn right on the level path and at 3.45 miles, cross the wooden bridge to reach the Wayside Overflow parking lot. Turn left to get back to the Canyon Meadow Staging Area.

LADYBUGS HIBERNATING ON THE TRAIL

From December to March, millions of ladybugs gather along the Stream Trail to find shelter under fallen leaves and ground litter near the stream when the weather is cold. As you walk along the Stream Trail, look carefully for red clusters looking like berries on the ground. The Stream Trail/Prince Trail junction is a particularly good ladybug-spotting area. The ladybugs keep warm together until the temperature reaches 55 degrees Fahrenheit so they can fly away. Some areas have so many of them that the ladybugs turn the tree stumps red. After rains, look for ladybugs under leaves and shrubs.

Clusters of ladybugs overwinter at Redwood Regional Park.

HAYWARD REGIONAL SHORELINE

BEFORE YOU GO
Maps: USGS Hayward. Map at Hayward Shoreline Interpretive Center.
Information: Park office (510) 783-1066. East Bay Regional Park District, www.ebparks.org.

ABOUT THE HIKE
Day hike; Moderate; Year round
5.5 miles, round-trip
Hiking time: 2–3 hours
High point/elevation gain: 30 feet/30 feet

GETTING THERE
- From I-880, take CA-92 west toward the San Mateo Bridge in Hayward.
- From I-280 or US 101, take CA-92 east toward the San Mateo Bridge and cross the bridge.
- Exit onto Clawiter Road/Eden Landing Road. Go straight through the light and turn left onto Breakwater Avenue.
- Park at the Hayward Shoreline Interpretive Center, at the end of the road on your right.
- There is no public transit.

ON THE TRAIL
Hayward Regional Shoreline provides a gorgeous walk along the South Bay to see egrets, herons, gulls, and many other shorebirds. On Fridays, Saturdays, and Sundays from 10:00 AM to 5:00 PM, kids can start their exploration with a visit to the Hayward Shoreline Interpretive Center. Perched on stilts, the center is designed as an introduction to the ecology of San Francisco Bay. Check the calendar for kids' programs (www.hayward rec.org/hayshore.html).

Be prepared for strong winds and many bird sightings, two staples of this marsh ecosystem! For better shorebird sightings, bird experts recommend late afternoon.

Around the interpretive center, look for cliff swallows. They will be flying and nesting in the spring and summer. Get on the wide, level path and head toward the bay. On your right, a slough separates you from

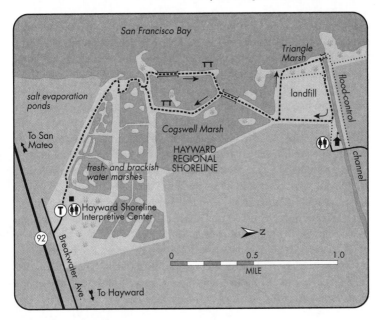

a marsh used by shorebirds. On your left, a pickleweed marsh was set aside as habitat for the endangered salt marsh harvest mouse. Around here the marsh may be smelly, but it gets better closer to the bay, especially if it's windy. The path bends right.

At 0.5 mile, look for a large marsh next to the bridge. No longer in use, these salt evaporation ponds illustrate Hayward's days as one of the largest salt-producing places in the world. Here, up to seventeen companies harvested 17,000 tons of salt each year. Imagine fields of white glittering salt raked by hand before being milled locally and shipped from the bay landings around the world. This was the area's landscape before intense restoration efforts resulted in the marshes you are visiting today, truer to the rich natural environment the Ohlone people lived in. The Ohlone people were a Native American people of the central California coast.

At 0.8 mile, you reach the bay and meander right and left to follow the levee tops, passing a bench with outstanding views of the South Bay. At 1.15 miles in front of a gate, turn left (west) to follow the bay on the gravel trail and over a bridge. Ground squirrels dart on both sides of the trail, stopping just long enough to look at you with their beady eyes before retreating to the riprap or low vegetation. Look for American avocets sweeping the mudflats with their long beaks to catch their prey. Other birds visiting the marshes or the bay shores include mallards, herons, grebes, terns, egrets, sandpipers, and gadwalls.

At 1.7 miles, the trail intersects with the trail that leads along Cogswell Marsh. Straight ahead, a long wooden bridge extends over the bay waters. Continue on the trail until you reach a raised platform, the only bump in this otherwise flat landscape. At 2.1 miles, turn left to loop around the landfill, now planted with coyote brush and wild fennel.

At 2.4 miles, the path veers right next to a bench and follows Triangle Marsh with a rocky beach on the left. Turn right after the marsh at 2.7 miles and right again at 2.8 miles to cross the flood-control channel. Bear left around the landfill and after the bend at 3.4 miles, head right at the sign for the marsh to cross the landfill.

Back at the landfill junction at 3.8 miles, go straight to return to the interpretive center but rather than going along the bay shore, take a left turn after the wooden bridge to explore Cogswell Marsh. At the end of this marsh, retrace your steps to the parking lot.

Families and school groups visit the interpretive center on their way to the marsh.

COYOTE HILLS REGIONAL PARK

BEFORE YOU GO
Maps: USGS Newark. Free map at the park and online.
Information: East Bay Regional Park District (510) 562-PARK. www.ebparks.org

ABOUT THE HIKE
Day hike; Moderate; Year round
4.2 miles, loop
Hiking time: 2–3 hours
High point/elevation gain: 270 feet/270 feet

GETTING THERE

- From CA-84 east of the Dumbarton Bridge in Fremont, exit at Paseo Padre Parkway.
- Turn right and drive north about 1 mile.
- Turn left on Patterson Ranch Road, the entrace road to Coyote Hills Regional Park. Park near the picnic areas and visitor center, by the marsh on the right.
- For information on public transit, visit www.transitandtrails .org/trailheads/279/.

ON THE TRAIL

With a freshwater marsh, an Ohlone shell mound and village, a visitor center with a reconstructed Ohlone cattail house, nature and culture exhibits, a butterfly garden, and a portion of the Bay Trail, Coyote Hills has enough to keep you coming back several times throughout the year. Summer is particularly full with family programs, so be sure to check them out. Since most of the trails are flat and wide, strollers are a common sight whether with parents or grandparents behind the wheels.

This grand loop combines views of the marsh with views of San Francisco Bay, but you can customize the route according to your needs. Note that there is no shade at all in this park, and it can get pretty windy by the bay.

From the parking lot, head east on the paved Bayview Trail, a multi-use trail that runs along the marsh. Look for waterfowl playing peekaboo or just basking in the open. As you might guess from a visit to the visitor center, this park is known for birding. At 0.25 mile you pass the Muskrat Trail, an elevated boardwalk cutting through the

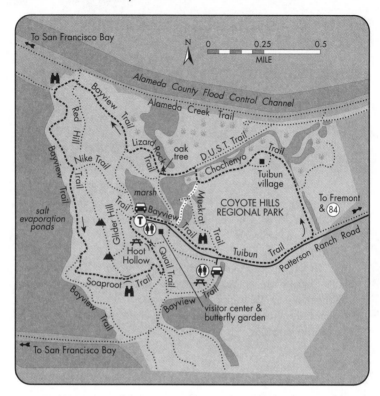

high reeds of the marsh. Save it for later: kids love that boardwalk and the feeling of adventure it brings. Continue along the marsh as the Bayview Trail gives way to the Tuibun Trail, heading toward the entrance kiosk. This level trail gives you a good idea of the size and pattern of the marsh.

At 0.7 mile the trail dips to a gravel area. Turn left on the Chochenyo Trail to continue circling around the marsh, now approaching a thick stand of willows. At 0.94 mile, keep straight to stay on the Chochenyo Trail as the paved road now slowly curves left.

At the fork, take a right to walk around the Tuibun village site, a 2500-year-old Ohlone village that features four partially constructed structures on an archaeological site. You won't see it from the trail and it is closed to the public except for special events (see the park's schedule), but school field trips visit the site for its historical and cultural significance.

Coyote Hills' trails are gentle enough to appeal to all ages.

When the Chochenyo Trail meets the Muskrat Trail at 1.5 miles, turn right to go over the marsh and left to head west toward the hills. From this point of view, the network of marshes and sloughs is quite impressive. At 1.7 miles, make a right on the Lizard Rock Trail to a big oak tree. Gently the trail starts to rise above the wetlands. At 2 miles, the trail dead-ends into the Bayview Trail. Turn right and leave freshwater lands for the salty side of the bay.

This paved trail continues to rise. At the northern end of the park, the Bayview Trail crosses a junction for the Alameda Creek Trail, which leads to the Pelican Trail, a narrow stretch of land running on a dirt levee. This area is a wildlife refuge where no dogs are allowed. Continue on the Bayview Trail, and around the bend discover the gracious curves of the Coyote Hills diving into the bay as well as the salt evaporation ponds separated by levees. These salt ponds—and others along the bay—support a five-year process of solar evaporation that yields 600,000 tons of salt a year.

At 3.4 miles, bear left on a dirt trail that rises up the hill, the Soaproot Trail. This short section takes you to the ridgeline from which you can see the marshes and the bay, before going down the hill. Look for signs of erosion due to cattle grazing and weather on the slopes. After a hairpin turn the trail intersects with the Quail Trail. Turn left and, past the Hoot Hollow picnic area, drop down to the visitor center. You can finish your visit by strolling through the butterfly garden (best time to see butterflies, spring and summer) or exploring the exhibits at the visitor center.

ARDENWOOD HISTORIC FARM

BEFORE YOU GO
Maps: USGS Niles. Map at entrance kiosk.
Information: Park office (510) 796-0199. East Bay Regional Park District, www .ebparks.org. Note: Closed on Mondays.

ABOUT THE HIKE
Day hike; Easy; Year round
0.8 mile, loop
Hiking time: 30 minutes–1 hour
High point/elevation gain: 0 feet/0 feet

GETTING THERE

■ From I-880 in Fremont, merge into CA-84. Exit at Ardenwood/ Newark Boulevard, and head north on Ardenwood Boulevard.

■ The entrance to Ardenwood Historic Farm is just north of CA-84. Proceed to the parking lot next to the entrance kiosk.

■ AC Transit bus 214 connects with the Union City BART station and stops on Newark Boulevard under the freeway.

ON THE TRAIL

Where can kids harvest hay, spot monarch butterflies on eucalyptus trees, sample cookies hot off a wood-burning stove, ride a steam train, feed sheep and goats, find corn kernels for popping, and see a tractor-powered grinding mill? Ardenwood Historic Farm Regional Preserve is one of the best family secrets of Alameda County. As a working farm and nature center, it also provides year-round family programs based on the seasons, so each visit will be different.

This 205-acre park is all that remains of a 6000-acre ranch created by George Washington Patterson in 1854. Named after the mythical Forest of Arden in Shakespeare's *As You like It*, Ardenwood is surrounded by wide, level paths that are ideal for strollers or wheelchairs.

From the entrance kiosk, go straight on the wide paved road past the station where horse-drawn and steam trains depart for Deer Park. The train operates from 10:15 AM to 3:30 PM Thursdays, Fridays, and Sundays (www.spcrr.org). At the lamppost junction at 0.1 mile, turn left toward Deer Park and walk on a tree-shaded path past the pool site and the large meadows in front of Patterson House. The house was built in

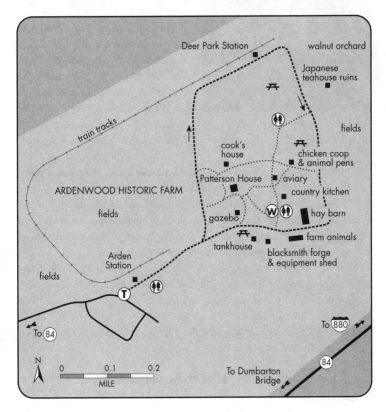

Deer Park Station   walnut orchard

Japanese
teahouse ruins

train tracks

fields

cook's
house

chicken coop
& animal pens

ARDENWOOD HISTORIC FARM

Patterson House   aviary

country kitchen

fields

gazebo

W   hay barn

farm animals

tankhouse

blacksmith forge
& equipment shed

Arden
Station

fields

T

To (84)

To (880)

N

0   0.1   0.2

MILE

To Dumbarton
Bridge

(84)

1853 and remodeled in 1889 and 1915. Check the family programs for visits open to children.

Keep straight and follow the road as it bends right at 0.3 mile, sweeping past tea gardens and fields, running parallel to the railroad tracks. Kids may want to explore the Victorian tea garden and re-create scenes from *Alice in Wonderland*. Continue on the path, now flanked by the forest on the left and picnic areas on the right.

At 0.4 mile, the path turns right and heads toward the farm buildings with a large walnut orchard on your left. Under a large live oak tree stands an interpretive sign on the ruins of a Japanese teahouse. Why a Japanese teahouse at a Victorian ranch? In 1915, the Panama Pacific International Exposition focused the world's attention on San Francisco. At the end of the exhibition in 1916, all buildings were to be destroyed, but San Francisco's Palace of Fine Arts survived, and Mrs. Clara

The Patterson House's meadows are made for running!

Patterson Layson purchased the 4185-square-foot building used as the Japanese Commissioners' Office. She had it shipped down the bay to her farm by barge. It burned in 1941, but the grassy meadow makes an appropriately silent testimonial to a woman's love for Japanese architecture.

Continue along the path to reach the tractor shed, the animal pens, and the chicken coop. Time to let the kids loose! Explore the area, then continue straight and turn right at 0.6 mile toward the hay barn and blacksmith forge. Demonstrations are held at the blacksmith forge from 10:00 AM to 4:00 PM on Thursdays, Fridays, Sundays, select Saturdays, and special events (www.ardenwoodforge.com).

You are likely to encounter feathery inhabitants of the farm here, strutting peacocks and peahens that would have been perfectly in harmony with the Victorian gardens. Get kids to pump water at the hand pump in the farmyard and check out the water tank before returning to the parking lot, going straight past the Farmyard Café on the main path back to the entrance gate.

31 SUNOL REGIONAL WILDERNESS

BEFORE YOU GO
Maps: USGS La Costa Valley. Free map at the trailhead.
Information: East Bay Regional Park District (510) 544-3249. www.ebparks.org

ABOUT THE HIKE
Day hike; Easy; Spring, Fall, Winter
1 mile, round-trip
Hiking time: 30 minutes–1 hour
High point/elevation gain: 500 feet/100 feet

GETTING THERE
- From I-680 south of the town of Sunol, exit at Calaveras Road/CA-84.

- Turn left onto Calaveras Road and drive 4 miles to Geary Road.

- Turn into the park entrance and park by the visitor center/green barn.
- There is no public transit.

ON THE TRAIL

Spring and early summer are the times of the year when Sunol Regional Wilderness beats any outdoor family experience where you can let kids be kids. With picnic grounds along Alameda Creek, kids can enjoy hours of splashing, lizard hunting, and rock studying, before or after embarking on this gentle nature trail. Let this be your entryway to other wilderness landmarks of Sunol, known for its Little Yosemite scenic gorge, cave rocks, Little Yosemite Falls, and the 28-mile long Sunol Wilderness Trail. Oh, and the grazing mammals, too.

Tucked smack in the continental part of the East Bay, Sunol is best avoided during the summer. It gets very hot very quickly here. With strollers, the 1.5-mile-wide gravel road along the creek to Little

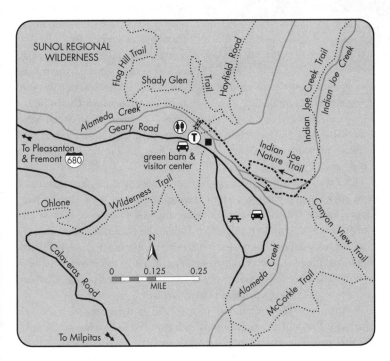

Sunol offers gentle trails as well as heart-pumping climbs.

Yosemite Falls is a better alternative. If the quaint green barn is open, check out the exhibits and borrow a self-guided brochure for the Indian Joe Nature Trail, as well as a wildflower identification kit if you visit in the spring.

From the green barn, head right (east) to a footbridge that crosses Alameda Creek. After the creek at 0.1 mile, turn right on the Canyon View Trail. This level dirt path winds through oak-lined meadows along the burbling creek. In the spring it might even jump a brook over a few rocks. Around you, rolling hills covered with a scenic oak savannah invite photo ops at every step.

At 0.25 mile after a creek crossing, turn left onto the Indian Joe Nature Trail, a narrow dirt trail that rises into the hills. Indian Joe Creek was named after one of the last Native Americans who worked this land when it was a ranch owned by Pat Geary. Indian Joe lived in a milk shed near the creek until the 1950s.

The trail leads you west up over the valley, lined by buckeye trees and sticky monkey flowers whose dark green leaves were used as bandages by the Ohlone people. Entering the oak woodland, look at the curly leaves of coast live oaks. At 0.4 mile, the trail rises more sharply and curves left until it crosses the creek and heads for the hills. Walking along the fence, you might see cows grazing in the meadows. These rolling hills were used exclusively as ranch land after the Gold Rush up until the park was opened in the early 1960s.

Continue on the Indian Joe Nature Trail as it merges with a ranch road at 0.7 mile. Turn right and then left to the footbridge at 0.8 mile. Retrace your steps to the parking lot.

SYCAMORE GROVE PARK

BEFORE YOU GO
Maps: USGS Altamont. Map online at www.larpd.dst.ca.us.
Information: Livermore Area Parks and Recreation District (925) 373-5700.
www.larpd.dst.ca.us/open _space/sycamore.html

ABOUT THE HIKE
Day hike; Moderate; Spring, Fall, Winter
4.6 miles, loop
Hiking time: 2–3 hours
High point/elevation gain: 450 feet/50 feet

GETTING THERE

- From I-580 in Livermore, exit at Airway Boulevard/CA-84. Go south past the airport and follow CA-84 right at Kittyhawk. Turn left onto Concannon Boulevard and right on Holmes. Turn left on Wetmore and keep going to Arroyo Road.
- From I-680 northbound before Pleasanton, exit at CA-84/ Vallecitos Road. After about 6 miles, make a right to stay on Vallecitos, then right on Wetmore and keep going to Arroyo Road.
- Turn right on Arroyo Road and park at the south entrance on your right, the entrance for Veterans Park (Sycamore Grove Park and Veterans Park are two ends of the same park).
- From I-680 southbound in Dublin, exit at I-580 and drive east.
- Follow the directions for I-580.
- There is no public transit.

ON THE TRAIL

One of the largest native-sycamore groves south of Livermore, criss-crossed by family-friendly trails on former agricultural land, the Olivina estate was founded in 1884 by J. P. Smith, a businessman who made his fortune by packaging borax in small boxes with his brother and selling it as household cleaner under the name 20 Mule Team Borax. Here, Lucques-variety olive trees were planted between rows of grapes and harvested for pickling. The land also produced almonds, walnuts, and brandy in a Mediterranean-type climate. In 1967 the Livermore Area Recreation and Park District acquired the 32 acres that comprise

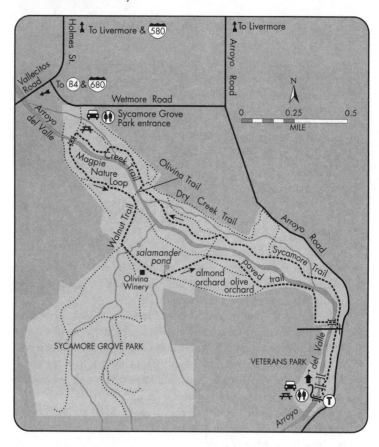

Veterans Park for public use, and in 1974 purchased a section of the old Olivina estate to establish Sycamore Grove Park. In 1999 the district acquired an additional 370 acres, including the old winery and distillery. Though Veterans Park and Sycamore Park are essentially two ends of the same park, the bigger portion belongs to Sycamore Park. The remains of the Olivina Winery still exist in the park, including the ruined winery building, a park residence, walnut lanes, and an arched gateway.

If the kids are ready for more local history and an apple orchard, the Ravenswood Historical Site (www.larpd.dst.ca.us), 2.4 miles north on Arroyo Road, is a romantic Victorian house museum where rangers organize a summer ice cream social, an autumn apple festival, and a winter yuletide celebration.

A hidden gem in Livermore, Sycamore Grove Park is great for hikers and bike riders.

Sycamore Grove is traversed by Arroyo del Valle, and the only bridge to cross the creek is exactly midway through the loop. With strollers, an out-and-back hike on the paved path from the north park entrance is easier.

From the parking lot, begin on the Sycamore Trail, a paved path that goes underneath a bridge and bears slightly left. At the second bridge at 0.1 mile, follow the dirt trail on the left. At 0.3 mile, walk past an elevated bridge and keep straight on the Sycamore Trail, now a wide dirt-and-gravel trail. The path loosely parallels the course of the creek and crosses oak meadows. At 0.5 mile, turn left at the fork to stay on the Sycamore Trail where tall sycamore trees grow. Despite views of newly planted vineyards across the road, the trail retains an open-space feeling.

Keep straight at the next junction at 0.9 mile and follow the path as it angles right to merge with another dirt trail along the park boundary. At 1.5 miles you reach a four-way junction. Turn right on the Olivina Trail and left on the Creek Trail, a narrow dirt track that follows the creek and becomes the Magpie Nature Loop. At 2.3 miles, you reach the bridge near the northern entrance of the park.

Cross the wooden bridge and get on the unnamed paved trail. The path is very popular with bikers, so expect to share the road. At 2.7 miles, turn right on the Walnut Trail, a dirt track that heads southwest for the hills. At the junction at 2.9 miles, turn left to follow the wooden fence and stay straight as the road forks almost immediately. The hollowed-out Olivina Winery appears at 3.2 miles, a fenced-in two-level building. Veer left at 3.4 miles to come back to the paved trail through a wide dirt-and-gravel road. Turn right at 3.5 miles and enjoy some of the prettiest views of this park, passing the almond orchards first and then the olive orchards on raised hills at 3.7 miles. Continue on the meandering path and cross the elevated bridge to return to the Sycamore Trail. Turn right into Veterans Park and retrace your steps to the parking lot.

 LAKE DEL VALLE

BEFORE YOU GO
Maps: USGS Altamont. Free map at trailhead.
Information: Del Valle information (925) 373-0332. East Bay Regional Park District, www.ebparks.org

ABOUT THE HIKE
Day hike; Year round; Easy/Moderate
2.2 miles, round-trip
Hiking time: 1–2 hours
High point/elevation gain: 50 feet/50 feet

GETTING THERE

- From I-580 in Livermore, exit at North Livermore Avenue and head south on Livermore Avenue until it turns into Tesla Road.
- At 3.7 miles, Tesla Road meets Mines Road. Turn right on Mines Road and drive 3.6 miles to a junction with Del Valle Road.
- Go straight on Del Valle Road to the Del Valle Regional Park entrance. Turn right (north) and drive just over 0.5 mile to the boat launch parking lot.
- There is no public transit.

ON THE TRAIL

A major summer swimming and boating destination for Bay Area families, Del Valle Regional Park offers miles of hiking trails, with a more developed trail system on Lake del Valle's eastern shore. If you want to stay overnight, the park features drive-in family campsites with connections to park trails.

To enjoy a gentle stroll with the little ones, this hike to Badger Cove is as family-friendly as it gets: a level, wide path suitable for jogging strollers and little legs, short stretches offering varied views, and swimming beaches at the end of the hike.

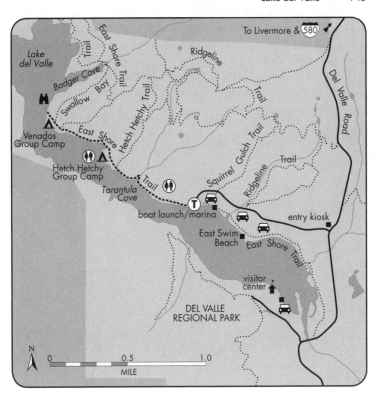

From the parking lot for the boat launch, walk northwest to a metal gate where the East Shore Trail begins. This dirt trail follows the edge of the lake 6 miles to the dam, but our hike stops way before. Hiking past interior live oaks, gray pines, and white alders, you may see groups fishing on the lake. At 0.4 mile the path goes inland around a cove opposite Tarantula Cove. If you come in late summer through the fall, you might get lucky and see tarantulas on these trails. Be gentle and simply observe.

At 0.64 mile continue straight, passing a restroom building, to Hetch Hetchy Group Camp; campers can either hike in or arrive by

Exploring trails along Lake del Valle

boat. The trail rises slightly as it meets two trails that explore the ridge-line. Continue straight past Venados Group Camp until the path dips down to Badger Cove at 1.1 miles.

Enjoy the views and retrace your steps on the same trail. At the end of the hike, you can walk past the marina to East Swim Beach for some water fun!

Opposite: *Family fun on Morgan Territory trails*

CONTRA COSTA COUNTY

POINT PINOLE REGIONAL SHORELINE

BEFORE YOU GO
Maps: USGS Richmond. Free map at trailhead.
Information: Park office (888) 327-2757, option 3, ext. 4551. East Bay Regional Park District, www.ebparks .org/parks/pt_pinole

ABOUT THE HIKE
Day hike; Easy/Moderate; Year round
3.3 miles, loop
Hiking time: 1–2 hours
High point/elevation gain: 100 feet/75 feet

GETTING THERE

- From I-80 in Richmond, take the Richmond Parkway exit and go west toward the bay.
- Cross San Pablo Avenue and watch for the Point Pinole/Giant Highway exit. Turn right (north) at Giant Highway.
- From I-580 east of the Richmond–San Rafael Bridge, exit at Richmond Parkway/Castro Street and go north. Exit at Giant Highway and turn right.
- The Point Pinole park entrance is on the left, past the railroad tracks.
- AC Transit line 70 serves Point Pinole daily and connects with the Richmond BART station and the Richmond Parkway Transit Center.

ON THE TRAIL

Hiking at Point Pinole? It's dynamite! Literally, this park used to be the site of several gunpowder and dynamite plants up until the 1960s. Just the trail names and landmarks seem right out of a superhero comic book: Nitro Trail, Black Powder Press, Angel Buggy, Dynamite Blast, and Burning Bunker. They stand out next to the more pedestrian (no pun intended) Marsh Trail and Bay View Trail.

Rescued from years of industrial abuse and slowly massaged back to its current state, Point Pinole is a daily escape for dog lovers, a Sunday trip for families who take the shuttle to the pier, a quiet spot for anglers, and a maze of short, easy trails for the birding hiker armed

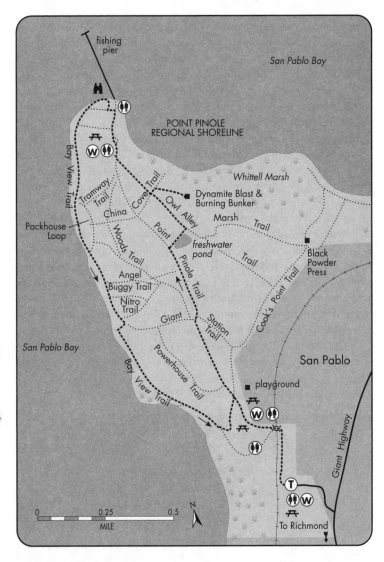

with binoculars. Pack sun hats and sunscreen—all the trails are in full sun.

From the parking lot, head north on the paved trail that parallels the railroad. At 0.2 mile, the trail bends left across the tracks, leading into the park itself. The change of scenery is dramatic. Point Pinole opens up on expansive meadows interrupted by eucalyptus trees that are amazingly straight compared to the horizontal landscape. These trees were planted to buffer explosions all around the park.

At 0.4 mile you reach a large children's play area with fields, sandboxes, and picnic tables shaded by trees. This area is popular with school outings. Continue on the Point Pinole Trail, a paved trail that cuts across grassland, winding along the route of the former dynamite trucking road. At 0.96 mile an unmarked dirt trail takes you to the freshwater pond. Turn right on that trail, enjoy the pond and its water-loving residents, and make a left on the Owl Alley Trail at 1.05 miles. This gravel service road offers views of San Pablo Bay.

At 1.2 miles, make a right on the China Cove Trail and find an unmaintained grassy path that heads right (east) to a promontory. Surprise, the promontory opens up into a semi-open crater that was used to blast dynamite and test explosives in a safe environment with a dirt shelter built all around. It'd be hard to tell today, now that grasses have colonized the mound. Note the eerily solitary picnic table sitting in the circular ground area. Return to the Owl Alley Trail (or check out China Cove quickly) and continue northwest toward the point.

At 1.66 miles, the trail rejoins the Point Pinole Trail and leads to a roundabout that serves as the terminal point for the shuttle bus.

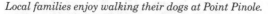

Local families enjoy walking their dogs at Point Pinole.

Continue right toward the pier. The old pilings are remains of the shipping docks of the Atlas Powder Company, where shallow-bottomed barges loaded with dynamite were wheeled from the factory on electric locomotives. The current fishing pier juts 1200 feet into the bay.

Connect to the Bay View Trail by turning left onto a path that reaches windswept bluffs. Turn left (south) and continue to the end of the aptly named Bay View Trail, passing several short trails, rail tracks, and wooden foundations. At 2.75 miles turn left to find the children's play area and the bridge. Retrace your steps to the parking lot.

TILDEN REGIONAL PARK

BEFORE YOU GO
Maps: USGS Richmond. Free map at trailhead.
Information: Park office (888) 327-2757, option 3, ext. 4562. East Bay Regional Park District www.ebparks .org/parks/tilden

ABOUT THE HIKE
Day hike; Moderate/Difficult; Spring, Summer, Fall
3.1 miles, loop
Hiking time: 2–3 hours
High point/elevation gain: 1000 feet/500 feet

GETTING THERE

■ From I-80 in Berkeley, take the Buchanan Avenue exit and go east on Buchanan. Stay straight onto Marin Avenue. Turn left on Spruce Street and cross Grizzly Peak Boulevard to turn left immediately on Canon Drive.

■ From CA-24 in Oakland east of the Caldecott Tunnel, take the Fish Ranch Road exit and drive uphill. Turn right on Grizzly Peak Boulevard and continue to Wildcat Canyon Road. Turn right on Wildcat Canyon Road and immediately left on Canon Drive.

■ Proceed to the Lone Oak parking lot next to the Blue Gum Group Camp.

■ On weekends and holidays, AC Transit line 67 runs from the Berkeley BART station into the park at Canon Drive and Wildcat Canyon Road, roughly 0.6 mile from the trailhead.

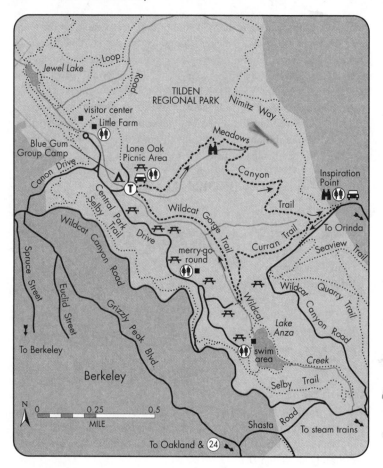

ON THE TRAIL

Tilden Regional Park is a world unto itself. With an antique merry-go-round, a steam train, botanical gardens, Lake Anza's swim area, and an educational farm and environmental center, it's easy to understand why families flock here year round. Covering over 2000 acres of hills, canyons, and ridges in Berkeley, Tilden is an incredible place to hike and get away from it all.

Before the featured hike, grab celery, lettuce, and carrots from your fridge so you can relax at the Little Farm after the hike and feed the cows and sheep. You can even push on to Jewel Lake (0.25 mile by level trail) and have lunch by the water so kids can spot turtles and ducks. Check the environmental education center for more information about the farm programs (www.ebparks.org/parks/vc/tna). In the summer, you can also pack swim gear and head to Lake Anza, a mile south of the trailhead, for a refreshing splash.

Note that after rain, even jogging strollers would be challenged by some very muddy sections on the trail, so it's best to wait until they dry out. The rest of the time it's a hike well worth the climb to enjoy spectacular views.

From the trailhead, get on the Meadows Canyon Trail, a dirt fire road that soon rises out of the forest into the canyon. Surrounded on both sides by low chaparral, the trail enjoys full sun exposure all the way to the top, rising with a gentle grade. For the first 0.5 mile, the trail follows the course of a creek that flows under a forest of willows. From the creek onward, it follows a mostly level course. Continue on the Meadows Canyon Trail until you reach a junction with the Curran Trail at 1.4 miles.

Turn left to reach Inspiration Point 0.13 mile north of the junction and enjoy one of the best views on the ridges of Tilden Park at the top, by Wildcat Canyon Road. After you've enjoyed the views and rested, return to the junction with the Meadows Canyon Trail (1.7 miles) and start your descent on the Curran Trail, heading southwest. Another trail will soon start on the left, but stay straight to stick to the Curran Trail. Descending through groves of tall eucalyptus trees, the Curran Trail is a lot steeper than the Meadows Canyon Trail but on hot days, it provides welcome shade thanks to a dense tree cover. At 2.3 miles, turn right on the Wildcat Gorge Trail, a narrow dirt trail that can be eroded in places. This level stretch follows Wildcat Creek under arching rows of oak trees, before reaching lovely redwood

Just above Berkeley, Tilden Park provides a nature escape with a plethora of child-friendly activities around.

groves where the creek transforms into soft waterfalls (after the rains). Continue as the trail emerges into open meadows to reach the parking lot at 3.1 miles.

 BRIONES REGIONAL PARK

BEFORE YOU GO
Maps: USGS Briones Valley. Free map at the entrance kiosk and trailhead.
Information: Ranger office (888) 327-2757, option 3, extension 4508. East Bay Regional Park District www .ebparks.org

ABOUT THE HIKE
Day hike; Difficult; Spring, Fall, Winter
6.7 miles, loop
Hiking time: 4–6 hours
High point/elevation gain: 1300 feet/600 feet

GETTING THERE

- From CA-24 in Orinda, take the Orinda/Camino Pablo exit and head northwest toward Richmond for 2.2 miles.
- Turn right on Bear Creek Road and drive 5 miles to the staging area on the right. Continue to the last parking lot.
- There is no public transit.

ON THE TRAIL

With over 6000 acres of open land comprising rolling hills, peaks, valleys, and ridges, Briones Regional Park is a must-go destination for many Bay Area hikers. Good for seasoned older hikers (ages six and up), this hike connects several ridges around the park and provides rewarding views from many vantage spots, including a lone bench with a spectacular view to enjoy a picnic lunch.

If your kids are interested in California newts, the park's vernal pools are great observation spots. The best time to see these amphibians is in the winter (December–January), but in that case, go in rain boots—trails turn to sticky mud when wet.

From the parking lot, walk past the gate on the Old Briones Road Trail and bear right at 0.1 mile on the Seaborg Trail. After crossing Bear Creek, the trail goes down a wide, shady road lined with bay laurel

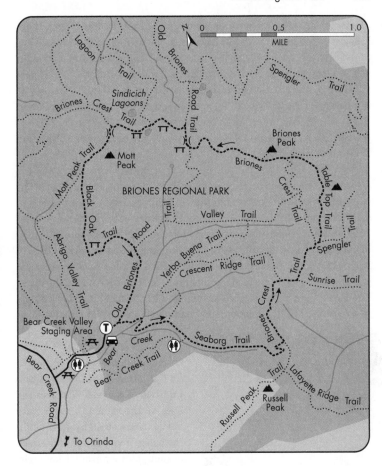

and live oaks. On both sides, poison hemlock and poison oak thrive, so keep to the trail and make sure plants are left alone.

Past a cattle gate you reach an open valley at the base of partly forested hills. At 0.6 mile, bear right to keep to the Seaborg Trail along Bear Creek, flowing between rows of willow trees. Look at the hills above and note dozens of parallel cattle trails rippling down the slopes. Briones Regional Park is open to grazing cattle, as you may see on your hike—or at least evidenced by the potholed state of the wide roads.

At 1.2 miles the trail rises moderately up the canyon, then steeply underneath an oak canopy. Two gates on the ridge announce a junction. At 1.7 miles, turn left onto the Briones Crest Trail, a spectacular roller coaster of a trail with wide views on both sides. In the spring, these hills are a kaleidoscope of wildflowers. In the winter or after rains, have the kids walk in front and look for animal tracks. Continue straight at the junction with the Crescent Ridge Trail and slightly left (almost straight) at the junction with the Sunrise Trail at 2.3 miles, keeping to the Briones Crest Trail. At the next junction, leave the Briones Crest Trail temporarily to get onto the Spengler Trail/Table Top Trail. While the Spengler Trail will make a hard right, your route on the Table Top Trail continues straight.

The Table Top Trail passes right by a peak that culminates at 1433 feet and a less poetic power station with TV antennas. Continue on the path and take in the panoramic views of Suisun Bay, Carquinez Strait, and Livermore. At 3.3 miles, your route merges with the Briones Crest Trail and traverses wide, grassy meadows, giving you an incredible feeling of remoteness. Another 0.7 mile takes you past the narrow trail to Briones Peak and brings you to a junction at 4.1 miles. Look up ahead of you and find a lone bench on a promontory on the other side of the fence. The views from this spot are amazing and invite at least a snack stop.

Come back to the junction and head north on the Old Briones Road Trail shortly before turning left onto the Briones Crest Trail at 4.5 miles. This uphill trail passes the California newt area with the Sindicich Lagoons. Follow the fence on the right to a cattle gate and continue straight up the hill. The bench above the trail is a nice lookout point for ground squirrels.

At 5.1 miles, turn left onto the Mott Peak Trail and then left on the Black Oak Trail. The latter curves around the hillside to take you down to the valley floor. At 6.4 miles, turn left to come back to the parking lot on the Old Briones Road Trail.

View from the ridge on Briones Crest Trail

HUCKLEBERRY BOTANIC REGIONAL PRESERVE

BEFORE YOU GO
Maps: USGS Richmond. Free map at trailhead.
Information: Park office (888) 327-2757, option 3, ext. 4532. East Bay Regional Park District, www.ebparks .org/parks/huckleberry

ABOUT THE HIKE
Day hike; Easy/Moderate; Year round
1.7 miles, loop
Hiking time: 1–2 hours
High point/elevation gain: 1265 feet/325 feet

GETTING THERE

- From CA-24 in Oakland east of the Caldecott Tunnel, take the Fish Ranch Road exit and drive uphill to Grizzly Peak Boulevard.
- Turn left, then left again at Skyline Boulevard.
- The Huckleberry Botanic Regional Preserve entrance is 0.5 mile down Skyline Boulevard, past Sibley Volcanic Regional Preserve (Hike 38).
- There is no public transit.

ON THE TRAIL

As tempting as the name sounds, Huckleberry Preserve is not something you spread on toast but a wonderful self-guided nature path in the Oakland hills. For a quick hike with a few ups and downs, head to Huckleberry on a free morning or afternoon. This mostly shaded park hosts an incredible variety of plants on canyon slopes and ridges, making it a great outing for all seasons. In the summer the trail will stay cool, and in the cold season you can sit on benches on any of the three exposed ridges to take in views all the way to Mount Diablo.

Before you start, grab a free brochure at the trailhead for a self-guided tour of the preserve. The Huckleberry Path angles right, then immediately reaches a junction; bear left down a slope. This shaded path plunges into a forest where oaks and ferns are at home, along with wild cucumber vines intertwined in the vegetation. Short switchbacks take you to the lower trail at 0.2 mile, where trail marker 1 awaits you in front of a Pacific madrone. Continue along this dirt path where you learn about ferns. Under the hazelnut tree at marker 2,

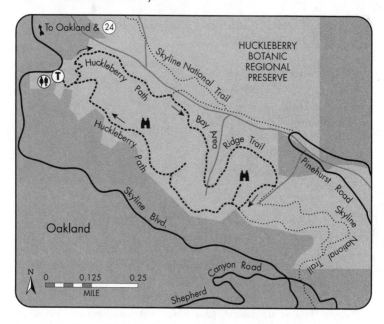

have the kids look for empty nuts on the ground, maybe under layers of leaves.

Continue on a gentler slope and notice how ferns give way to hazelnuts and bay laurels. Soil erosion exposes entire laurel root systems, a delicate balancing act on the slopes for these massive trees. At 0.32 mile, the path intersects with two major hiking trails. Coming from the left is the Skyline National Trail, a 32-mile-long trail that crosses six East Bay parks and at this point comes from Sibley Volcanic Regional Preserve (Hike 38). To the right is the Bay Area Ridge Trail, a project to connect 550 contiguous miles of ridgeline trails in the Bay Area. Head uphill (right) on the Bay Area Ridge Trail. Kids will enter a fern universe where sword ferns are prevalent. Just turn any leaf and look at the pattern of the spores underneath. If your kids have a sketchbook or a nature journal, they can try copying the design. Right before you reach the ridge, the trail gets steeper and dips like a roller coaster.

At 0.93 mile, turn right up the hill on a steep connector trail and at 1.04 miles, right again on the Huckleberry Path. Now's the time to pay attention to the two short side trips the preserve offers you. The first one (to trail marker 6) offers beautiful views of the Oakland hills and Sibley Volcanic Regional Preserve. The bench and open bare areas make a good rest or picnic stop so kids can roam around. The second side trip, at trail marker 8, leads to a manzanita world, but with a smaller footprint and no views, it won't keep you as long as the previous ridge unless kids start playing treehouse under the manzanita bushes.

Come back on the main path and travel through open tunnels of huckleberry, following a level line to an overlook with a bench. The trail, now level, curves left and returns to the trailhead at 1.7 miles.

Huckleberry bushes give their name to this park.

 SIBLEY VOLCANIC REGIONAL PRESERVE

BEFORE YOU GO
Maps: USGS Richmond. Free map online at the park and online.
Information: East Bay Regional Park District (510) 562-PARK. www.ebparks.org

ABOUT THE HIKE
Day hike; Easy/Moderate; Year round
1.6 miles, loop
Hiking time: 1–2 hours
High point/elevation gain: 1600 feet/200 feet

GETTING THERE

■ From CA-24 in Oakland east of the Caldecott Tunnel, take the Fish Ranch exit.

■ Drive 0.8 mile to Grizzly Peak Boulevard.

■ Turn left and continue 2.4 miles to Skyline Boulevard.

■ Turn left onto Skyline Boulevard. The park's entrance is 0.25 mile farther on the left.

■ For public transit options, visit www.transitandtrails.org/trail heads/187.

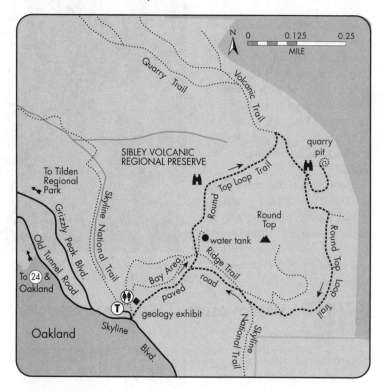

ON THE TRAIL

Who would have thought there was a volcano in Oakland? While this is not exactly Kilauea—the volcano was active 11 million years ago—you will hike around an extinct volcano called Round Top. The highlight of the trip for children will probably not be a reclining volcano, as exciting as that sounds, but a rock maze at the bottom of a quarry.

From the parking lot, pick up a map and walk east (right) to the gate. Get on the Round Top Loop Trail, a paved road with a gentle grade that curves underneath eucalyptus trees. Just before 0.2 mile, the road forks; the right fork leads up to a water tank and to the south is the trail portion you'll be coming back on. Bear left on a gentler grade to keep on the main trail, which circles clockwise around the volcano. Bear left again along a grove of eucalyptus trees. You are now on a wide gravel-and-dirt road that stays mostly level and enters the volcanic area with panoramic views of the surrounding hills. West of the road, you can see the Skyline National

The park's maze is a fun feature for all ages.

Trail (part of the Bay Area Ridge Trail) crossing a smooth ridgeline, the result of tectonic plates having pushed Round Top onto its side.

At 0.6 mile the trail angles left and reaches a junction where the Volcanic Trail leaves the Round Top Loop Trail. Before you make a sharp right to stay on the Round Top Loop Trail, look for exposed rock to the west above the Volcanic Trail. Embedded in the hillside are quartz rocks called amygdules that look like milky-clear marbles. These are essentially fossil gas bubbles trapped in lava flows that filled with minerals when the lava cooled down. As the volcanic layers erode, these compact bubbles surface at the edges of exposed rocky surfaces.

Turn right on the Round Top Loop Trail and make your way to a fence overlooking a steep drop. At the bottom is the quarry pit your children will love. This quarry pit was started in 1947, and natural water accumulation has left a seasonal pond that becomes a marsh in the summer.

At 0.7 mile, turn left to find the service road that goes down to the bottom of the quarry pit. Walk past the wooden sign to reach the labyrinth. Although supposedly this serpentine maze was made for spiritual walking, most children seem to run through its curving lines. At the edge of the maze, after the wet season, the pond is habitat for the red-legged frog, garter snakes, and newts. Pollywogs ripple the water in the spring.

On the hills right below the fence, look for three diagonal bands that indicate different lava flows. This rock layer crumbles easily, which explains the existence of the gravel quarry.

When your children know the labyrinth inside out, you can climb back up the service road to the Round Top Loop Trail and make a left. The trail curves right around the 1-mile mark, then goes uphill and traverses the eastern slopes of Round Top. The trail soon enters a dense mixed pine forest, passes a metal gate, and meanders quietly around the top of the volcano (although you never see it directly).

At 1.35 miles you come to a junction with the Bay Area Ridge Trail. Walk uphill to reach the paved road at 1.65 miles and follow it downhill (west) to return to the parking lot.

 JOHN MUIR NATIONAL HISTORIC SITE/ MOUNT WANDA

BEFORE YOU GO
Maps: USGS Benicia. Free map at ranger station of the John Muir National Historic Site across CA-4.
Information: Visitor center (925) 228-8860. www.nps .gov/jomu

ABOUT THE HIKE
Day hike; Moderate/Difficult; Spring, Fall, Winter
2.3 miles, round-trip
Hiking time: 2 hours
High point/elevation gain: 660 feet/660 feet

GETTING THERE

- Going eastbound on I-80, exit on CA-4E toward Stockton.
- Going northbound or southbound on I-680, exit on CA-4 westbound.
- Exit at Alhambra Avenue, turning right at the bottom of the ramp.
- From the John Muir National Historic Site, drive south on Alhambra Avenue and go under the freeway.
- The Mount Wanda parking lot is immediately to your right at the corner of Alhambra Avenue and Franklin Canyon Road.
- From the Martinez Amtrak station, or the Pleasant Hill and Walnut Creek BART stations, County Connection buses run to Alhambra Avenue and Walnut.

ON THE TRAIL
John Muir, who lived in Martinez on a 2600-acre orchard from 1890 to his death in 1914, was the doting father of two daughters. After he named a hill behind their house after his eldest daughter, Wanda, the second one protested; thus the twin hill was named Mount Helen. The property became a national historic site in 1964 and now preserves the house where Muir lived, the surrounding orchard, and 365 acres of oak hills. Also at the site, the Martinez Adobe has an exhibition on Juan

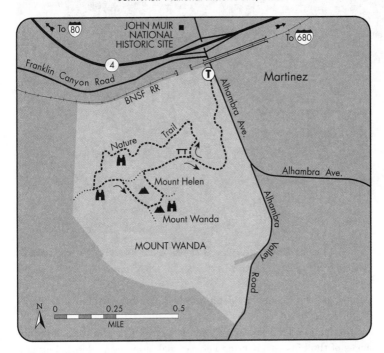

Bautista de Anza, a Spanish explorer who found the first overland route to San Francisco Bay in 1776. Now separated from the Muir house by CA-4 and encircled by homes and industries, the oak and grass woodlands of Mount Wanda stand in stark contrast to their surroundings. However, do combine this hike with a visit to John Muir's house to visit his home and gardens. You will get a sense of who the spiritual father of our national parks really was.

From the parking lot, walk along Franklin Canyon Road and up a few steps to the trailhead on the left to get on the main fire road. Beyond the gate, a signboard displays a map as well as local information on trail use and plants. Note that this entrance is the only way out of the park. The roads that branch off the trail are all dead ends apart from the Nature Trail.

The fire road climbs a solid 400 feet over the next 0.5 mile, getting you around the hill and, for the most part, away from the city's traffic noise. Black oak, coast live oak, and bay laurel line the trail. After this harrowing climb at 0.5 mile, turn right at the junction with the Nature Trail and take a well-deserved rest on a bench. Pick up a laminated self-

Pick up a self-guided brochure at the start of the Nature Trail.

guided tour for insights on John Muir's life and the wildlife and plants on the trail.

The Nature Trail is a mostly level narrow dirt trail that skirts the edges of the hills, meandering between oak groves and descending at a slight grade. Past a bridge and before trail marker 5, watch out for a beehive inside an oak tree on the right side of the trail, 8 feet above the ground. The trail keeps going down and crosses another bridge before finally going up steep sides on tall wooden steps. The steps soon give way to a regular trail that rises out of the oak forest, offering panoramic views of the grassy slopes right below Mount Wanda. A bench allows you to catch your breath and to contemplate what's coming ahead. Marker 9 is the last on the Nature Trail and leads you to the next trail junction at 1.1 miles.

Turn left on the service road. At the ridgetop, the road forks without any signs or directions. Bear right on the service road for the last (gentle) part of the climb. At 1.3 miles Mount Wanda is up the small trail that departs on the left, right across from Mount Helen at the same elevation; twin summits for two sisters. Though Mount Wanda's top is marked by a small concrete base with a metallic post, the views from the Diablo Range all the way to Carquinez Strait are stunning.

Look for a narrow grassy trail north of the summit and descend the slope to a service road. Turn left to connect with the main road. Turn right to retrace your steps to the parking lot.

MARTINEZ REGIONAL SHORELINE

BEFORE YOU GO
Maps: USGS Benicia. Free map at trailhead.
Information: East Bay Regional Park District (888) 327-2757 option 3, ext. 4542. www.ebparks.org

ABOUT THE HIKE
Day hike; Easy; Year round
2 miles, round-trip
Hiking time: 1 hour
High point/elevation gain: 0 feet/negligible

GETTING THERE

■ From CA-4 in Martinez, exit at Alhambra Avenue and go north to Escobar Street. Turn right on Escobar, then left on Ferry Street. Go over the railroad tracks and turn right on Joe Di Maggio Drive, then left on North Court Street. Continue straight to the Martinez Regional Shoreline Ferry Point parking lot on the left by the waterfront.

■ From I-680 in Martinez, exit at Marina Vista and go west. Turn right on Ferry Street into the park.

■ The Martinez Amtrak station borders the park. Exit on Marina Vista Avenue heading north, turn left on Ferry Street, and keep going to the waterfront.

■ Western Contra Costa Transit Authority line 30Z connects with El Cerrito del Norte BART. County Connection buses 108 and 116 connect with North Concord/Martinez BART. County Connection bus 116 connects with Walnut Street BART.

ON THE TRAIL

This bayside family-oriented park along Carquinez Strait is split into a natural habitat marsh, recreational lawns, playgrounds, and picnic areas. Enjoying a full sun (or fog) exposure with bay breezes, this easy hike is for all ages.

From the parking lot, follow the shoreline, heading west on a gravel path leading to the Duck Pond Trail. Colonies of geese and ducks call this pond home, providing endless hours of bird-viewing pleasure for little ones—and making the pond's sand beach a bird-poop minefield best avoided.

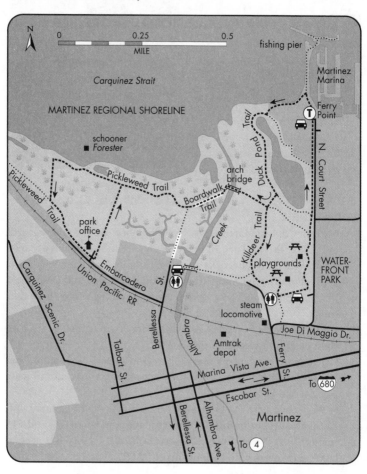

Progressing between the pond and a natural wildlife refuge for migratory birds, you'll find a walkway over the marsh at 0.3 mile. Turn right on the Boardwalk Trail and right again on the flat gravel road that leads toward a wooden bridge. Arching gracefully over Alhambra Creek, the bridge is one of the distinctive landmarks of this park. Get on the elevated boardwalk to explore the wildlife diversity of this marsh that was extensively restored to provide critical habitat for the delta smelt and the winter-run chinook salmon. You can now see a maze of sloughs connecting with Alhambra Creek and, farther away, mudflats

The remains of the schooner Forester *are close to shore.*

that regularly get flooded with tides. If you are lucky you will spot the salt marsh harvest mouse, but this tiny rodent is a shy animal that prefers to wander at night.

From time to time the sound of trains on the tracks reminds you that this park sits at the edge of an urban environment. However, its bayside trails feel very removed.

Continue on the Pickleweed Trail and look for egrets, geese, and pheasants. At 0.7 mile, the trail is so close to the shoreline that you can relax on a small beach with a big stump behind the interpretive sign for the schooner *Forester*. In front of you a few feet offshore, the sunken hull contemplates the passage of time. This 105-year-old wooden skeleton is now an organic part of the bay's mudflats. Just look at the plants growing on it! However, from 1900 to the Second World War, this 217-foot-long four-masted ship carried lumber over the Pacific Ocean to China, Peru, and the South Pacific islands.

Continue past a dark sandy cove as the Pickleweed Trail bends sharply to the right then left just before the next junction toward the train tracks. At this junction, bear left. The path goes behind the park's office buildings, and exits through the parking lot. Walk north to return to the Pickleweed Trail and retrace your steps until you find the Kill-deer Trail across from the walkway at 1.4 miles.

Turn right to circle around the green lawns on a paved path, pass-ing restrooms, a small play structure, and picnic tables. Turn left after the parking lot to head toward the duck pond and back to the Ferry Point parking lot. On Ferry Street on your way out, admire the shiny Southern Pacific steam locomotive built in 1921 and its wooden Santa Fe boxcar and caboose.

 FERNANDEZ RANCH

<table>
<tr><td>

BEFORE YOU GO
Maps: USGS Mare Island/
Richmond. Free map at the
trailhead.
Information: Muir Heritage
Land Trust (925) 228-5460.
Bay Area Ridge Trail,
www.ridgetrail.org

</td><td>

ABOUT THE HIKE
Day hike; Moderate; Spring,
Fall, Winter
3.6 miles, loop
Hiking time: 2–3 hours
**High point/elevation
loss:** 680 feet/410 feet

</td></tr>
</table>

GETTING THERE

- From CA-4 westbound after Martinez, take the Franklin Canyon exit. Turn left and merge onto CA-4 eastbound.
- From CA-4 eastbound, take the first exit after the Franklin Canyon Golf Course onto Christie Road. (Use caution: Christie Road is a minor exit off CA-4.)
- Fernandez Ranch is 0.7 mile down Christie Road on your right.
- There is no public transit.

ON THE TRAIL

Opened to the public in 2010, this historic ranch combines 702 acres of open hills, woodlands, and creeks between Hercules and Martinez. Add-ing a segment to the Bay Ridge Trail, the ranch provides an opportunity for hikers to continue exploring the parks and watershed in a corridor that stretches on both sides of CA-4. Your hike will provide scenic views of the surrounding hills and up-close scrutiny of the underwood in the search for local rodents.

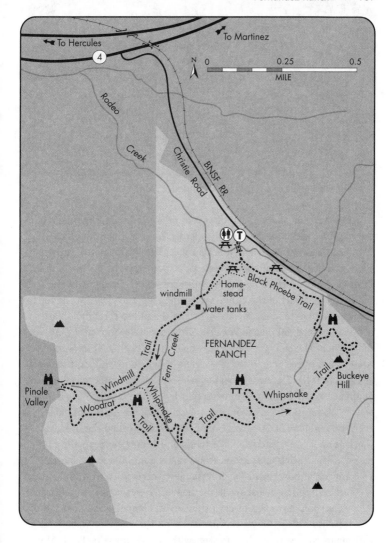

From the parking lot, cross the 156-foot-long bridge over Rodeo Creek to reach a multiple trail junction. Turn right on the Windmill Trail, a wide dirt road that leads to a cattle gate. Though the grasses around you seem safe, make sure children stick to the trails and watch where they step, as the park is home to the endangered Alameda whip snake or striped racer, a yellow- or orange-striped snake with a black or dark brown body. Garter snakes are common here, too.

Looking for snakes and raptors at Fernandez Ranch

After 0.2 mile you will see the windmill on your right against a backdrop of live oaks and grassy hills, across from water tanks. The Windmill Trail soon reaches the junction with the Whipsnake Trail, at the edge of a buckeye and oak forest. Continue straight on the Windmill Trail as it climbs the ridge, first under tree cover, then out in the open. While the last part of the climb will seem steep, the views at the top are gorgeous and extend on the other side of the hill to the Pinole Valley.

Make a hard left on the Woodrat Trail, a smaller dirt trail that skirts the hillside. The change from grassy open ridge to shaded tree-lined trail is abrupt and welcome. After the ascent, it is nice to walk on this mostly level path. Tell children to quiet down because if they talk too loudly, they might scare away the little rodents that live in these hills. They'll have to be very observant to see them, because gophers are quick animals. However, the real star of this trail is a sneaky rodent called the dusky-footed woodrat that builds nests out of twigs and branches. Scan the hills for messy-looking stick piles; chances are they might be woodrat nests.

Canyons of bay laurels with ferns now surround you; this habitat is soon interrupted by a boardwalk that leads across a riparian area to more laurel canyons. As you get out of this forest, enjoy the splendid views of the opposite hills. Alternating meadows and mixed oak woodland, you will make your way to the junction with the Whipsnake Trail. Make a hard right on the Whipsnake Trail to get to the most scenic part of the park. For a little while you will follow the bed of Fern Creek, but you will leave it for a steep ascent of the next ridge. Again, watch for little rodents on the trailsides, as well as garter snakes once you reach the grassy hills.

In the distance you see a lone oak sitting on the hill. It is a blue oak, and the two benches below provide a great spot to stop for a snack while enjoying views of the surrounding hills. After you resume your walk, the trail keeps climbing gradually through open grassland until you reach the highest point of the hike, marked by a single bench at 680 feet. Down below you can see—and hear—CA-4, as well as rolling hills, an electric power station, and Carquinez Strait. If you look closely you will even be able to see the parking lot.

Good news for little ones: the trail is now all downhill. Once you reach the bottom of Buckeye Hill, make a left to go through a cattle gate and follow the Black Phoebe Trail back to the parking lot. Black phoebes are little black birds with white bellies that build nests of mud and grass over or near water. This is why your best chance to spot this bird is on this trail, following the creek.

 MOUNT DIABLO STATE PARK/MITCHELL CANYON

BEFORE YOU GO
Maps: USGS Walnut Creek. Map available for purchase at the Mitchell Canyon Interpretive Center (open weekends, www.mdia.org).
Information: Mount Diablo State Park (925) 837-2525. California State Parks, www.parks.ca.gov

ABOUT THE HIKE
Day hike; Easy/Moderate; Year round
2.15 miles, round-trip
Hiking time: 1–2 hours
High point/elevation gain: 800 feet/200 feet

GETTING THERE

■ From I-680 in Walnut Creek or CA-24 eastbound (before merging with I-680), take the Ygnacio Valley Road exit (right), and drive 7 miles on Ygnacio Valley Road.

■ Turn right onto Clayton Road and right again onto Mitchell Canyon Road. The visitor center is at the end of Mitchell Canyon Road.

■ Mount Diablo State Park's Mitchell Canyon Staging Area is accessible from the Walnut Creek BART Station with a bus connection that stops 0.6 mile from the trailhead. Check www.transit andtrails.org/trailheads/99/ for details.

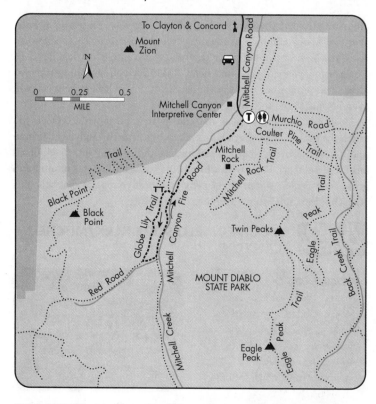

ON THE TRAIL

Towering above the Bay Area from its summit at 3849 feet, Mount Diablo is a major landmark with an extensive trail system. Mitchell Canyon, at the northern edge of the park, is the epicenter of nature education in the park and a hot spot for tarantulas. In the winter, birds are a big attraction, as this side of the mountain is known for winter migrations. Even at the parking lot, you can spot permanent residents such as the acorn woodpecker or the western wood pewee. Spring is wildflower season, and Bay Area enthusiasts come from all over to scout these hills for ephemeral blooms. Summers are hot and sunny, but the shade in the canyon cools off dry days. Fall is best for crimson foliage on the trails and Mount Diablo's iconic eight-legged creature, the hairy tarantula. If you hike between August and October, be on the lookout for the crawlies during mating season. If you are lucky, you'll spot a male scurrying on trails and roads to find a female to court in her burrow.

For a more plant-oriented tour, pick up a self-guided brochure for the Mitchell Canyon Trail inside the Mitchell Canyon Interpretive Center, where children can find displays about various aspects of Mount Diablo State Park, such as geology, wildlife, trails, and plant life.

In terms of signage, the naming of markers differs from other Bay Area parks and can be confusing to the uninitiated. For example, a marker will say BLACK POINT ROAD TO RED ROAD, giving you both the immediate trail and the final destination at once. The trail you are currently *on* is marked in small type, horizontally. The name of the trail or road you are heading *to* is marked in big type, vertically. The big letters do not indicate your location, only your destination. Be vigilant in reading the signs carefully to get used to this format.

From the parking lot, head southwest on Mitchell Canyon Fire Road, an oak-lined fire road that rises slightly on the flanks of the mountain. Wild grapevines and poison oak are common plants along the trail, as are coffeeberry and sagebrush. Following the bottom of the canyon, the road is mostly level.

At 0.6 mile at a junction, a bench under an oak tree provides welcome respite from the sun if you are hiking in the summer. Turn right on the Black Point Trail, a dirt path that climbs in gentle switchbacks. At 0.7 mile, turn left on the Globe Lily Trail, a narrow dirt trail that skirts the edges of a canyon before meeting Red Road at 1.12 miles. Along the trail, look for small round burrows in the hillside; they might be tarantula hangouts. At 1.12 miles, turn left on Red Road and left again on Mitchell Canyon Fire Road at 1.2 miles.

The road goes slightly downhill along a seasonal creek that allows diverse vegetation to grow here. Continue straight until you reach the bench at 1.55 miles and straight again to reach the Mitchell Canyon trailhead at 2.15 miles.

Tarantula hikes are one of the best ways to enjoy Mitchell Canyon after summer has passed.

TARANTULAS

North America's largest spider, the tarantula, is a light and fragile creature that roams the hills of Mount Diablo in the fall. A tarantula spends most of its life in and around its underground dirt burrow. Male tarantulas only come out of their burrows once they've reached maturity—between seven and ten years—and start searching for females by scent. From that moment, they only have a year left to live as they slowly starve to death—or get eaten by hungry females or their main predator, the tarantula hawk wasp. To learn more about these fascinating creatures, children will love to join tarantula hikes in the fall (check the schedule of the Mount Diablo Interpretive Association at www.mdia.org).

BLACK DIAMOND MINES REGIONAL PRESERVE

BEFORE YOU GO
Map: USGS Antioch South. Free map at the trailhead.
Information: Ranger office (925) 757-2620. East Bay Regional Park District, www.ebparks.com

ABOUT THE HIKE
Day hike; Moderate/Difficult; Spring, Fall, Winter
2.3 miles, loop
Hiking time: 2–3 hours
High point/elevation gain: 1200 feet/460 feet

GETTING THERE

■ From CA-4, take the Somersville Road exit in Antioch. Drive south (away from the Sacramento River) on Somersville Road to the Black Diamond Mines Regional Preserve entrance.

■ Continue 0.9 mile farther to a parking lot by a large picnic area, where the hike begins. This is also where the Hazel Atlas Mine tours start.

■ There is no public transit.

ON THE TRAIL

Black Diamond Mines Regional Preserve is an absolute must-see in the East Bay park system (except in the summer when it's blazing hot). You will be blown away by the serene beauty of the landscapes and the

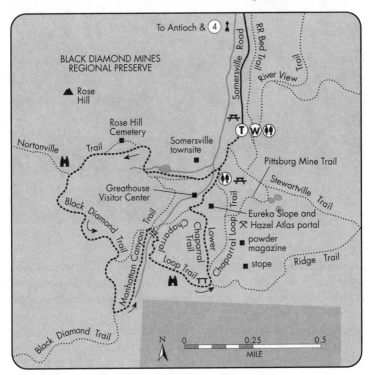

rich mining history. Did you realize there were mines in the Bay Area? "Black diamond" refers to coal, and in the 1860s there were five coal-mining towns housing 900 people in the preserve, making the area the largest coal-mining operation in California. Up to four million pounds of coal were extracted from these hills, and miners and their families suffered the hard life and plights of coal mining.

The only mine you can visit with your children (ages seven and above) is the Hazel Atlas Mine, which supplied silica-rich sand for quality glassmaking (e.g., ketchup bottles) and steel foundries. Even if you don't visit the mine, walking the trails of this beautiful preserve will let you discover remains of these long-deserted mining towns. This hike will lead you through a pioneer cemetery, up a grassy ridge, down some manzanita-covered rocky slopes, and past two mine shafts where you can peek down through metal gates.

From the parking lot, head straight up the Nortonville Trail, a paved road at this point. The rolling hills around you are dotted with dark

Lunar landscapes and mining history blend at Black Diamond Mines.

green oak trees. Down the small hill, stay right on the Nortonville Trail toward the Rose Hill Cemetery. This wide dirt road slowly gains elevation through grassy meadows and buckeye trees. At the fork, bear right and make your way up a wide S cutting across the hillside. The pond on your right is home to many frogs, newts, and birds.

Up above, the iconic pencil shape of cypress trees announces the cemetery. Though the cypress is exotic and was imported, this tree has fascinating historical connections. Used in ancient Egypt to make sarcophagi, cypress trees were planted all around the Mediterranean in cemeteries and symbolized life after death. In the 1860s, when this cemetery was started, the cypress tradition was still very strong.

As the trail angles right, look for a rusty old trough under the trees. On your way up, take a good look at the ring of bald hills in front of you. The way their parallel lines etch themselves against the sky is pure nature art. To visit the cemetery, turn right at the unsigned dirt road. It is well worth a detour (see sidebar), a poignant testament to the hard living conditions and epidemics of the Victorian era.

Continue up the road all the way to Nortonville Pass and enjoy sweeping vistas north and west of the upper Kirker Creek watershed and the valley where Nortonville, one of the five coal-mining towns, was located. Raptors revel in the powerlines overhead as their towers provide perfect observation platforms for small mammals.

Turn left on the Black Diamond Trail, a wide dirt road that climbs steeply through blue oaks. After a short but challenging section, the trail levels out and climbs again, though more moderately. Blue oaks and toyon provide much-welcomed shade. On windy days, listen to the ruffle of the leaves in trees. After a gentle descent, walk past cattle gates and descend through low chaparral. At the next trail junction with the Manhattan Canyon Trail, continue straight on the Black Diamond Trail.

The sandstone walls above the trail are part of a specific geological formation called the Domengine Formation. Millions of years ago when this land was under an ocean, decomposed vegetation accumulated at the bottom of the sea and turned into peat while being covered by silica-rich sediments eroding from the Sierras. Fast forward a few million years, with a drop in sea level and tectonic upheaval. The carbon in the peat converted to coal and the compressed sediments formed sandstone. This explains the presence of coal and sand mines at the same park, as well as sandstone formations throughout the hillsides.

Continue, and before the next gate, turn left on the Manhattan Canyon Trail, a single-track dirt trail that steeply descends the ridge, with a few sharp drops. Notice how the opposite hill seems close and how narrow the canyon is. You will reach a flight of steps going down near the bottom of the gully. At the intersection with the Chaparral Loop Trail, keep straight and then turn right on the wooden bridge. The Chaparral Loop Trail's climb to the ridgetop has some heart-pumping stretches, but the short level ones will let you catch your breath. You may scent whiffs of yerba santa and aromatic sage bushes along the trail. When you finally reach the top of the hill with its tufts of paintbrush, enjoy its rugged beauty under a power tower. The Chaparral Loop Trail keeps on straight, lined with manzanita and chamise and offering great views of the rocky ridge ahead.

At the next intersection, turn left to stay on Chaparral Loop Trail, coming down the hillside on exposed rock, still among a picturesque blend of manzanita, toyon, and Coulter pine. A bench under a pine tree provides a well-deserved resting spot in the shade. At the next junction, take a slight left on the Lower Chaparral Trail and continue your descent on rocky patches of clay and sand. Use caution in tricky spots. Sticky monkey flowers and sage cover the sides of the trail. As you hit a flight of stairs, turn right and go down the steps to an open gravel area.

At the bottom the angular entrance awning of the Eureka Slope juts out of the mountainside. On a hot day, it feels wonderful to get close and enjoy the cold air coming out of the shaft. Peek through the gates and see how steeply the tunnel digs into the earth. The Eureka Mine was a coal mine. Across from the Eureka Slope, walk down another flight of stairs to the entrance of the Greathouse Visitor Center, the original portal (opening) into the Hazel Atlas sand mine.

Walk down to the picnic area and straight down to the parking lot.

VISIT A SAND MINE!

For children ages seven and above, the tour of the Hazel Atlas underground silica sand mine is a must, but you need to get your timing right. Tours are offered weekends only from March to November. Check www.ebparks.org to find out the days and hours of these tours. It is a great educational experience with hard hats, flashlights, and the opportunity to see a portion of the mine as it existed when it was still operational. Visitors take a 950-foot walk into the mine to see mine workings, ore chutes, the shifter's office (mine boss), and ancient geological features.

THE ROSE HILL CEMETERY

The Rose Hill Cemetery is the resting place of almost two hundred Protestants, many of them Welsh, and is still being restored after years of vandalism. Walking between the graves, notice how shockingly white the gravestones are. They look almost new, but they were carved out of white marble more than a hundred years ago. Low rainfall allows them to withstand the passage of time without lichen or mold.

For children, a sculpture art scavenger hunt of the cemetery is a non-spooky way to understand symbols associated with saying goodbye to a loved one. If you can, grab a cemetery interpretive brochure so you can correlate your findings to people's actual biographies. Have children walk around and look for carved headstones. A carved decoration of a lamb designates a child, as does a tiny hand on a bed of roses. Clasped hands mean saying good-bye. Lilies are a symbol of death and were placed on graves of young innocents. Tulips are the symbol of undying love. Look for more symbols and decipher their hidden meaning.

MORGAN TERRITORY REGIONAL PRESERVE

BEFORE YOU GO
Maps: USGS Altamont. Free map at trailhead.
Information: Morgan Territory Rangers (888) 327-2757, option 3, extension 4546. East Bay Regional Park District, www.ebparks.org

ABOUT THE HIKE
Day hike; Moderate/Difficult; Spring, Fall, Winter
4.7 miles, loop; 5.95 miles including Bob Walker Ridge
Hiking time: 2–3 hours
High point/elevation gain: 2030 feet/600 feet

GETTING THERE

- From I-580 in Livermore, exit at North Livermore Ave-nue and head north for 4 miles. North Livermore Avenue becomes Manning Road.
- Turn right onto Morgan Territory Road and drive 5.5 miles to the park entrance. (The last 4 miles are on a single-lane road.)
- There is no public transit.

ON THE TRAIL

Spreading from Mount Diablo to the Contra Costa watershed, Morgan Territory Regional Preserve is the place to feel far from it all only minutes from bustling Livermore. Named after Jeremiah Morgan who bought this ranch in 1847 to hunt grizzly bears, Morgan Territory was the traditional land of a Bay Miwok-speaking group called the Volvon people.

Because of the steep and narrow last leg of the route, this hike is best for parents with walking children or with child carriers. Strollers would only be able to do an out-and-back on the Volvon and Blue Oak trails to the junction with the Corral Trail.

At the trailhead, kids can see the cattle corral still used by cows grazing in the park, next to the picnic tables and restrooms. Head right on the Volvon Trail and walk past a cattle gate. The trail creeps up a hill and turns left on a wide ranch road. After another hill, the trail starts a slow meandering descent across grassy slopes and oak woodland. At 0.3 mile, the trail merges with a gravel road that snakes like a gray ribbon between oak and buckeye trees.

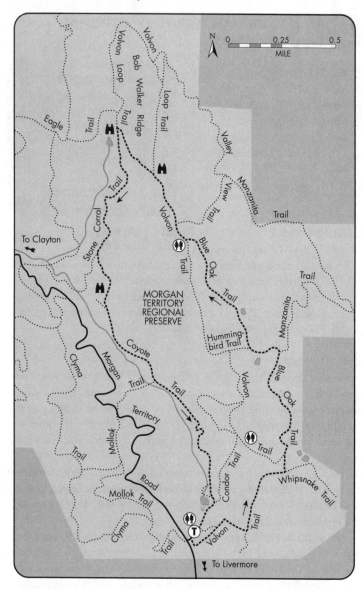

Turn left at 0.6 mile to get on the Blue Oak Trail, a beautiful wide road lined with the eponymous tree. Have your kids look at the waxy blue leaves of blue oak trees. Growing all along the trail, these trees yielded up to 500

pounds of acorns per year, ready to be used as mush or cakes by the Volvon people. High in protein and fiber, acorns were a very important food source for the California Native Americans and harvested in the fall. For details on how the Coast Miwok processed acorns into flour and the essential leaching out of tannins, see Hike 45. Try acorn muffins at home, they're tasty!

Enjoying a picnic lunch amidst the never-ending hills of the Morgan Territory

Turn left at 1.2 miles to stay on the Blue Oak Trail and look for a sag pond on your right around 1.6 miles. Green balls of mistletoe grow on many trees, their parasite existence spread on blue and valley oak trees by birds that eat its sticky fruit and poop the seeds on the trees' branches. A restroom graces the intersection at 1.9 miles where you turn right, past a gate, on the Volvon Trail. Miles of oak savannah on rolling hills unfold with views of Mount Diablo to the west.

At 2.3 miles, the Volvon Trail bears left on a ridge where the Volvon Loop Trail takes off on the right. This ridge between two valleys is the ideal spot for a picnic lunch. Climb on the promontory across from the trail marker to enjoy higher views, and a flat area. To prolong these views, you can add 1.25 miles to this loop by heading north on the Volvon Loop Trail and circling around Bob Walker Ridge. At the south junction between the Volvon Trail and the Volvon Loop Trail, turn left (west) onto the wide Volvon Trail, going down a lovely valley with a pond. As the trail bends, you can see the coming hairpin trail junction. At 2.9 miles, make a sharp left on the Stone Corral Trail.

Going down the valley, you progressively leave the grassland for more wooded areas where poison oak is abundant in the understory. At 3.3 miles, turn left on the Coyote Trail, a narrow dirt track taking you to the foothill. At the edge of the forest, if you come across a strong vinegar or turpentine smell, look for a small minty plant with blue flowers called tarweed.

Past the cattle gate (be careful of the barbed wire), the trail goes down to a creek and follows its bed upstream. After a big jumble of rocks and an open vista on the valley, the trail climbs steeply in the shade of the forest and crosses the creek before reaching the open and a pond. Frog jumping contests! Continue right at the junction where the Condor Trail arrives from the left and return to the parking lot.

POINT REYES/KULE LOKLO TRAIL

BEFORE YOU GO
Maps: USGS Inverness. Free Point Reyes map/brochure at the Bear Valley Visitor Center.
Information: Point Reyes National Seashore Visitor Center (415) 464-5100. U.S. National Park Service, www.nps.gov/pore/

ABOUT THE HIKE
Day hike; Easy; Year round
0.9 mile, round-trip
Hiking time: 1 hour
High point/elevation gain: 150 feet/50 feet

GETTING THERE
- From CA-1 northbound in Olema, just north of the junction with Sir Francis Drake Boulevard, turn left on Bear Valley Road.
- From CA-1 southbound in Point Reyes Station, go 0.2 mile from the end of the town's main street to Sir Francis Drake Boulevard. Turn right on Bear Valley Road.
- The Point Reyes National Seashore park entrance is on the left. Park by the Bear Valley Visitor Center.
- West Marin Stagecoach services the Bear Valley Visitor Center from Inverness and San Rafael.

ON THE TRAIL
The best place to begin your exploration of Point Reyes National Seashore is the Bear Valley Visitor Center, an information center that includes a store and a natural history museum where younger ones can discover the local wildlife and history through exhibits and displays. (If you have older children, ask about the Junior Ranger program.) From the visitor center you can pick up one of three easy interpretive trails, all good choices for children because they are under a mile and almost completely flat. Picnic tables and benches provide ample places to rest for a snack.

Opposite: *Stairs go up a steep mile along Cataract Falls.*

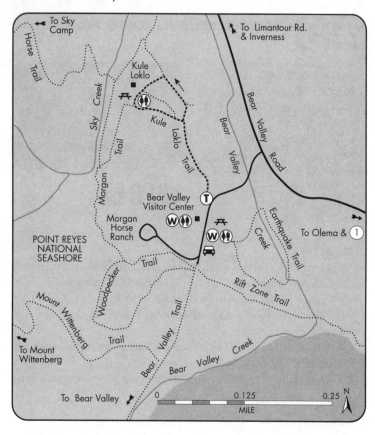

Kule Loklo means "Bear Valley" and is the name of a reconstructed Coast Miwok village maintained by volunteers (www.kuleloklo.com). Each July, a Big Time Festival brings the village to life. Before Europeans, beginning with the Spanish, came to California, the coast of what we call today Marin County was inhabited by the Coast Miwok people. Used for educational purposes and more rarely for ritual celebrations, the village dwellings you are going to see are not remnants of an old site but relatively new constructions dating from the 1970s. Because the site is secluded and away from the visitor center's main buildings, it is easy to imagine what life was like here 300 years ago.

Find the Kule Loklo Trail about 100 yards north of the visitor center, heading up among tanoak and coast live oak trees. Stop in front of the tanoak stump and try to imagine what the oak trees were used for. Acorns were one of the main sources of food of the Coast Miwok. Gathered in the fall, the nuts were stored in granaries for later use throughout the year. Boys went up in the trees to shake the branches, and the falling acorns were then gathered in mats woven of tule or cattail.

Keep moving on the trail and look for miner's lettuce and elderberry. The blue variety of elderberry is edible, and the Coast Miwok brewed tea from its blossoms, using it as a medicine for fever. Ask your children to find in the bushes sticks that they think would make good shafts for arrows and spears.

At 0.1 mile find an interpretive sign about baskets entitled OUR WORLD IS ALIVE. Did you know that the Coast Miwok could weave baskets tight enough to hold water?

Kids get to play traditional Miwok games during ranger-led hikes.

At 0.3 mile, turn right toward Kule Loklo under a line of eucalyptus trees of the south blue gum variety. Those did not exist in the days of the Coast Miwok but were planted by Europeans. From March to July, they host a small population of Bullock's orioles and other overwintering birds.

At 0.45 mile you reach the village. The site for the Kule Loklo reconstructed village was chosen because it could have been, many moons ago, an ideal site for a village: forest nearby, stream on the other side of the hill, meadows around. Look for a grinding stone at the far end of the village. To the left is an acorn granary, used to store acorns. Can you see it? Lined with redwood or Douglas fir bark, it protected the nuts from raccoons, and was topped with buckskin to protect them from the rain.

The location of the grinding stone and granary was not arbitrary. Acorn processing usually entailed grinding acorns into flour and leaching the flour down by the stream to remove the bitter tannic acid (tannins, once used to tan hides) present in most types of acorns.

A cool trick to show your kids is to ask them to lie down foot-to-foot on the ground. This is how the Miwoks decided the circumference of each structure. They had the two tallest members of the household lie down foot-to-foot.

185

To visit the roundhouse, you need to be part of a ranger program. This half-buried structure is charged with meaning and symbols for the Coast Miwoks. Pay attention to etiquette rules about traffic and gestures inside the roundhouse, what you can and cannot touch.

Continue around the loop, then retrace your steps to the parking lot.

THE COAST MIWOKS AND THE SEASONS

Relying on nature's bounty as their sole source of food and other raw materials, the Coast Miwok had a deep understanding of the seasons. While the ocean provided food year round through sea animals and plants, forests and meadows provided food from the spring (grasses, greens, wild berries) through the summer (seeds) and into the fall (acorns, buckeye nuts, hazelnuts . . .). If you can, join the Spring Festival to celebrate strawberries, the Big Time Festival in July to celebrate culture and traditions, or the Acorn Festival in the fall to celebrate the fall harvest.

 POINT REYES/PALOMARIN NATURE TRAIL

BEFORE YOU GO
Maps: USGS Inverness. Free Point Reyes map/brochure at the Bear Valley Visitor Center.
Information: Point Reyes National Seashore Visitor Center (415) 464-5100. U.S. National Park Service, www.nps.gov/pore/

ABOUT THE HIKE
Day hike; Easy; Year round
1 mile, loop
Hiking time: 1 hour
High point/elevation loss: 200 feet/200 feet

GETTING THERE

▪ From CA-1 northbound past Stinson Beach, look for the Bolinas Lagoon on your left. At the north end of the lagoon, turn left on the Bolinas–Fairfax Road (the sign might be missing, because Bolinas residents frequently remove it).

▪ Turn left on Olema–Bolinas Road, heading around the other side of the lagoon toward Bolinas.

■ From CA-1 southbound in Olema, drive about 8 miles and look for an unmarked paved road (Olema–Bolinas Road) on your right across from a white farmhouse, just before the Bolinas Lagoon.
■ Turn right.
■ Drive 0.5 mile down Olema–Bolinas Road and turn left at the first stop sign. The second stop sign will be Mesa Road.
■ Take a right and continue 4 miles on Mesa Road to Point Reyes Bird Observatory (PRBO). (The paved road changes to dirt at about 3.25 miles.)
■ Follow the dirt road until you see the sign for PRBO on your left.
■ Turn in at the driveway on your left; the parking lot is on the right.
■ West Marin Stagecoach provides public transportation between Marin City and Bolinas.

ON THE TRAIL

At the southern tip of the Point Reyes peninsula lies the Palomarin Staging Area, a quieter side of Point Reyes with serious trails leading to

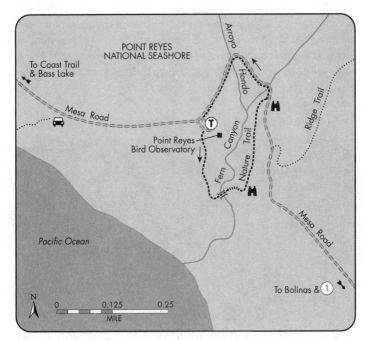

spectacular coastal views. From Bass Lake where you can swim, to the Alamere waterfall gushing 400 feet down to a dark sand beach, and the remote Wildcat Camp right on the beach, this area has a lot to offer. For children, this short hike explores a lush fern canyon with meadows to roam around. Palomarin's Point Reyes Bird Observatory is a must for bird lovers.

From the parking lot, find a narrow grass-and-dirt path that heads west at the sign NATURE TRAIL. You start with a gentle descent through coastal scrub and arrive at a grassy meadow. In the spring, the meadow and trailsides are dotted with wild irises and other wildflowers. At 0.1 mile you get under tree cover surrounded by oak trees whose branches are green with moss. The trail is now lined with ferns on both sides, and this is only the beginning. Green is the dominant color of this hike, thanks to the freshwater creek that runs below.

At 0.2 mile a series of wooden steps descends into the canyon, getting closer to the distant gurgle of the creek. At 0.3 mile, walk across a wooden bridge at the bottom of the narrow canyon. Don't go up just yet—look for three steps going down the trail on your left after the bridge. Have children walk down the steps and look straight ahead. On the tiny packed-dirt ledge 2 feet above water level, the milky waters of the creek run over a bed of red rocks. On the vertical wall in front of you, hundreds of ferns grow, their dark green "hands" hanging above the creek. Farther up toward the ridge, light filters through twisted branches of buckeye trees, adding an eerie feeling to the scenery.

At the bottom of the canyon, there are walls of ferns above the creek.

After exploration time is over, walk up the stairs to continue on the trail. Going up the canyon is steep, but the sights from up above by the wooden fence are rewarding. As the slope gets gentler, the trail winds through grassy woods before opening up on a bright green circular meadow at 0.5 mile. The trail meanders through the meadow and reaches two wooden posts. Look for the tree with old-man's beard dripping from the branches. This is a type of lichen (usnea) that does not damage the tree. The trail continues through the forest and hits a second pair of wooden posts right before a gorgeous ceanothus tree arching over the trail. Have the kids look inside the posts; they are hollow tree stumps.

Head straight through meadows and follow the dirt trail. (After rains, some parts of the trail can become inundated and require waterproof shoes.) A last grove of trees leads you to another view of the canyon before you climb up to Mesa Road. At 0.8 mile, turn left and follow Mesa Road back to the parking lot.

 MARTIN GRIFFIN PRESERVE

BEFORE YOU GO
Maps: USGS Bolinas. Map at visitor center.
Information: Audubon Canyon Ranch Headquarters (415) 868-9244. www.egret.org. Open weekends and holidays from mid-March to mid-July (check website for dates).

ABOUT THE HIKE
Day hike; Easy/Moderate; Spring, Summer
1 mile, loop
Hiking time: 30 minutes–1 hour
High point/elevation gain: 240 feet/240 feet

GETTING THERE

■ From US 101 north from San Francisco or south from San Rafael, take the CA-1/Stinson Beach exit. Follow CA-1 for approximately 12 miles to Stinson Beach and continue 3.5 miles north to Bolinas Lagoon. The Martin Griffin Preserve gate is on the right side of the highway.

■ From US 101 north from San Francisco or south from San Rafael, take the Sir Francis Drake Boulevard exit and drive northwest on

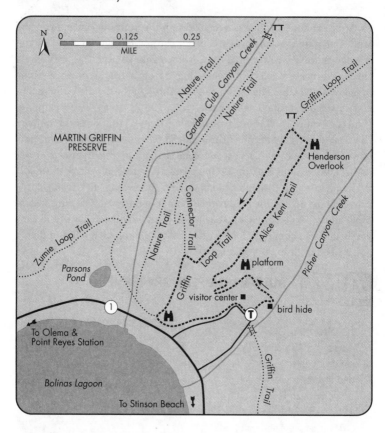

Sir Francis Drake Boulevard for about 21 miles to Olema. Turn south (left) on CA-1 and follow it for about 10 miles to Bolinas Lagoon. The preserve is approximately 1 mile farther on the left.

■ Accessible via the West Marin Stagecoach on a limited basis.

ON THE TRAIL

Formerly known as Audubon Canyon Ranch, Martin Griffin Preserve is only open six months a year to coincide with the nesting of blue herons and white egrets. Take this easy hike to an observation platform so kids can watch snowy white egrets roosting inside old-growth redwood trees. To make this a day, explore the nearby city of Bolinas or enjoy the long, sandy stretch at Stinson Beach.

Binoculars allow ample observation of nesting egrets across the canyon.

Before starting the hike, stop at the preserve's bookstore and ask if they can lend you a telescope. They have a limited number, but a scope will come in handy to see the egrets in the trees.

From the parking lot, don't start your hike immediately. Instead, head out to the garden and ask the kids to find a hut with a roof made of grass. Step inside without making any noise and through blinds, kids will be able to spy on birds as they would at the aquarium for fish. Located beside Picher Canyon Creek, the bird-feeding area is a lush environment of hanging birdhouses and feeding tubes where rodents sometimes like to think they can enjoy the same grainy diet as their feathery friends. This bird hide is a fun place to start to get kids excited about birds.

Back in the garden, find the Alice Kent Trail by a wooden fence. This trail rises up the canyon on dirt and needles under a mixed forest of oaks and bay laurels. Steps lead to a first viewing platform at 0.1 mile. Scan the trees opposite the canyon for any white spots. Depending on the month of your visit, you will see courting birds, nesting birds (quiet time), chicks recently hatched (more chaotic) or taking their first flight (playtime).

Continue on the trail until you reach the Henderson Overlook at 0.4 mile. Docents help out with questions and some preset binoculars facilitate bird-spotting. In any given year, you could view as many as 100 active bird nests in the redwood trees below you. It's exhilarating spotting your first egret, because then you realize how many more there are around. Some trees are high-rises for birds, with several levels of branches taken up for lodging. In addition to the bird show, the view that extends until the lagoon and beyond that, the ocean, is sublime.

After you've had time to enjoy the views, go up a few steps and turn left at the trail junction on the Griffin Loop Trail. Going down on an easy grade, the path is shaded and smooth. After a long wooden bench at 0.7 mile, the trail bends right and then passes a laurel tree with a "mushroomy" base. At 0.8 mile, turn left toward the ranch yard. The trail narrows down to a single track and reaches a viewing platform above the lagoon. Keep going straight to reach the parking lot at 1 mile.

 MUIR WOODS

BEFORE YOU GO
Maps: USGS San Rafael. Map at ranger station.
Information: Ranger station (415) 388-2595. U.S. National Park Service, www.nps.gov/muwo

ABOUT THE HIKE
Day hike; Moderate; Year round
3.6 miles, round-trip
Hiking time: 2.5–3 hours
High point/elevation gain: 300 feet/90 feet

GETTING THERE

■ From US 101 in Mill Valley, exit at CA-1/Stinson Beach and follow CA-1 northbound about 0.5 mile.

■ At the stoplight, turn left and drive about 2.7 miles, following the signs for Muir Woods.

■ At the top of the hill, turn right onto the Panoramic Highway toward Muir Woods/Mount Tamalpais and drive about 0.8 mile.

■ At the four-way intersection where Sequoia Valley Road goes down to Mill Valley, turn left (west) on Muir Woods Road. Continue down the hill about 1.6 miles. The Muir Woods parking lots will be at the bottom of the hill, on a sharp turn, on your right.

■ There is no direct public transit, but Golden Gate Transit bus 63 runs on weekends and holidays and makes stops at the Mountain Home Inn, Pantoll, and Bootjack on the Panoramic Highway—all 1 to 1.8 miles away from Muir Woods.

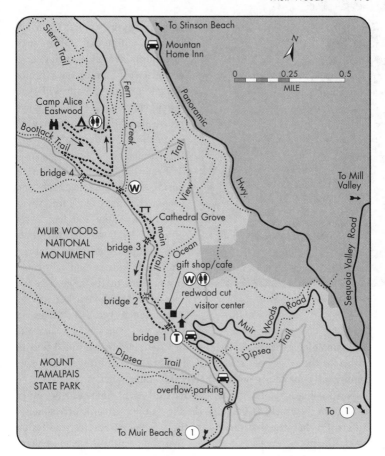

ON THE TRAIL

Only 12 miles north of San Francisco lies the remnant of an ancient redwood forest, a grove tucked in the shadows of Mount Tamalpais that Theodore Roosevelt chose to protect by declaring it a national monument in 1908. Named after conservationist John Muir (see Hike 39 for the John Muir National Historic Site), the park features a creek-side stroll on a succession of boardwalks, dirt trails, and paved trails. Walking through the redwood forest is a meditative experience, but children may view the wide trails, bridges, and nooks and crannies as fodder for a game of tag or hide-and-seek. When nature is fun, you know the day's a success. If things get on the wild side, channel the

Feel tiny in the redwoods.

kids' energy by having them follow the self-guided nature trail (brochures available at the ranger station) or sign up for a Junior Ranger program. Both will help them explore and learn about the redwoods at the same time, with a pinch of nature stewardship thrown in.

From the ranger station, walk past the imposing log arch and get on the main trail, initially a boardwalk. After 200 feet a set of stairs leads to the gift shop, café, and restrooms. Just past the stairs, the kids can enjoy a time-travel game by the huge redwood tree cut with time markers. At 0.1 mile, bridge 1 crosses Redwood Creek on your left. A parallel trail runs along the creek until bridge 3, so if children decided to trail off across the creek, you still meet them at the next bridge—and view them at all times since both trails are 0.05 mile apart.

Keep going straight and follow the trail as it momentarily curves away from the creek. At 0.2 mile, the Pinchot and Emerson trees honor Gifford Pinchot, the first director of the U.S. Forest Service, and Ralph Waldo Emerson, a poet and essayist instrumental in the transcendentalist movement of the mid-nineteenth century. At 0.21 mile, the Ocean View Trail spurs off on your right, a trail initially created as a fire line in the forest. Have children look for fungi on the fallen stump on the right. At 0.25 mile, walk past bridge 2 and a plaza under the redwoods where ranger-led activities sometimes take place and a box full of maps awaits visitors. If you forgot to pick up a trail map at the entrance, here is your last chance.

Continue past bridge 3 at 0.4 mile and tell everybody to stop. You are about to enter the quiet zone of the park. This zone was created so visitors could enjoy the sounds of the forest without human-caused noises. Hush hush, walk softly, and go around Cathedral Grove on the right side. A series of wide benches is an open invitation for children to sit down and get their sketch pads out.

At 0.7 mile, cross a bridge above Fern Creek, a mountain stream that flows into Redwood Creek. You are about to enter the quieter reaches of Muir Woods, paths where crowds thin out. At 0.8 mile, bear right on the Camp Eastwood Trail for a little adventure. This stage road was a busy intersection in 1906 when a branch of the Mount Tamalpais and Muir Woods Scenic Railway was built to transport visitors by steam train from Mill Valley to the Muir Inn. The inn overlooked Redwood Canyon, the former name of Muir Woods, and was surrounded by cabins. At 0.9 mile, look for a bench at the junction of the Camp Eastwood Trail and the Plevin Cut, and continue straight on the Plevin Cut. This narrower trail cuts through the slope in 0.2 mile to join the location of the former Muir Inn, now known as a group campsite, Camp Alice Eastwood, at 1.1 miles.

From Camp Alice Eastwood, cross the parking lot and walk past the gate to continue west on the Camp Eastwood Trail. At 1.3 miles, this is your chance to enjoy a view over Muir Woods. Capture it in your mind or with a camera, as the trail soon reenters dense tree cover looping back around the hill along the old stage road. At 1.8 miles, turn right on the Bootjack Trail to skirt the canyon and come down at creek level upstream from bridge 4. At 2 miles, make a sharp left to follow the creek trail. A few wide spots are good places for an impromptu picnic lunch. Retrace your steps to the entrance, opting to walk down the west-side trails at Cathedral Grove and across the creek, so you get a full experience of Muir Woods.

CELEBRATE THE SOLSTICES AT MUIR WOODS

Twice a year, the rangers at Muir Woods National Monument organize activities, songs, and games to celebrate the solstices. On June 21, visitors gather at Muir Beach and spread blankets on the sand around a bonfire to listen to stories and sing songs for the longest day of the year. On December 21, families join Muir Woods rangers for nature crafts and wait for night to fall, when the forest paths are lit by luminaria and you can walk among the redwoods after sunset. Activities, games, and music celebrate the longest night of the year, and the event takes place rain or shine.

OLOMPALI STATE HISTORIC PARK

BEFORE YOU GO
Maps: USGS Petaluma River.
Map at visitor center.
Information: Park office
(415) 892-3383. California
State Parks, www.parks.ca.gov

ABOUT THE HIKE
Day hike; Easy; Year round
0.6 mile, round-trip
Hiking time: 30 minutes–
1 hour
**High point/elevation
gain:** 200 feet/90 feet

GETTING THERE

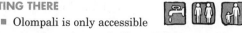

■ Olompali is only accessible coming from the north. From US 101 southbound after Petaluma and before Novato, turn right into the park entrance.

■ From US 101 northbound 3 miles after Novato and before Petaluma, pass the Olompali State Historic Park entrance and turn around at the nearest safest exit.

■ Coming down US 101, the park entrance will be on your right.

■ Proceed to the parking lot.

■ There is no public transit.

ON THE TRAIL

Where else in the Bay Area do you combine Coast Miwok culture with Victorian gardens and a Grateful Dead retreat? Olompali State Historic Park holds a special place among Marin County's parks, partly due to its odd access, but mostly because of its low profile despite unusual natural and cultural offerings. The 700-acre park stretches from Mount Burdell's summit to its bowl-shaped lower flanks. This easy hike meanders through the lower areas where kids can roam on open meadows and play at the re-created Miwok village.

From the parking lot, walk up the gravel road toward the ranch area. The big yellow building across the meadow houses the visitor center. Down the stairs on your right are the terraced Victorian gardens landscaped by Mary Burdell in the 1870s, now ghosts of an elegant past. At its height, the Burdell Garden featured two rockeries, a spectacular spraying fountain with sculpted cranes, curving paths, a gazebo, a pond, and exotic plants. On your left, the burned two-level Burdell Mansion incorporated the earliest European building, a Spanish adobe,

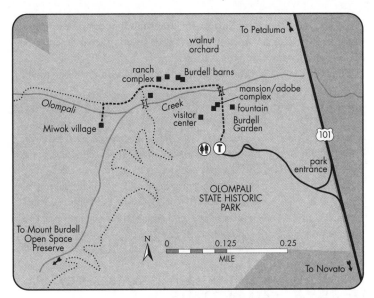

inside its structure. This is where the iconic band the Grateful Dead lived in the spring of 1966, just before they moved to 701 Ashbury.

Continue on the wide service road, which turns left at 0.1 mile and slowly rises up the hill. You pass a barn, the blacksmith forge, and grinding rocks. Entering a spotty oak forest, the road keeps rising and reaches the site of a reconstructed Miwok village at 0.3 mile. Here, kids can sit inside a *kotcha*, a redwood bark Coast Miwok dwelling, and look out on the oak trees that provided the staple mush of Coast Miwok people. Olompali Creek runs right by the village site. After shelling the acorns and grinding them into a fine meal, the Coast Miwoks spread the acorns on a sand plateau and poured the creek's water through branches to leach the bitter tannic acid out of the oak acorns. Only then could they prepare their daily acorn mush.

The round dirt area surrounded by rocks is a ritual dance circle where Coast Miwok ceremonies are held by present-day Miwok descendants. (To learn more about the Miwok, visit the Marin Museum

Olompali's reconstructed Miwok village invites free exploration.

of the American Indian in Novato; www.marinindian.com.) Sitting on the rocks, kids can look for western fence lizards running around, easily identifiable with their bright blue bellies.

To return to the parking lot, retrace your steps on the same road.

OLOMPALI DAY AND BAT NIGHT

To enjoy Olompali's uniqueness, two yearly events are must-sees. On the first Saturday in May, come learn about the Olompali people at the park's Heritage Day, where kids can play Miwok games, watch Pomo dances, or see blacksmithing demonstrations. On the first Saturday of August, families come to the park for an after-hours Bat Night. Play bat-based activities, enjoy bat s'mores, and watch as bats come out of one of the park's structures to eat insects.

 MOUNT TAMALPAIS WATERSHED/ CATARACT FALLS

BEFORE YOU GO
Maps: USGS San Rafael. Map online at www.marin water.org/documents/201 0.10.20_VstrMap_color.pdf
Information: Sky Oaks Ranger Station (415) 945-1181.

ABOUT THE HIKE
Day hike; Moderate/Difficult; Spring, Summer, Winter
3.2 miles, round-trip
Hiking time: 2–3 hours
High point/elevation gain: 1670 feet/1000 feet

GETTING THERE

▪ From US-101 northbound near San Rafael, take the San Anselmo exit, which curves left and takes you to Sir Francis Drake Boulevard.

▪ Drive about 5 miles west to Fairfax. After a small hill as you head down, turn left on Pacheco Street.

▪ At the stop sign, turn right onto Broadway and left onto Bolinas Road. Drive 7.8 miles on Bolinas–Fairfax Road.

▪ Just beyond Alpine Dam, the road curves sharply in a hairpin. Park on the sides of the curve.

▪ For public transit information, visit www.transitandtrails.org /trailheads/90.

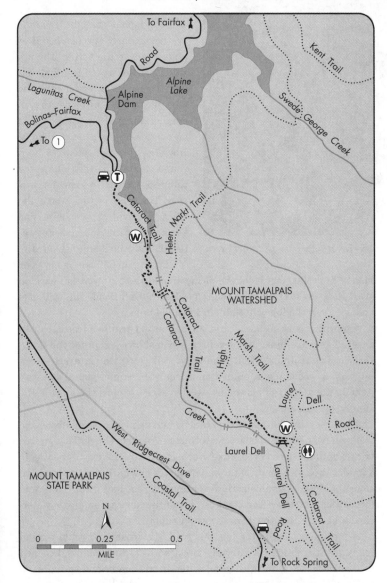

ON THE TRAIL

Cataract Falls is the rock star of Marin County waterfalls for a good reason. This waterfall is actually a series of seven to nine separate waterfalls spread out over a steep mile, each one flowing freely into the next—

Several bridges cross Cataract Creek.

a photographer's delight. The falls are particularly spectacular after a good rain in the spring. The upside: once you reach the first waterfall, you are never far from the next level. The downside: the elevation gain and the tricky footing on narrow steps on the way down! However, fear not. Families with young children do this hike every rainy season and return the next year. The trail is well worth the effort. You will have a hard time keeping up with the number of waterfalls, but you'll enjoy them all.

If going up 650 feet is not your idea of fun (1000 feet is for the picnic area at the top), you can park on West Ridgecrest Drive near the top of Laurel Dell Road. This will give you access to the top waterfall after just 0.4 mile.

From the parking area, find an unmarked trailhead next to two covered garbage bins. This level trail soon shows a sign for the Cataract Trail and Laurel Dell—the only trail going up Cataract Creek anyway. A wooden sign pinned on a tree will remind you of the way. At 0.3 mile a bridge followed by wooden stairs signals the start of the steady zigzag climb.

Underneath a dense redwood canopy and lined by graceful ferns, the trail is a beauty and reaches the bottom of Cataract Creek. Though this trickle of water doesn't seem like much, it actually travels all the way to Tomales Bay, with many of the watercourses flowing down the northern slopes of Mount Tamalpais. However tempting the idea, keep hands and feet out of the water. The creek is part of the Mount Tamalpais watershed and feeds into the domestic water supply.

From the bottom to the top, this trail is a dream and could remind many a little child of a fairytale forest with its lush plants, lichened trees, mossy rocks, and glistening water. In the winter and spring, even the light that filters through the trees has a storybook quality. If you can lend a camera to your child, let them take photos.

Bringing you back to realities, steps show you the way uphill. This is a rare trail where steps outnumber path distances. Though the ascent is steep, the many switchbacks and platforms allow you to pause and get ready for the next stretch. At 0.5 mile, after a bridge at the junction with the Helen Markt Trail, keep right to stay on the Cataract Trail.

Around 1 mile, the trail levels before picking up again, with some eroded trail portions that will make you watch your kids closely. As the terrain gets steeper, handrails assist hikers up the steps. The largest waterfall is at 1.3 miles and can be easily admired from a viewing platform right off the trail. If you want to sit down for lunch, push another 0.3 mile up the hill to Laurel Dell, an open meadow with picnic tables, grills, and restrooms.

Retrace your steps the way you came, being careful not to go too fast. The trail is tricky and slippery going down.

 MOUNT TAMALPAIS WATERSHED/ BON TEMPE LAKE

BEFORE YOU GO
Maps: USGS San Rafael. Map online at www.marin water.org/documents
Information: Sky Oaks Ranger Station (415) 945-1181.

ABOUT THE HIKE
Day hike; Moderate; Year round
3.8 miles, loop
Hiking time: 2 hours
High point/elevation gain: 750 feet/minimal

GETTING THERE

■ From US-101 northbound near San Rafael, take the San Anselmo exit, which curves left and takes you to Sir Francis Drake Boulevard.

■ Drive about 5 miles west to Fairfax. After a small hill as you head down, turn left on Pacheco Street.

■ At the stop sign, turn right onto Broadway and left onto Bolinas–Fairfax Road. Drive roughly 1.5 miles.

■ Turn left on Sky Oaks Road at the sign LAKE LAGUNITAS and drive 0.3 mile to the Sky Oaks Watershed Headquarters on the left.

■ Once past the entrance kiosk, drive about 0.4 mile and turn right to Bon Tempe Lake at a signed junction onto a gravel road. Drive about 0.3 mile, then bear left (unsigned) to the trailhead.

■ For public transit information, visit www.transitandtrails.org /trailheads/89.

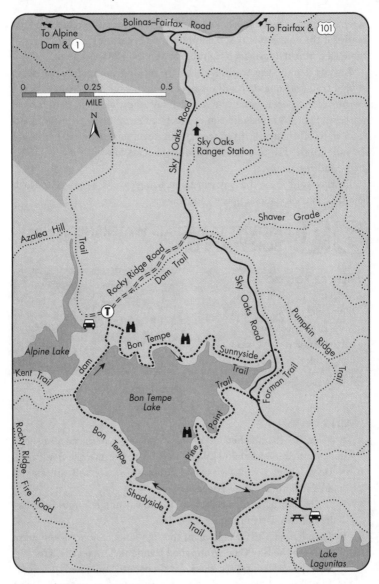

ON THE TRAIL

Mount Tamalpais's north flanks host four major reservoirs whose shores invite scenic strolls and fishing opportunities. Because it offers

Circling Bon Tempe Lake provides incredible views of Mount Tamalpais.

lake views almost all around the trail, Bon Tempe is a perfect family hike. It will also interest curious young engineers as the trail goes over two dam spillways, a fun opportunity to explain the mechanics of dams. After your hike, hit downtown Fairfax for an ice cream or a hot chocolate, depending on the season.

From the parking lot, cross the gate and follow the wide dirt trail going up the hill. Bear left at the fork to follow the Bon Tempe Sunnyside Trail. Over the hill, take in the majestic views of Mount Tamalpais towering 1800 feet over Bon Tempe Lake. At your feet 140 acres of blue waters spread out, surrounded by redwoods, madrones, and ferns. The only ripples troubling the water's surface are those created by breathing rainbow trout and bass stocking the lake for the fishing season.

Go down to the lakeside and turn left to keep on the Sunnyside Trail, the wide dirt trail facing south, hence the name Sunnyside (the opposite trail is called Shadyside for a good reason). This open trail is right on the shore and follows the lake closely over the next mile until it rises at the northeastern shore of the lake to meet a paved road.

At 1 mile, cross Sky Oaks Road with caution and turn right on the Forman Trail, a narrow dirt trail that snakes under stooping oak trees and runs parallel to the road. At 1.3 miles, make a right on the Pine Point Trail, which traces the shore of the aptly named peninsula, ending up on a paved road. At the junction with Sky Oaks Road, turn right toward the Lagunitas parking lot and picnic area, and right again before the gate onto the Bon Tempe Shadyside Trail.

As much as the Sunnyside Trail is in full sun and a mostly wide trail, the Shadyside Trail is a narrow path that meanders through redwood forests and stays under cover until you hit the dam. Along the way, count three little bridges going over seasonal creeks.

At 3.5 miles, you reach the western end of the dam. Turn right to walk over the dam, a wide gravel road lined with grass. Don't forget to look down on the valley below where Alpine Lake forms fjord-like valleys. The spillway is at the eastern end right before you leave the dam, a fantastic waterslide that fascinates all ages. Continue straight back to the parking lot.

 MOUNT TAMALPAIS STATE PARK/ EAST PEAK

BEFORE YOU GO
Maps: USGS San Rafael. Brochure with trail map online at www.parks.ca.gov.
Information: Ranger office (415) 388-2070. California State Parks, www.parks.ca.gov

ABOUT THE HIKE
Day hike; Easy; Spring, Fall, Winter
1.4 miles, loop
Hiking time: 1–2 hours
High point/elevation gain: 2570 feet/350 feet

GETTING THERE
- From US 101 in Mill Valley, take the CA-1/Stinson Beach exit and turn left on Shoreline Highway (CA-1).
- Turn right on Panoramic Highway and follow the signs for Mount Tamalpais State Park.
- At Pantoll Road, turn right on East Ridgecrest Boulevard and park at the visitor center lot at the end of the road.
- You can get to Mount Tamalpais by public transportation but not as far as East Peak. West Marin Stagecoach bus 61 stops at the Pantoll Ranger Station, 3 miles from the trailhead. For details, check www.marintransit.org/stage.html.

ON THE TRAIL
Dominating Marin County from the top of its 2574 feet, Mount Tamalpais is iconic of the Marin ridgeline. With Muir Woods' ancient redwood forests at the base, coastal chaparral on its slopes, lakes in the dips, and killer views of the coast from the fire lookouts, Mount Tamalpais offers a beautiful day excursion from anywhere in the Bay Area.

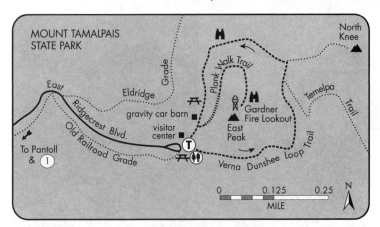

From the parking lot, find the trailhead on the right with the sign for the Verna Dunshee Loop Trail. The paved trail starts lined with low stone walls beyond which grow chamise, manzanita, lupine bushes, paintbrush, and sticky monkey flowers. On damp days (fog, rain), look for slithering yellow-eyed ensatinas. These red-body cousins of California newts ambush and catch their prey with a super-sticky tongue.

Continue on the trail where moss-covered trees and low-lying bushes lend a more "wilderness" feel to the walk. Down below, green valleys and hills are crisscrossed with the park's dense trail network. Bridges, benches, and platforms along the trail allow you to circle the peak while enjoying spectacular views.

At 0.4 mile, the Temelpa Trail departs down rocky steps to the right. Continue on the Verna Dunshee Loop Trail where wooden benches offer rest stops. On the north side of the trail, you can see Bon Tempe Lake (Hike 51), Lake Lagunitas, and farther west, Alpine Lake.

At 0.7 mile you reach picnic tables next to the barn of the old gravity car. Usually staffed on weekends, the barn contains displays on the open gravity car that took crowds down the mountain after a day of hiking on the trails, dinner at the tavern, and dancing at the pavilion. The way gravity cars worked is that open passenger cars were pulled up the slope by small geared locomotives (Shays and Heislers) to the top of Mount Tamalpais, from where passenger cars then coasted down the mountain led by gravity alone. Operated between 1896 and 1930, the steam train and gravity car zigzagged up and down the mountain's steep slopes on tracks known as "the crookedest railroad in the world."

The lookout on top of East Peak

Imagine your train car coming down 281 turns at full speed to end up at the Mill Valley Depot. What a ride!

If you feel like exploring the Gardner Fire Lookout on top of East Peak, turn left at 0.8 mile on the Plank Walk Trail. This moderately graded path rises up a trail whose wooden steps are planks recycled from the gravity car tracks. At the wooden post at a rocky junction, turn right to summit the peak at 1.1 miles. Don't follow the trail beyond the fire lookout; it is not safe. Retrace your steps to the parking lot.

EXPERIENCE MOUNT TAM THROUGH ART, FOOD, AND NATURE

The "Mount Tam" experience wouldn't be complete without two seasonal events that make this trailhead a choice destination for families. First, feed the mind: Each spring a professional theater group organizes a big outdoor play (www.mountainplay.org) at the Mountain Theater. Families come with picnic baskets and make it a day outing. Second, feed the body: From spring through the fall, the West Point Inn (www.westpointinn.com) organizes monthly pancake breakfasts at the inn, only accessible via hiking trails. Both are within easy reach of East Peak. To find out about wildflower walks, astronomy nights, or full moon hikes, check out the Mount Tamalpais Interpretive Association (www.mttam.net)—a fantastic resource and organizer of docent-led activities.

MARIN HEADLANDS/WOLF RIDGE

BEFORE YOU GO
Maps: USGS Point Bonita.
Free trail map at the Marin
Headlands Visitor Center.
Information: Marin Headlands Visitor Center (415)
331-1540. U.S. National
Park Service, www.nps.gov
/goga

ABOUT THE HIKE
Day hike; Difficult; Year round
5.2 miles, loop
Hiking time: 3.5 hours
**High point/elevation
gain:** 960 feet/900 feet

GETTING THERE

- On US 101 from San Francisco, take the Alexander Avenue exit, keeping right.
- From US 101 south after the Waldo Tunnel, take the Sausalito exit just before the Golden Gate Bridge and turn right to pass under US 101. At the stop sign, go straight onto Alexander Avenue.
- Turn left on Bunker Road (a brown sign says MARIN HEADLANDS VISITOR CENTER) and go through the one-way tunnel.
- Turn left onto Field Road and park by the Marin Headlands Visitor Center on the right.
- Muni bus 76 connects the Golden Gate Bridge and downtown San Francisco to the Marin Headlands Visitor Center. It runs on Sundays and certain holidays.

ON THE TRAIL

Right outside the Golden Gate, the Marin Headlands combine local history and spectacular scenery with child-friendly features. The army bunkers, active lighthouse, and marine mammal hospital are a chronological map to the area's conversion from military site to protected coastal lands. This hike along Wolf Ridge and Hill 88, a ridgetop leading to an abandoned military air base, provides a great aerial view of the area, then descends to a surfers' beach next to a lagoon.

Inside the visitor center (see sidebar), pick up a free Junior Ranger booklet to keep kids spirited through the effort.

From the parking lot, walk northeast on Bunker Road, watching for a wooden bridge on your left at 0.2 mile. Turn left and cross the bridge

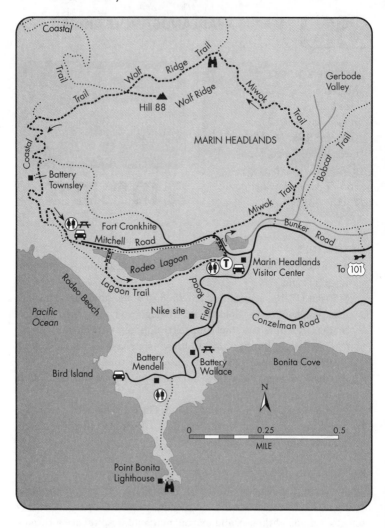

over a small creek. The path then leads you under a thicket of willows to grassy meadows.

After you cross the bridge, look for horsetail, also known as the dinosaur or Lego plant. These plants look like stacked-up green umbrellas or miniature bamboos. Survivors from the age of the dinosaurs, these plants have needle-like leaves that are hollow. Take two apart and put them back together—they really are like Legos. The surrounding grassland is dotted by coyote brush, bush lupine, and wild fennel. Turn right onto the Miwok Trail. At 0.3 mile, go straight to keep to the Miwok Trail.

So far level, the fire road now rises gradually. It's a long and steady ascent looking down on the Gerbode Valley. Alongside the road ask your children to find scat. Besides the "eeww" factor, scat is a

Fire roads make climbing easy at the start of the hike.

fantastic way of tracking animals in the wild. The Marin Headlands are home to coyotes and deer, and roadsides are good places to look for coyote poop; it looks like medium-sized canine poop only with more fibers. When you find it, break it with a stick and don't be shy, check it out. What do you think the animal ate? The only other tracks you are likely to see are footprints in the dirt.

At 1.6 miles, the Wolf Ridge Trail starts on the left. This is the perfect spot for kids to sit down, get out their journals, and take a few minutes to rest and snack. In the spring, this ridgetop between the Gerbode and Tennessee valleys is covered with tiny flowers, and you can admire several little streams rolling down the deep green, sunny hillsides.

Ahead of you comes the steep portion of the trail. The Wolf Ridge Trail skirts the north side of the hill through thickets of blackberry bushes and coastal chaparral. You will see shooting stars, milkmaids, umbrella-shaped cow parsnip, miner's lettuce, and sticky monkey flower. The latter produces an orange flower that some people think looks like a grinning monkey face. Ask your child to pinch a leaf between two fingers and count until ten. Let go. The leaf should stick like tape to fingers!

The closer you get to the next trail junction, the harder the climb will be. Stick to your guns and play games with your children to keep them engaged.

At 2.1 miles, you reach a paved road. Turn left toward Hill 88, going uphill on a road half consumed by blackberry bushes until you see barbed-wire fences. At 2.3 miles, you reach a military base in a state of arrested decay with empty guardhouses, two platforms in ruins, and broken ladders for a radar site that was never used—all that is Hill 88. Cool by daylight, the place can be creepy at night despite the prime stargazing location. Walk to the concrete platform with the best views on the Marin Headlands and take a lunch break. Rodeo Beach stretches south to a white rock called Bird Island, a series of rock outcroppings covered by bird guano.

Descend from Hill 88 on the paved road and at 2.5 miles, instead of turning right onto the Wolf Ridge Trail, simply go straight on the Coastal Trail. Make sure children walk in the middle of the road, as poison oak thrives on these trails. Look for mission butterflies, a native species of butterfly particularly fond of blue lupine pollen. Overhead, turkey vultures scan the hills for carrion to "clean."

At 3.7 miles the paved road ends with a fence. Follow the detour on the right toward Battery Townsley. For a fun detour, keep to the right, following the Pacific Coast Trail sign to explore this underground fort that in its glory days in 1940 could fire a one-ton shell to a battleship 25 miles away. Otherwise bear left and climb down a series of log stairs to a service road, go right, and turn left down more rock and log stairs. After the trail meets up with the paved road again, turn left and follow it to Rodeo Beach at 4.1 miles. When the waves come in, you can't miss the surfers waiting for waves like bobbing sea lions in the frigid ocean waters.

Walk on the right side of the road, cross the wooden bridge, and continue until you reach the other side of the beach, sinking in rainbow-colored sand. At the far end to your left, look for a dirt trail that climbs parallel to the lagoon (not the trail straight up the hill going to Battery Smith-Guthrie). The Lagoon Trail brings you back to the visitor center after a colorful display of plants and flowers.

THE MARIN HEADLANDS VISITOR CENTER

Before or after the hike, peek inside the visitor center. It used to be a chapel. Not only will you find exhibits on the cultural history of the area—including a small Miwok hut that children can crawl into to listen to a prerecorded story—but the interactive exhibits for children at the back are lots of fun. From the various stones and bones you can touch, to the clear glass flasks containing essences of wild roses or skunks to smell, it speaks to budding naturalists. On cold days, you can get a cup of hot cocoa, tea, or coffee for a small donation at the back of the building.

MARIN HEADLANDS/RODEO BEACH

BEFORE YOU GO
Maps: USGS Point Bonita.
Free brochure at the Marin
Headlands Visitor Center.
Information: Marin Head-
lands Visitor Center (415)
331-1540. U.S. National
Park Service, www.nps.gov
/goga

ABOUT THE HIKE
Day hike; Easy/Moderate;
Year round
2 miles, loop
Hiking time: 2 hours
**High point/elevation
gain:** 0 feet/50 feet

GETTING THERE

■ On US 101 from San Francisco, take the Alexander Avenue exit, keeping right.

■ From US 101 south after the Waldo Tunnel, take the Sausalito exit just before the Golden Gate Bridge and turn right to pass under US 101. At the stop sign, go straight onto Alexander Avenue. Turn left on Bunker Road (a brown sign says MARIN HEADLANDS VISITOR CENTER) and go through the one-way tunnel.

■ Turn left onto Field Road and park by the Marin Headlands Visitor Center on the right.

■ Muni bus 76 connects the Golden Gate Bridge and downtown San Francisco to the Marin Headlands Visitor Center. It runs on Sundays and certain holidays.

ON THE TRAIL

Just over the Golden Gate Bridge, the Marin Headlands recreation area offers some of the prettiest and easiest hikes close to San Francisco. The area used to be an army base until the 1960s and is peppered with buried bunkers and coast-side forts (see Hike 53 for an abandoned army base exploration). However, the real attraction lies in miles of coastal chaparral, a lagoon, and a beach, favorites for local families. On weekends and certain days, a visit to Point Bonita, an 1855 lighthouse that still guards the entrance to the Golden Gate, is a must for its breathtaking views (see sidebar). Come on any given day and enjoy the biggest urban recreation area in the United States.

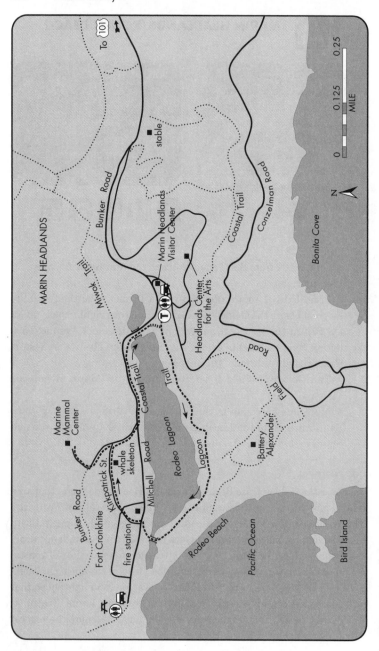

From the west end of the parking lot of the Marin Headlands Visitor Center, find the Coastal Trail past the metal gate and descend a gentle grade on gravel and dirt. Where the Coastal Trail turns right toward the lagoon, continue straight on the Lagoon Trail to keep to the south side of the lagoon. The path features quintessential coastal scrub plants such as coyote brush, wild fennel, sagebrush, wild mustard, blackberries, and poison oak—the latter grows in abundance on the trail, so make sure children walk in the middle of the trail and don't touch any plants. A big eucalyptus tree with low-hanging branches makes for a fun climbing structure before you enter a shaded portion of the trail lined with willows.

At 0.5 mile, log steps climb a dirt hill with lupine bushes—see if you can spot the endangered mission blue butterfly, one of forty-four butterfly species that call these hills home. The trail narrows as you reach the top of the trail, with miner's lettuce, thistles, and blackberries growing in abundance. At the top, enjoy full views of the lagoon and the beach. The lagoon, fed by streams coming down the hills, sometimes fills with waves from the ocean when winter storms wash over the strip of sand. Notice how abruptly you leave the coastal scrub to find sand under your feet and blankets of ice plant (also called fig plant, a South Africa native that was imported to stabilize sand dunes) around you.

At 0.7 mile, Rodeo Beach is much more than meets the eye. Obviously it's a great water playground for kids, and the northern end of the beach is a choice spot for local surfers. It is also filled with "rainbow sand." If kids get on their bellies and examine the sand closely, they should understand why. Look at the hills around you and see if you can find the same colors. From reddish chert to greenstone, serpentine, and jasper, you will find all shades from green, brown, gray, to red. One of the rare colors on the beach is the iridescent orange-red of carnelians. The closer to the waterline, the bigger the sand. These are actually tiny pebbles the size of a bead.

Walk to the other end of the beach and cross the wooden bridge over the lagoon to reach Mitchell Road. At 1.1 miles cross Mitchell Road to go up the street of the fire station. Turn right into the second

Splashing in the waves at Rodeo Beach is one of the rewards of this hike.

street, Kirkpatrick Street. At 1.3 miles past the Marin Headlands Nursery, look for the skeleton of a blue whale displayed on a terrace below the road. It washed ashore in 1988 and now serves as an educational skeleton.

At 1.5 miles, turn left on Bunker Road to reach the Marine Mammal Center (www.marinemammalcenter.org) on your right. Open all year from 10:00 AM to 5:00 PM except Thanksgiving, Christmas, and New Year's Day, it is free. Go inside and start your visit with the upstairs viewing platform on your left. It is a fantastic place to teach children about animal rescue on the coast—the center is responsible for 600 miles of California coast. Keep exploring, and don't forget to peek inside the fish kitchen where staff blend fish milkshakes for sick animals.

After the center, walk down Bunker Road to the junction with Mitchell Road and cross—with caution—so you can walk toward the visitor center on the other side of the railing on the dirt path. Keep following the path as it curves above the lagoon. At 1.9 miles, turn right onto the Lagoon Trail/Coastal Trail where a series of steps takes you between ferns back on the Coastal Trail. Turn left to get back to the parking lot.

POINT BONITA LIGHTHOUSE

From the Point Bonita trailhead (accessible by car, 0.5 mile south of the visitor center via Field Road; park on Conzelman Road), the Point Bonita Lighthouse stands at the end of a 0.5-mile trail that goes through an 118-foot-long hand-dug tunnel, skirts the edges of a steep cliff, and crosses a suspension bridge 124 feet over raging waters. For its dramatic windswept vistas and eagle-nest location, Point Bonita is a sight not to be missed. The cliff is so steep that the lighthouse keeper, who lived across the suspension bridge with his family, built harnesses to tether his young children and prevent them from falling. This Marin Headlands landmark still guides ships through the often-foggy Golden Gate strait.

Have kids count the number of seconds between each rotation of the Fresnel lens. If the bridge is open, walk around the white 56-foot-tall lighthouse and look for wild cabbages. They are offspring-gone-wild of the lighthouse keeper's garden, now clinging to rocky soil above precipitous drops.

MARIN HEADLANDS/TENNESSEE VALLEY

BEFORE YOU GO
Maps: USGS Point Bonita.
Free map at trailhead.
Information: Marin Head-
lands Visitor Center (415)
331-1540. U.S. National
Park Service, www.nps.gov
/goga

ABOUT THE HIKE
Day hike; Moderate/Difficult;
Year round
4.4 miles, loop
Hiking time: 2–3 hours
**High point/elevation
gain:** 1000 feet/800 feet

GETTING THERE

- From US 101 in San Francisco, take the CA-1 exit. Keep straight toward Mill Valley.
- After about 0.5 mile, turn west onto Tennessee Valley Road.
- The Tennessee Valley parking lot is 1.5 miles down the road.
- There is no direct public transit.

ON THE TRAIL

Part of the Marin Headlands (see Hikes 53 and 54), Tennessee Valley is considered a must-see valley for San Francisco families. From the trail-head, a fire road takes you along a creek, past a pond, down to sandy Tennessee Beach, flanked by dramatic cliffs. The ending is gorgeous, and this 2.6-mile hike is the route 95 percent of people do. If you feel adventurous, head for the hills instead!

From the parking lot, find the trailhead for the Miwok Trail, south of the restrooms. This dirt trail gently descends before crossing a bridge and rising among coyote brush, blackberry bushes, and sticky monkey flowers. The trail levels before a grove of eucalyptus trees, but past the grove it's all uphill until the ridge. Pace yourself—the grade is moderate, and the rolling hills are a sweet visual reward until you can feast your eyes on the ocean. At 0.5 mile, the trail crests near a grove of cypresses, a good spot to recuperate. Continue straight to stay on the Miwok Trail.

You will pass through a thick grove of eucalyptus trees before curving left (do not go straight, Marin Drive is a private driveway) to a water tank and turning to the hills above Marin City. At this point, the Miwok Trail is a wide service road and after the bend you are looking down

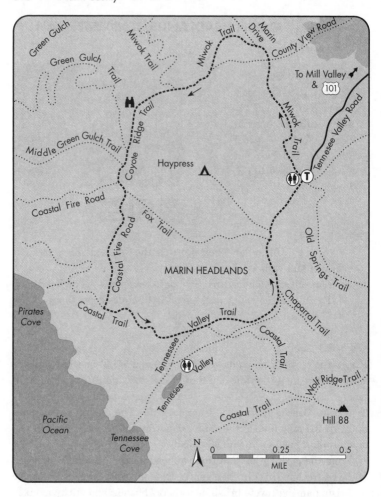

on Green Gulch. The green fields and buildings down below are the beautiful orchards and produce fields of Green Gulch Farm, a farm that supplies Greens Restaurant with organic produce. The buildings are all part of the Zen Center, whose gardens are well worth a family stroll.

At 1.1 miles, turn left on the Coyote Ridge Trail and start a steady ascent for the ridgeline from which you will have amazing views (unless it's a foggy day) of the Marin Headlands, the bay, and the ocean. Be warned, the ridge is windy and keeping a hat on anyone's head can be a challenge. Small rabbits and quail families call these bushes home,

Views of Tennessee Valley from above

patrolled by turkey vultures overhead. The Coyote Ridge Trail being a multi-use trail, you will meet bikers as well as equestrians.

At 2 miles, turn left onto Coastal Fire Road and bear right to stay on that trail, going down gently toward the ocean. At 3 miles, this road dead-ends into the Coastal Trail. Your route goes left (south), but if you're looking to spice up the hike with an extra adventure, turn right for Pirates Cove. This challenging descent is only for adults and older children, as the steep trail disappears into a gully and you'll need to scramble down to beach level on rocks and roots. It's a wild secluded cove with dark rocks, but the only pirates here are of the waterfowl kind. Pirates Cove would add 1 mile to your hike.

Southbound on the Coastal Trail, you are now headed to Tennessee Cove, named for the SS *Tennessee*, a steamship that ran aground in 1853 and disintegrated into the surf after two weeks of unabating waves. Going down, the trail hugs the coast before heading toward the valley floor away from the beach. Look for red jasper along the sides of the trail.

At 3.6 miles, the Coastal Trail crosses the Tennessee Valley Trail. If you want to include beach time in this hike, turn right and count an additional out-and-back mile (mostly level) to beautiful Tennessee Cove and Beach. Otherwise, turn left to return to the parking lot on the wide service road, exploring the valley floor and looking up at the hills you just conquered. Along the creek the silvery green foliage of willow trees offers a stark visual contrast against the slopes behind.

ANGEL ISLAND

BEFORE YOU GO
Maps: USGS San Quentin.
Trail map for sale at the gift
shop.
Information: State park
information (415) 435-5390.
www.parks.ca.gov. Angel
Island Association,
www.angelisland.com

ABOUT THE HIKE
Day hike; Moderate; Year round
2.6 miles, round-trip
Hiking time: 2–3 hours
**High point/elevation
gain:** 200 feet/200 feet

GETTING THERE

■ Angel Island is accessible by private boat or ferry departing from San Francisco, Tiburon, and occasionally, Oakland and Alameda. Visit www.blueandgoldfleet.com and www.angelislandferry.com for details.

ON THE TRAIL

Close enough that you can leave in the morning and be back midafternoon, Angel Island still requires a 10–30-minute ferry ride to reach the trailhead, which in itself is pretty neat. This gorgeous 1.2-square-mile mountain island can be explored via a perimeter road and dirt paths that lead to its central peak, Mount Livermore (796 feet). The island also features structures left from its human occupation, such as camps, garrisons, and immigration stations.

When the ferry docks at Ayala Cove, you are greeted with views of the marina and lush lawns peppered with picnic tables in front of the visitor center. From the cove, you can enjoy a splash at the beach, bike around the island, or tour it with a tram. However, hiking is the only way you can experience quiet spots where nobody else goes, and enjoy breathtaking views of the bay. So lace up your shoes and hit the trails for this unique Civil War–era adventure.

From Ayala Cove, walk along the cove to the picnic area and look for a boardwalk past the beach next to the restrooms. It heads uphill across a grassy hillside and leads to a wide path under oak woodland. The path turns into stairs and at 0.4 mile meets Perimeter Road south of

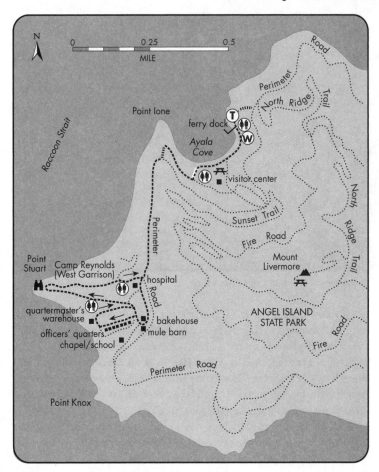

Point Ione. The aptly named Perimeter Road, a paved road that circles the island, is where all things on wheels go. Turn right, heading south on Perimeter Road. At 1 mile, you find a red 1904 structure that served as the third hospital for the troops stationed at Camp Reynolds. It is closed, as are most of the Camp Reynolds buildings, but still a nice history marker. Right after the hospital, leave Perimeter Road and bear right on a dirt road lined with eucalyptus trees, heading down the hill to a group of buildings dating back to the Civil War era.

Created in 1863 to prevent Confederates from entering through the Golden Gate, Camp Reynolds houses the largest collection of Civil War–

Relax on the beach at Camp Reynolds.

era wooden buildings in the United States. The dirt road snakes through eucalyptus groves to the top of oval parade grounds and lands in front of the laundresses' quarters, an officers' house, and the bakehouse. The latter is a restored kitchen where Bay Area students bake bread and dress like soldiers in the late 1800s as part of the environmental living program during school field trips. If the bakehouse is open, pop inside to show the wood-burning stove to your kids.

Walk down toward the shore along the officers' quarters (closed to visits), circling the parade grounds clockwise. This gently graded path leads down to a brick warehouse where the dock used to be at 1.2 miles. Several benches and picnic tables make rest spots for young ones, and the open area along the shore is ideal to roam around. North of the warehouse, a low wall leads to a wide sandy beach in front of the remaining pillars of a jetty. This beach is a good splash spot, and if you are lucky you might see kayaks too.

Walk back up to the top of Camp Reynolds and swerve left on a level service road. This road slowly rises over the bay to Point Stuart where views embrace Raccoon Strait and San Francisco, from San Francisco's financial district to Mount Tamalpais. Follow the single-track path uphill to a ridge, through an oak forest, and down to the red brick hospital. Retrace your steps to Ayala Cove.

IMMIGRATION STATION AND MOUNT LIVERMORE

If you have a stroller, another option is exploring the eastern side of the island. Carry the stroller up the wooden stairs of the North Ridge Trail (140 steps) and turn left on paved Perimeter Road to visit the U.S. Immigration Station that earned Angel Island its nickname of "Ellis Island of the West." This 2.4-mile round-trip combines cultural and historical exploration. If you would rather leave the stroller behind, the area behind the gift shop can be used to store strollers. Confirm with rangers when you arrive. More ambitious walkers can climb to Mount Livermore by following the North Ridge Trail to the top (2.1 miles and 780 feet elevation gain from Ayala Cove).

SALT POINT STATE PARK

BEFORE YOU GO
Maps: USGS Plantation.
Free park brochure with map
online.
Information: Salt Point
State Park (707) 8473221.
www.parks.ca.gov

ABOUT THE HIKE
Day hike; Moderate/Difficult;
Year round
3.8 miles, loop
Hiking time: 2 hours
**High point/elevation
gain:** 1000 feet/575 feet

GETTING THERE

- On CA-1 north of Jenner, drive 18 miles to the Salt Point State Park entrance.
- Turn east into Woodside Campground. Park at the day-use parking lot next to the park's headquarters.
- There is no public transit.

ON THE TRAIL

Salt Point State Park is a jewel in the California state park system. Hugging the coast between Jenner and Gualala, this 6000-acre park includes a marine conservation area, a state marine reserve with a bull kelp forest, miles of rugged coast, rare tafoni rock formations, redwood forests, a prairie where elk used to roam, and a pygmy forest. In addition to its nature features, the park provides an introduction to Kashaya Pomo culture through interpretive signs on the main trail. To better explore the park, two campgrounds are located within the park, each featuring family campsites. While Gerstle Cove Campground sits above the ocean bluffs, Woodside Campground is on the other side of the highway in the forest.

Though Salt Point is a good hiking park year round, seasons can have a significant impact on your experience. Winter rains easily turn trails into puddles, so wear rain boots after the rain. Springtime is a high point for mushroom foraging. Late spring to early summer is blooming season at the nearby Kruse Rhododendron State Natural Reserve, a brilliant pink flower extravaganza. Summer is foggy and cool

Opposite: *Plucking blackberries on the trail is a summertime pleasure.*

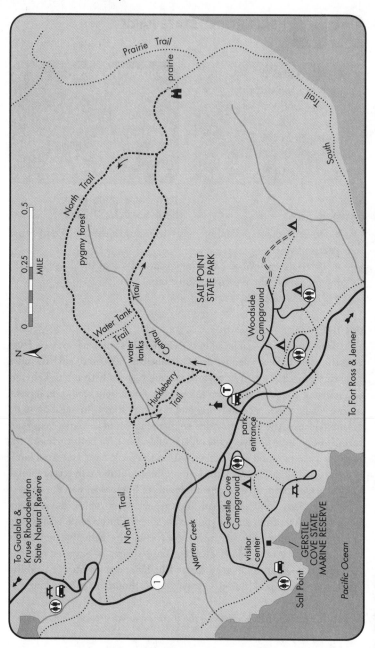

and the water is dark green with seaweeds providing habitat for rockfish. Autumn is gentle and berry season for the local wildlife.

From the north end of the parking lot, walk past the gate on an old logging road. The Central Trail starts off with a steep and steady climb in a coastal mixed forest. Walk at your kids' pace and stop at the interpretive signs ex-

Enjoy Salt Point's prairie before entering the pygmy forest.

plaining the use of native plants by the Kashaya Pomo. Children should enjoy the sign about the sour-face game (which they can replicate at home with sour foods such as citrus) played by native children.

Stay on the Central Trail at the next two junctions. You will walk past four big water tanks where kids can calculate with giant rulers the water level in each tank. Continue up the trail as it gradually becomes gentler. After your long ascent through a dense forest, the trail finally levels out and you reach a sign indicating PRAIRIE. You are at the junction with the North Trail, but keep on until you get to a wide prairie surrounded by a pine forest. The prairie, one of the nature wonders of Salt Point, is an open grassy expanse where elk once grazed. Follow the trail along the prairie 0.2 mile for a good sense of space. Views of the grasses swaying with the wind and raptors flying overhead transport you to another world. This is a good place to spread out your picnic blanket since you are at the top of the hike and halfway through. Don't forget to check for ticks.

Turn back and look for a right turn on the North Trail, a narrow dirt path going north toward the pygmy forest. The vegetation arches graciously over the trail and gives it a green hallway feel, only the tree size is imperceptibly going to shrink until you reach the pygmy forest on sandy soil. A shallow layer of graywacke sandstone combined with highly acidic soils make it impossible for trees to grow to a normal size. Though they are still taller than you, the cypress, redwoods, manzanitas, and Bishop pines around you are dwarves compared to their regular cousins.

Rather abruptly the pygmy forest gives way to a coast redwood habitat as the North Trail descends more steeply, now running parallel to Warren Creek. Kids will love standing next to the mossy-covered tree stump that's burnt inside and rises tall on the right (north) side of the

225

trail. During the wet season, the undergrowth is covered in colorful mushrooms, and if you can identify them, mushroom gathering is allowed at this park with a five-pound limit per person.

You will pass the other end of a connector trail that leads to the water tanks, but wait for the second junction to turn left on the Huckleberry Trail. After 0.3 mile you connect with the Central Trail. Make a right to find the parking lot 0.1 mile down the road.

 FORT ROSS STATE HISTORIC PARK

BEFORE YOU GO
Maps: USGS Fort Ross. Free brochure with map at the park.
Information: Fort Ross State Historic Park (707) 847-3286. www.fortrossstatepark .org California State Parks, www.parks.ca.gov

ABOUT THE HIKE
Day hike; Easy/Moderate; Year round
1 mile, round-trip
Hiking time: 1 hour
High point/elevation loss: 120 feet/120 feet

GETTING THERE
■ On CA-1 north of Jenner, drive 11 miles to the Fort Ross State Historic Park entrance.
■ Turn west on the park's main entrance road. Park at the visitor center parking lot.
■ There is no public transit.

ON THE TRAIL
Fort Ross State Historic Park stands tall as a living reminder of Russian America, a century of Russian settlements ranging from Alaska to California, trading mainly in sea otter pelts. The southernmost colony of this commercial enterprise was Fort Ross, a fort built in 1812 on the site of Metini, a Kashaya Pomo native village. It was supposed to supply northern Russian colonies with fresh food but met mixed fortunes and progressively declined until 1841 when it was sold to John Sutter of Sutter's Mill fame. Sutter was also the owner of the Sierras sawmill where James Marshall discovered gold in 1848, triggering the Gold Rush. After Fort Ross left Russian hands, it became known as the Call Ranch.

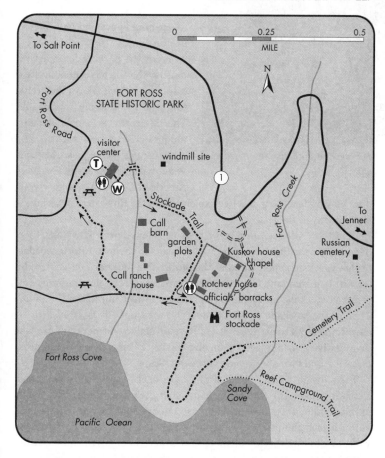

Schoolchildren from the whole Bay Area come to this fort to experience a day in the life of 1800s Russian America. For details on special events, history, and educational programs, consult the exellent Fort Ross Interpretive Association website (www.fortrossinterpretive.org); for more regional information and children's history, the Fort Ross State Historic Park website addresses all questions of prospective visitors and volunteers (www.fortrossstatepark.org). For the real thing, the fort organizes an elaborate living-history day the last Saturday of July each year.

Besides the unique historical interest of the site, Fort Ross offers easy trails around the fort, including a Russian orchard, and this coastal hike to a white sandy beach where Fort Ross Creek empties into the sea. As this hike features the inside of buildings, call the rangers to check

The coast at Fort Ross is rugged and wild.

on opening hours and days before heading out.

From the parking lot, start by touring the visitor center and its displays on the Kashaya Pomo culture and the Russian way of life. The interpretive panels explain unique local aspects such as sea otter fishing techniques, Kashaya Pomo basketry, and the Russian-American Company. Younger children may prefer to skip to a live exploration of the Russian colony's buildings directly at the fort.

Exit the visitor center out the back door and down some steps, then head left on the Stockade Trail, which leads to the fort. After a wooden bridge you reach open views of the bluffs. The Call barn on your right (south) is a remnant from the fort's ranching era. Soon the imposing redwood stockade enclosing the fort rises 15 feet tall above the plain. Though the stockade is pretty much isolated nowadays, it used to be surrounded by a thriving village of Russian sailors, farmers, and tradesmen, native Alaskan fishermen, and Kashaya Pomo people. Windmills, bakeries, and farms were part of the landscape.

Step inside the fort and, if they are open, visit the Kuskov and Rotchev houses, the Orthodox chapel, and the officials' barracks. Some of the buildings are furnished and used in living-history programs, providing a good glimpse of how the fort compound was organized. Kids will want to climb to the top of the guard towers to enjoy the views. After your fort exploration, walk out of the stockade and follow the wall down (southwest) toward the sea. At the trail junction with a wide gravel road, make a left toward Sandy Cove. The road cuts across windswept coastal bluffs. Make your way to the point. To the west is Fort Ross Cove where the steamer SS *Pomona* sank in 1908 and where divers can still explore the wrecked hull under 25 feet of water. To the east is Sandy Cove, your destination. Follow the road as it bends left to go down the hillside toward the beach.

Sandy Cove, protected from the wind and thus appropriate for onshore/offshore sea maneuvers, was used by Fort Ross workers for loading and unloading ships. Where the mouth of the creek meets the ocean, a shipyard, forge, tannery, boathouse, and storage house used to stand.

Now pelicans and other sea animals are the only inhabitants of these shores. Take some time to beachcomb and build sand castles before retracing your steps up the bluff and back to the parking lot by way of the Call ranch house and back across the stream. A nice picnic spot is the historical orchard where picnic tables are scattered on a grassy expanse that turns yellow with sour grass in the spring.

SONOMA COAST STATE PARK/ KORTUM TRAIL

BEFORE YOU GO
Maps: USGS Duncan Mills. Free map at Sonoma Coast State Park Visitor Center in Jenner and Duncan Mills, and at the Sonoma Coast Visitor Center in Bodega Bay. Free map online.
Information:
Sonoma Coast State Park
(707) 875-3483.
www.parks.ca.gov

ABOUT THE HIKE
Day hike; Moderate/Difficult; Year round
**5 miles, out and back;
1.5 miles round-trip to
Mammoth Rocks
Hiking time:** 2–3 hours
**High point/elevation
gain:** 280 feet/280 feet

GETTING THERE
- On CA-1, drive 7 miles north of Bodega Bay or 4.5 miles south of Jenner.
- Turn west into Sonoma Coast State Park's parking lot for Shell Beach.
- There is no public transit.

ON THE TRAIL
Sonoma Coast State Park spans 17 miles of the most gorgeous rugged coastline in California—cliffs, sea caves, coves, tidepools, and a spectacular nature show—all in true coastal fashion with rapidly changing weather, thick summer fog, and windy bluffs. Expect to have a ball, whether on a foggy or a sunny day, while discovering part of the Kortum Trail along the bold Pacific. This hike takes you from Shell Beach to Goat Rock at the end of Blind Beach, passing split rocks where mammoths

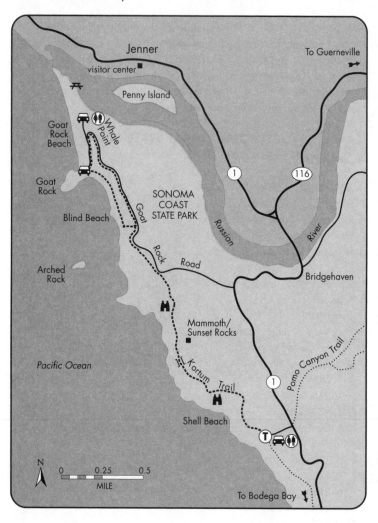

rubbed their fur to scratch their itches. At the end of Goat Rock Beach, at the mouth of the Russian River, colonies of harbor seals provide a year-round viewing treat for visitors. Note that swimming is absolutely not recommended at any of the beaches of the Sonoma Coast due to strong rip currents, sleeper waves, and cold water.

From the northwest side of the Shell Beach parking lot, pick up the Kortum Trail. This wide, level path was named after Bill Kortum, a Sonoma Coast environmental activist who fought to preserve these landscapes. Coastal scrub and large coastal prairies cover the bluffs as you leave behind the rocky crags and sandy shores of Shell Beach, a prime tidepooling beach for kids. For an overlook of Shell Beach, turn left at the trail junction and stay on the trail—these bluffs are unstable. On clear days, you can see down to Bodega Head to the south.

Get back on the trail and continue your exploration of the coast as the path three times becomes a narrow boardwalk, thus protecting wetlands and seasonal creeks and allowing for dry foot passage when the rain turns these prairies into marshes. If visiting during the dry season, you can spot creek beds by the willows growing alongside them. Thistles and cow parsnips line the path, followed by cascading native grasses.

Well marked, the path snakes between tall grasses and drier ground. Right off the coast, guano-covered rocks rise like tall towers above the sea and provide great opportunities to slip geology into your day hike. These sea stacks were formed by the constant wave action battling rock formations resulting from the collision of tectonic plates—the soft particles were washed away, leaving the hard rock standing on the ocean floor. Think of melted rocky road ice cream to get the idea. Now look to the right (east) of the trail and compare the big rock sitting on the prairie. It used to be a sea stack, too! You are hiking on a former sea terrace that was uplifted by one oceanic plate colliding with another.

A wooden bridge takes you down and up a gully, then straight on the bluffs, then down another depression over a creek. The trail bends right opposite a split rock formation, the highlight of this hike for budding archaeologists. Known as Sunset Rocks or Mammoth Rocks, these ancient sea stacks bear evidence of rubbing by large Ice Age mammals, a theory developed by senior state archaeologist E. Breck Parkman in 2001. In summary, 12,000 years ago sea levels were significantly lower and vast prairies stretched from the Golden Gate to the Farallon Islands. Mammoths, giant bison, and other Pleistocene mega-animals roamed the pastures of the Sonoma Coast where you are now. As part of their bathing and grooming activities, the

Floating stairs going down to Goat Rock Beach.

big mammals would wallow in mud and rub off their itchy hides on large boulders. Hence the rubbing marks on these rocks going up 14 feet, the size of an adult male mammoth.

If you have younger children, this is where you should turn around and come back to the Shell Beach parking lot. Otherwise, get ready for some exercise.

The path now leaves the coastal bluffs to ascend toward the hills, reaching superb views of Blind Beach and Goat Rock from the ridge. Coming down the hill, the trail will now hug the road until you reach the parking lot for Blind Beach. On the way, admire Arched Rock 200 feet from the shoreline, rising like a tall arched Lego piece above the waterline. The way down to the beach from the lot is steep and ends on a log ladder anchored in the sand. Wide and sandy with a few rocks, Blind Beach invites family strolls to the level and massive Goat Rock. For easier access, continue on the Kortum Trail all the way down to the Goat Rock parking lot at sea level.

When you are ready to come back, retrace your steps back to the Shell Beach parking lot.

 ARMSTRONG REDWOODS STATE NATURAL RESERVE

BEFORE YOU GO
Maps: USGS Guerneville. Map of Armstrong Redwoods State Reserve and Austin Creek State Recreation Area available at the park's visitor center.
Information:
Armstrong Redwoods State Natural Reserve (707) 869-2391. www.parks.ca.gov

ABOUT THE HIKE
Day hike; Easy; Year round
1.6 miles, round-trip
Hiking time: 1 hour
High point/elevation loss: 120 feet/120 feet

GETTING THERE
■ From the town of Guerneville on CA-116, turn north on Armstrong Redwoods Road.
■ Drive 2.5 miles to the park entrance station, and park by the visitor center.
■ There is no public transit.

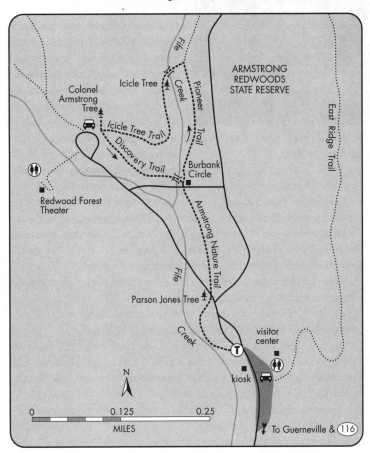

ON THE TRAIL

A typical trip to the Russian River Valley usually involves beach time or water sports, farm-fresh produce, art galleries, and winery tours. However, 3 miles removed from the Russian River at Guerneville stands an ancient coast redwood grove whose shaded trails invite quiet strolls and nature discovery. Ideal for relaxation, this easy hike is for all ages even if it's raining. Coast redwood forests are rain forests and love rain and fog.

Before you enter the grove, know that this forest was saved from logging by Colonel James B. Armstrong, the owner of a sawmill on the Russian River where millions of board feet of redwood were cut. Today, Armstrong Redwoods tells a story of nature survival.

Measuring time on a redwood's rings is no easy task!

Start at the visitor center and have kids look for (faint) white bear footprints on the ground. They lead you to the Armstrong Nature Trail, which starts on the west side of the entrance kiosk. The spongy trail is the result of several layers of redwood bark shavings and feels bouncy. Walking between wooden fences, ask your children to see how many kinds of leaves or twigs they can spot on the ground. Interestingly, redwood leaves have two types of needles: flat at lower levels and curved on the top so they can catch fog moisture.

At 0.1 mile the trail crosses the road near the Parson Jones Tree. It's the tallest tree in the park, towering at 310 feet, 10 feet taller than a football field upright in the air. Walk past the tree and find on the right a cross section of a redwood tree with history markers. School-aged kids are fascinated with the circular lines showing the age of the tree and can look for events they know, such as the 1906 earthquake. At 0.3 mile the path crosses another paved road and continues straight ahead.

On the right, Burbank Circle is a large "fairy ring," the name for young redwood trees growing from a parent tree now dead in the middle, usually a stump or a root. These sprouts use the same root system as the parent and are genetically identical. The fact that these sprouts create a ring around the parent tree is pure poetry. At the trail junction, go straight on the Pioneer Trail.

A fallen stump along the trail is a good place for children to "walk" the length of a redwood tree. At the next trail junction, turn left toward the Armstrong Tree on the Icicle Tree Trail. The Icicle Tree is such a famous tree that it is now protected by a fence. Go around it looking at the "icicles," burls that reproduce the tree downwards.

The path crosses the bed of Fife Creek on a wooden bridge and comes to a giant stump whose massive root system you can imagine. This dormant stump makes an imaginary theatre for junior explorers. Walk under an arching Douglas fir and continue.

At the trail junction, turn right to find the platform in front of the Colonel Armstrong Tree. Back at the trail junction, follow the Discovery Trail to the right (south) toward the ranger station. The Discovery Trail is a unique trail for the physically and visually disabled with signs in

Braille, a rope connecting the signs, and an ADA-accessible trail. Because the signs explain this forest in unusual ways for a specific audience, they provide a fresh view of your surroundings.

At the junction with the Pioneer Trail at Burbank Circle, turn right to get back to the parking lot.

 ## RIVERFRONT REGIONAL PARK/ LAKE BENOIST

BEFORE YOU GO
Maps: USGS Guerneville. Map posted at Redwood Grove picnic area. Printer-friendly map online.
Information: Sonoma County Parks (707) 565-2041. www.sonoma-county.org /parks/index.htm

ABOUT THE HIKE
Day hike; Easy; Spring, Summer, Fall
2 miles, loop
Hiking time: 1 hour
High point/elevation gain: 100 feet/100 feet

GETTING THERE

■ From US 101 north after Santa Rosa, exit at Central/Windsor and turn left on Old Redwood Highway, which becomes Windsor River Road. After 2 miles, turn left on Eastside Road.

■ From US 101 south after Healdsburg, exit at Old Redwood Highway. Drive 1.8 miles and turn right on Eastside Road.

■ The entrance of the park is 2 miles down on the right (west) side of the road.

■ Turn right, then left (south) at the end of the vineyards. Park at the Riverfront Regional Park parking lot next to a grove of redwood trees and a picnic area.

■ There is no public transit.

ON THE TRAIL

On the banks of the Russian River next to prestigious vineyards, Riverfront Regional Park is a family favorite because of its beautiful picnic areas and fishing opportunities. Formerly a gravel quarry, this 300-acre park comprises two lakes for recreational fishing with an easy trail circling Lake Benoist.

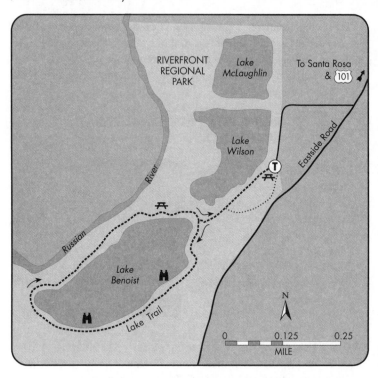

Start at the redwood grove and walk along the north side of the picnic area to find a large service road at two yellow posts. A wooden board displays an aerial map as well as information on local fish species. Follow the road as it levels out and curves around the redwood grove. The blue waters of Lake Wilson show through the trees on your right at 0.1 mile.

After 0.3 mile, you arrive at Lake Benoist and the Lake Trail. You can circle the lake clockwise or counterclockwise; the eastern shore is shaded and the western shore is in full sun. This hike goes clockwise.

Turn left on the Lake Trail, a large service road overlooking narrow dirt trails used by fishermen to access the lake's edges. For better views of the water, children may prefer the lakefront trails, but the higher trail is wider and easier to walk on as a group or with a stroller.

Lined with thistles, blackberry bushes, fennel, and coyote brush, the trail crosses a seasonal creek at 0.4 mile and continues through a short alley of redwood trees. At the foot of a hill on your left, look for

Lake Benoist is a hidden gem along the Russian River.

California spicebush. This native plant has leaves the size of an adult hand that are lime green in the spring and dark green in the summer. Its burgundy-maroon curly flowers bloom in the spring and summer. This is one of the few plants deer will leave alone. Why? Both the leaves and the flower have a spicy fragrance between cinnamon and nutmeg.

As the views open up, Mount Jackson rises tall across the lake, a mountain whose hills were mined for quicksilver (or mercury) from 1889 to 1972. The wind whispers quietly in the trees, now a mixed forest of redwood, live oaks, bay laurels, big-leaf maples, and willows. Giant vines cascade down the trees.

At 0.8 mile, you cross another seasonal creek. This end of the lake is protected habitat for nesting great blue herons, so from January to June be as quiet as you can. At 1 mile, the trail curves around the lake and passes a stone dam across from a level boat access. At this level, you are very close to the Russian River but the thick tree cover hides it from view. Note that swimming is not allowed in this lake. If this trail is flooded, look for higher ground. At 1.2 miles the trail rises. Bear left to continue the loop on the wider path (the lower path at lake level is used by fishermen) and continue around the lake, passing a group of picnic tables, to the junction where you came from at 1.7 miles. Turn left to retrace your steps on the wide dirt trail leading to the parking lot.

At 1.8 miles, a TRAIL sign points east to the forest. This narrow foot-path (closed to bicycles and horses) is another route to the parking lot. If you decide to go back this way, you'll climb sharply over the hill and finish on a wooden bridge at the redwood grove picnic area.

FOOTHILL REGIONAL PARK

BEFORE YOU GO
Maps: USGS Healdsburg.
Map of the trails posted at
entrance or available online
at www.sonoma-county.org
/parks
Information: Sonoma
County Parks (707) 565-
2041. www.sonoma-county
.org/parks

ABOUT THE HIKE
Day hike; Moderate; Spring,
Fall, Winter
**2.5 miles, loop; 2.8 miles
via Alta Vista**
Hiking time: 1–2 hours
**High point/elevation
gain:** 275 feet/275 feet

GETTING THERE

■ From US 101 in Santa Rosa heading north, drive 10 miles to Windsor.

■ Exit at Arata Lane and drive east 1.3 miles until Arata Lane becomes Hembree Lane.

■ The parking lot is on the north side of the road.

■ Sonoma County Transit operates bus line 66 in Windsor with a stop at the entrance of Foothill Regional Park.

ON THE TRAIL

Foothill Regional Park is something of a Sonoma secret. Hidden among new residential developments, this 211-acre park offers all a family could hope for on an outing: dog friendly, three ponds, rolling hills, restrooms and water at the trailhead, tons of benches and picnic tables, and views of the valley up on top. The longest trail is 2 miles long, and most of the dozen trails are fractions of a mile. Bring a picnic and enjoy this park, popular with jogging strollers and new parents' playgroups.

From the parking lot turn left (west) on the Westside Trail, a wide dirt trail that rises among manzanita and oak trees. At 0.1 mile the trail angles right along the park boundary and proceeds to rise up to the ridge. On the way you meet a trail that leads down to pond A, but keep going. Around 0.3 mile the trail levels up at the ridge. Turn right to stay on the Westside Trail, and at the intersection with the Bobcat Trail at 0.35 mile, keep straight.

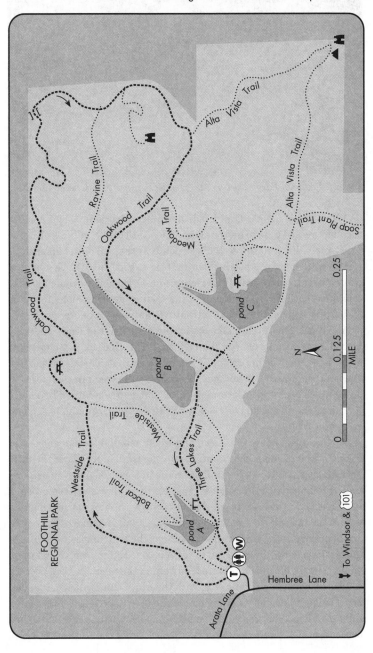

FOOTHILL
REGIONAL PARK

Oakwood Trail

Ravine Trail

Meadow Trail

Alta Vista Trail

Alta Vista Trail

Soap Plant Trail

Oakwood Trail

Westside Trail

Westside Trail

pond B

pond C

Three Lakes Trail

Bobcat Trail

pond A

N

0   0.125   0.25

MILE

Arata Lane

Hembree Lane

To Windsor & 101

Foothill Regional Park serves as the extended backyard of Sonoma families.

While the Westside Trail heads down between pond A and pond B, turn left at 0.44 mile to hop onto the Oakwood Trail for a full loop of the park. You will get to see each of the ponds at the end of the hike; now's the time to enjoy the heights. On that note, you will still be going up while the path curves east. The picturesque Oregon white and blue oaks combined with the snaky route of the trail contouring along a hilltop break this segment into small adventures for junior explorers.

You'll be able to tell blue oaks by the bluish tint of their shallowly lobed leaves, usually shorter than 3 inches. The blue oak is somewhat of a survivor tree: The bluish tint is a waxy layer that reflects the sun and keeps the leaves cool in summer. As a result, the tree can therefore endure severe heat—as in several weeks of 100-degree weather. To quench its thirst, the tree sends its roots down 80 feet underground to tap into the water table.

At the ridge, enjoy the views and break out the snacks and water at one of the picnic tables. Continue on the trail as it follows the hill's natural slope. Next to a log wall at around 0.8 mile, look for an oak tree that resembles a twisted ladder. Passing through a gorgeous grove of oak trees, the trail starts its slow descent with views of neighboring vineyards and oak ridges. A wooden bridge at 0.9 mile marks the northern boundary of the park. After the bridge, the trail angles right. At 1.1 miles, the narrow Ravine Trail enters on your right; keep straight and enjoy views of a pond on private land behind the fence.

The Oakwood Trail intersects with the Alta Vista Trail at 1.15 miles. For a longer hike and summit views of the park, turn left (southeast) on the Alta Vista Trail, reaching the park's highest point at 600 feet, then descend past the junction with the Soap Plant Trail to pond C where you pick up this hike on the Three Lakes Trail at the junction with the Oakwood Trail. This option adds 0.3 mile to the total distance.

To continue this hike, simply turn right to keep to the Oakwood Trail, now a wide dirt road out of the tree cover, and keep going as the road passes the Meadow Trail and winds its way down to the Three Lakes Trail at 2 miles. On your left stands pond C, on your right pond B. These artificial lakes are used for recreational fishing, but no swimming or wading is allowed.

Turn right on the Three Lakes Trail and follow it over the hill down to pond A. A bench on its southeast shore is a perfect dragonfly observation spot next to the tule reeds. From here, curve left along the trail back to the parking lot.

 SPRING LAKE REGIONAL PARK

BEFORE YOU GO

Maps: Map of the trails posted at entrance signboard. Printable map online at www.sonoma-county.org/parks.
Information: Sonoma County Parks (707) 565-2041.
www.sonoma-county.org/parks

ABOUT THE HIKE

Day hike; Easy; Year round
2.2 miles, loop
Hiking time: 1–2 hours
High point/elevation gain: 0 feet/0 feet

GETTING THERE

▪ From US 101 in Santa Rosa going north, take CA-12E/Sonoma.

▪ After 1.7 miles, turn left onto Farmers Lane and after 1 mile, right into 4th Street/CA-12W.

▪ After 1.1 miles turn right onto Mission Street and in two blocks, left on Montgomery Drive.

▪ After 3 miles, turn right onto Channel Drive and right again onto Violetti Road to reach the Spring Lake Park entrance, close to the Environmental Discovery Center. Park next to the swimming lagoon.

▪ Sonoma County Transit operates bus line 30 in Santa Rosa with a few stops about 1 mile from this entrance of Spring Lake Regional Park.

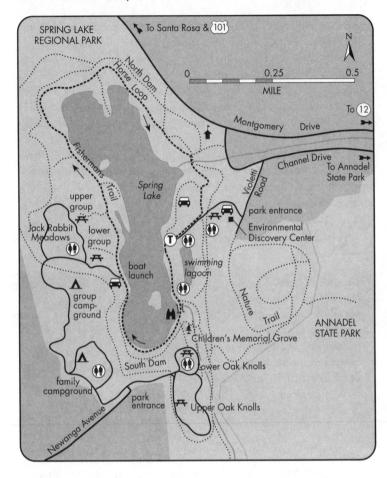

ON THE TRAIL

Rubbing shoulders with Howarth Memorial Park (with a farm, train rides, and play structures) and Annadel State Park, Spring Lake Regional Park is Santa Rosa's favorite park for an impromptu nature outing. At the edge of town in the Sonoma foothills, this 320-acre park is just the right combination of sun and shade with minimal elevation gain. The swimming lagoon and beach are an obvious summer highlight, but renting paddleboats to get out on the lake can be equally fun.

Since there is basically one trail going around the lake with a few variations, there's no need to worry if you get confused by unclear trail

Kids just can't resist peeking into the water from rocks above the lake.

markers as long as you stay close to the lake. Partly paved and partly dirt, this hike only requires comfortable walking shoes.

Even when it's not swimming season, you can enjoy the picnic tables, restrooms, and drinking fountains at the start of this hike. Plus, little ones can roam around easily on the lawns by the lagoon.

From the parking lot, find the paved multi-use trail leading right beyond the lagoon. Surrounded by landscaped lawns and willow trees, the scene seems right out of an urban planning magazine. After 0.1 mile, a small bridge crosses a Spring Creek diversion channel. Turn right onto the bridge and have your kids look for fish in the water. At the other end, you can see colorful stick-figure sculptures holding hands and a circular shelter. The Children's Memorial Grove is dedicated to Sonoma County children who have passed away and is a place of reflection with beautiful views of the lake.

Turn right on the paved path, walking by tall maple trees. Older children will get a kick out of the fitness circuit with stations all around the lake (though you need to stay on the paved trail to see them all).

At 0.4 mile, big rocks on the shore are good spots to get close to the water. Keep walking until you reach the boat launch parking area at 0.8 mile. A jetty forms another good vantage point for fish and duck observation. Your hike continues across the lot on the Fishermans Trail, a narrower dirt-and-gravel path with wilder natural surroundings. Close to the park's riparian habitats and dense tule reed shores, this trail is nicely shaded.

At 1.3 miles, turn right on the paved multi-use trail. After a bend where a massive oak tree is covered in a lichen called old-man's beard, find the Horse Loop (horse sign on a post). If you have a stroller, you may prefer to stay on the paved path, which runs along the North Dam. The horse trail runs parallel to the paved trail but is much less busy and more scenic. It also stays level when the paved path rises over a hill. Turn right at the next junction to cut through stands of blackberry bushes, and right again on the paved trail to return to the parking lot.

THE ENVIRONMENTAL DISCOVERY CENTER

Open to the public from Wednesdays through Sundays from noon to 5:00 PM (check hours on website, free with park admission), the Environmental Discovery Center (www.sonoma-county.org/parks/edc.htm) is a must-see part of the park, before or after your hike. Bring your little ones here and let them learn about the local animals of Sonoma County, and have some hands-on fun at the touch tidepool tank.

 ## ANNADEL STATE PARK/LAKE ILSANJO

BEFORE YOU GO
Maps: USGS Santa Rosa.
Trail map posted at trailhead.
Information: Ranger station
(707) 539-3911. www.parks
.ca.gov

ABOUT THE HIKE
Day hike; Moderate/Difficult;
Year round
5.3 miles, round-trip
Hiking time: 3–4 hours
**High point/elevation
gain:** 900 feet/550 feet

GETTING THERE

▪ From US 101 in Santa Rosa going north, take CA-12E/Sonoma.

▪ After 1.7 miles, turn left onto Farmers Lane and after 1 mile, right onto 4th Street/CA-12W.

▪ After 1.1 miles turn right onto Mission Street and in two blocks, left on Montgomery Drive.

▪ Keep straight past Violetti Road (which leads to Spring Lake Park, Hike 63) and drive into Annadel State Park. Proceed to the last parking lot on the right.

▪ There is no public transit.

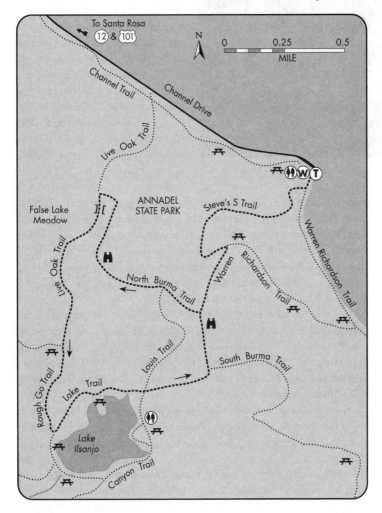

ON THE TRAIL

At the edge of Santa Rosa, Annadel State Park is at its best in the spring when the meadows are a lush green. The park features a man-made lake where fishing is allowed, as well as a marsh. For tiny nature lovers, the park is the perfect occasion to get down on all fours to explore the trailsides. Wildlife is also abundant, and you might see wild turkeys, jackrabbits, deer, and waterfowl.

From the parking area, head briefly onto the Warren Richardson Trail before turning right onto the hiking-only Steve's S Trail. Making your

Ceanothus blooms blue in the spring.

way up the hill through firs and oaks, look for shiny black shards on the trail. They are flakes of obsidian, a very important resource to the Southern Pomo and the Southern Wappo Native Americans who lived nearby and used this smooth, brittle glass to make scrapers, knives, arrow points, and spearheads.

As you meander between the trees, stop and tell your child you are going to play a nature detective game. Scan the surroundings for the tower-shaped nests of turret spiders. These fascinating California native crawlies build towers above their terrestrial silk-lined burrows and decorate them with available materials such as pine needles, moss, and lichen. As soon as you identify a nest, you'll be seeing dozens of them along the trail. The spiral design of the fir needles can be quite impressive.

At 0.8 mile you reach a junction with the Warren Richardson Trail next to a picnic table. Turn right on this wide service road that continues all the way to Lake Ilsanjo. Rather than cutting straight to the chase, turn right at 1.1 miles onto the North Burma Trail. Leaving the forest environment behind, you soon come upon open views of the Valley of the Moon ridges.

Passing several rocky jumbles, this narrow dirt trail takes you to one of the most scenic areas of this park, with expansive meadows and grand views. In the spring this place is a multicolor wildflower carpet. Madrone, ceanothus, and coyote brush line the trail. At 1.8 miles, the Live Oak Trail is marked with a wooden box with a map of the park. Turn left onto the Live Oak Trail, a roller coaster of a trail that keeps going up and down in the shade. Cross a wooden bridge and step out of the forest into the largest meadow of the park. Cutting through open grassland, you may regret that there is no campsite here to enjoy the place at night. A lone live oak tree drips with old-man's beard (usnea lichen), its low-lying branches a perfect jungle gym.

Up the slope you reach a picnic table under the trees by the junction with the Rough Go Trail at 2.7 miles. Continue straight on the Rough Go Trail. After 0.5 mile you reach Lake Ilsanjo at 3.2 miles. Turn left onto the Lake Trail and leisurely enjoy the lakeshore with its assortment of picnic tables and riparian areas where ducks and geese wade in groups.

Bear left beyond the lake onto the Warren Richardson Trail, ascending slightly on a wide fire road. At 3.8 miles, turn left to follow the signs to the parking lot, and enjoy your departing views of the meadows from higher ground. Bear right at the junction with the North Burma Trail and retrace your steps to the parking lot.

 JACK LONDON STATE HISTORIC PARK

BEFORE YOU GO
Maps: USGS Glen Ellen.
Free brochure at the park.
Information: Jack London
State Historic Park (707) 938-5216. www.jacklondonpark
.com. California State Parks,
www.parks.ca.gov

ABOUT THE HIKE
Day hike; Easy; Year round
0.8 mile, round-trip
Hiking time: 30 minutes–1 hour
**High point/elevation
gain:** 700 feet/740 feet

GETTING THERE

■ From CA-12 southbound from Kenwood, make a right on Arnold Drive southwest to Glen Ellen. From CA-12 northbound from Sonoma, turn left on Arnold Drive to Glen Ellen.

■ Turn right on London Ranch Road, following the signs to Jack London State Historic Park, and drive up to the entrance.

■ After the entrance kiosk, turn right to the upper parking lot for Beauty Ranch.

■ There is no public transit.

ON THE TRAIL

Jack London, one of the great names of early-twentieth-century literature and the author of the wilderness adventure books *White Fang* and *The Call of the Wild*, was born in downtown San Francisco. Oyster pirate, gold prospector, whale hunter, he lived a full yet tragic life and finished his days on a ranch he loved overlooking the Valley of the Moon—the Native American name for the Sonoma Valley. Though his books brought him fame, his final years were spent on a lesser-known

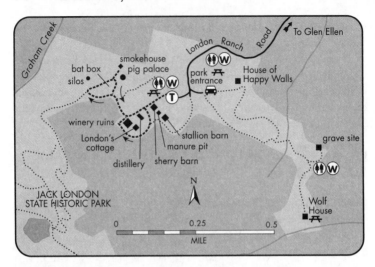

mission in which he invested all his energy: creating a model farm on his ranch. A pioneer farmer in many ways, London experimented with sustainable farming and higher-quality crops.

This hike will show you the practical side of Jack London, his love of the land, and a deluxe pig palace fit only for the best of hogs. On weekends, you can even visit the cottage where he wrote his later books. For a different hike in memory of the writer and the dark side of his life, head to the museum in the House of Happy Walls, his grave site, and the ruins of his dream house, Wolf House, a house he never got to live in as it burned down before he moved in.

From the parking lot, head up a gravel trail lined by tall eucalyptus trees to a picnic site and a map. Before you stretches Jack London's complex of farm buildings against a backdrop of sloping vineyards. Turn right toward Beauty Ranch and head to the sherry barn on your left where you can see an old horse-drawn firemen's carriage. This building, formerly used for making sherry, was converted by London into a barn for his shire horses. Go next door and explain to your kids that the manure pit was used to store animal poop to fertilize the fields. They should love the idea. London even dried the manure to retain its richness to spread it later.

Admire the stallion barn, the next building. London was not only a survivor of extreme outdoor conditions, he was also a serious rider and loved to wander the trails of his ranch on horseback. Now return to the sherry barn and turn left to walk between the cattle stalls before entering a stone-walled wide, grassy area. Though this may look more like a track field than a farm building, you are actually standing in the remains of an old winery. The walls around you formed the stone foundation of the Kohler & Frohling Winery; its upper wooden floors were destroyed by a fire in 1965. Now head out of the heart of the farm complex and turn left on the Lake Trail toward the pig palace/smokehouse. After you see the two silos on your right, get on the unmarked trail that cuts through the grasses up a small hill. Over 40 feet tall, the silos stand over the trail as gray stone ghosts of a glorious past. Continue past the silos and turn left to see the smokehouse made of stone and concrete. Fittingly, it is right next to the pig palace, ensuring a smooth transition from improved pigpen to table. Now backtrack just a bit and turn onto the small path for the pig palace, a circular building where pig families had their own apartment (see the enclosures with walls) with a front sun porch and sleek water troughs. Children will get a kick out of going inside the pig "apartments" with low, slanted ceilings and 3-foot-high walls allowing for observation across pens. Just outside the pig palace, look for a wooden structure on metal posts. It is a bat box, a maternity roost for bats dislodged in 2004 when the cottage was restored.

After you finish exploring the pig palace, head down the hill toward the vineyards and turn left on the Lake Trail to retrace your steps to the parking lot.

A former pioneer farm, Beauty Ranch is now fittingly surrounded by vineyards.

WOLF HOUSE RUINS

For a more dramatic hike at Jack London State Historic Park, start by exploring the House of Happy Walls. This museum is dedicated to the life and work of Jack London. The former home of London's second wife, Charmian, it features furnished rooms, photos, and short videos that give you an idea of the man he was. Outside the House of Happy Walls, head east on the trail to Wolf House. This 0.5-mile (one-way) trail takes you past a short spur to the hilltop where London's ashes were buried under a rock, following his written instructions. Continue on the trail to the charred ruins of the arts and crafts house Jack London planned in 1910. Surrounded by majestic redwood trees, the house would have been magnificent had it not burned down in August 1913, three days before completion. Retrace your steps the same way or come back on the Wolf House Service Road.

 SONOMA VALLEY REGIONAL PARK

BEFORE YOU GO
Map: USGS Glen Ellen. Printable map online at www .sonoma-county.org/parks.
Information: Sonoma County Parks (707) 565-2041. www.sonoma-county .org/parks

ABOUT THE HIKE
Day hike; Easy/Moderate; Spring, Fall, Winter
2.35 miles, loop
Hiking time: 1.5–2 hours
High point/elevation gain: 480 feet/120 feet

GETTING THERE

■ From CA-12 near Glen Ellen, 5.6 miles north of Sonoma and 16 miles south of Santa Rosa, turn west into Sonoma Valley Regional Park and proceed to the parking lot.

■ There is no public transit.

ON THE TRAIL

Across from the Bouverie Preserve and several neighboring hot springs, Sonoma Valley Regional Park is a 202-acre park that offers unexpected open space with outstanding oak woodlands right off CA-12. If you have

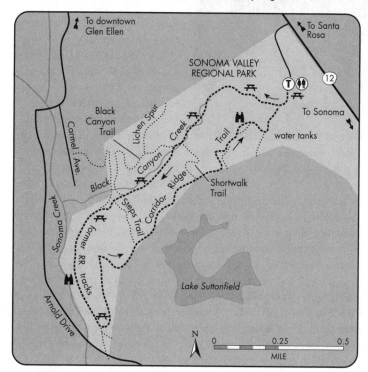

a stroller, you can simply go to the end of the multi-use trail and retrace your steps for a good 2.4-mile hike.

From the parking lot, walk past the gate and, leaving two big water tanks on your left, turn right down the main road that descends between grassy hills. Two picnic tables are on your right, the first of six picnic sites scattered along the trail, a feature that makes this park a weekend pleaser for families. Oak trees arch over the trail, their branches hanging with delicate lace-like silver green threads of old-man's beard. Combined with dark brown to green mossy trunks, the visual effect comes close to an impressionist nature painting.

Winding your way down the canyon, at 0.3 mile you reach the bed of Black Canyon Creek, a seasonal creek that feeds into Sonoma Creek at the western edge of the park. At 0.4 mile pass the junction for the Shortwalk Trail on your left and another for the Black Canyon Trail on your right; keep going on the main road.

At 0.6 mile reach another set of picnic tables next to an oak tree whose trunk has been oddly cut near the base. The reclining stump now makes a

Kids on wheels enjoy the main trail at Sonoma Valley Regional Park.

fun play structure for children, but beware of poison oak.

Looking right, you can see an elevated path that's completely horizontal. This used to be a narrow-gauge track constructed by the Sonoma and Santa Rosa Railroad around 1881–82. At that time Glen Ellen was becoming known as the finest wine-producing area in California. There used to be a bridge across the creek from a distillery building to a railroad siding and platform in what is now the park. The siding was called Chauvet Railway Siding after Joshua Chauvet, a native of France, who ran a large grist mill and made large quantities of wine and brandy. His operation was located at what is now the site of Jack London Village, a historic sawmill complex now converted into a shopping and dining area in Glen Ellen (explore the nearby Jack London State Historic Park in the Glen Ellen hills, Hike 65). On weekends as many as 3000 people would come from San Francisco by train and by ferry to picnic in Glen Ellen and the Sonoma Valley in the 1890s. The Northwestern Pacific rail line operated in the area until the late 1930s.

At 0.8 mile, your trail merges with the railroad track bed, then curves left and gets out in the open. As the noise from Arnold Drive rises to the trail, views open up of the mountains of Glen Ellen. Mostly hidden by thick tree cover, Sonoma Creek runs through the valley at the bottom.

At 1.1 miles the road rises and leaves the rail tracks curving in the vegetation. Look for a dirt trail that starts on your left and goes up the hill. The Corridor Ridge Trail climbs without hesitation until you are walking on the ridge, enjoying east and west views of the Sonoma Valley. At 1.5 miles, turn right at the junction with the Steps Trail, staying on the Corridor Ridge Trail to follow the fence of an old ranch. The trail stays mostly level and passes the other end of the Shortwalk Trail; continue straight on the Corridor Ridge Trail, heading east.

After the waters of Lake Suttonfield appear through the trees (looking south), the Corridor Ridge Trail crests a ridge from which you see the big water tanks visible from the parking lot. Benches under oak trees provide good vista points. At the next two junctions, go straight to go down the hill and get to the road behind the water tanks. Turn left to get back to the parking lot.

 SUGARLOAF RIDGE STATE PARK

BEFORE YOU GO
Maps: USGS Kenwood. Free map at the kiosk.
Information: Sugarloaf State Park (707) 833-5712.
www.parks.ca.gov

ABOUT THE HIKE
Day hike; Moderate; Year round
3.3 miles, loop
Hiking time: 2–3 hours
High point/elevation gain: 1500 feet/300 feet

GETTING THERE

■ From CA-12 northbound, turn right on Adobe Canyon Road just after Kenwood.

■ From CA-12 southbound, turn left on Adobe Canyon Road (after you see Lawndale on your right).

■ Drive 3.4 miles northeast to the Sugarloaf Ridge State Park entrance kiosk. Keep straight and park on the left at the trailhead for Lower Bald Mountain.

■ There is no public transit.

ON THE TRAIL

Minutes away from Kenwood sits a green oasis that provides a nature break with a unique science angle in the middle of the Sonoma Valley. Sugarloaf Ridge State Park offers great hiking opportunities year round, even on hot summer days, thanks to its location above the valley floor. Families come here to camp and wade in Sonoma Creek in the early summer (the creek may dry out later in the year). Dominated by Bald Mountain, a 2729-foot summit that offers views all the way to San Francisco on clear days, Sugarloaf Ridge State Park is also home to the only observatory in the Napa–Sonoma area. Interestingly enough, the observatory is not located on a ridge but on the valley floor so that the surrounding ring of hills protects the telescopes from city light pollution.

The Robert Ferguson Observatory set up the solar system–inspired Planet Walk, part of which you will follow on this hike. The trail also gives a good overview of the meadows and peaks surrounding the park.

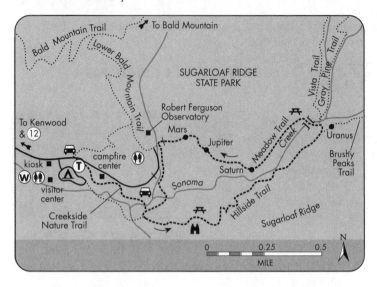

From the parking lot, cross the road and begin on the Creekside Nature Trail to the right of the picnic area. This is a mostly level path that follows the gentle curves of Sonoma Creek upstream and skirts the edges of the campground. The numbered posts on the trail correspond to a self-guided nature trail created by the Youth Conservation Corps in 1977, with a descriptive brochure available at the visitor center.

After the campfire center and a bridge that leads into the campground, you will be walking through grassy meadows along the creek. At 0.3 mile, cross the creek carefully, as the stones can be slippery. You will pass a trail to the horse stables; keep straight.

Climb the hill until you reach the Hillside Trail at 0.5 mile; turn right on this service road. As you reach blackberry bushes, look to your left for the white dome of the Robert Ferguson Observatory. A picnic table and drinking fountain on your left provide a great view on the surrounding peaks. Watch for a short pile of bricks, remains of outdoor facilities that Sonoma State Hospital built for its clients in the 1920s. There were small cabins in the backcountry, which explain fruiting trees and other non-native plants.

The Hillside Trail continues its way up the flanks of Sugarloaf Ridge, passing wild rose bushes and water tanks and alternating between shady oak trees and exposed grassy meadows. Though the descent is interrupted by several brief uphill episodes, you are definitely headed to the valley floor but not done yet with the climbing.

At 1.5 miles, turn right on the Brushy Peaks Trail. Junior astrono-mers will get a kick out of this part of the hike: At 1.6 miles on a rugged dirt trail, a marker for the planet Uranus comes up on the trailside. This marker is one of nine markers in the park, part of an ambitious scale model of the solar system designed to fit within Sugarloaf Ridge State Park. This Planet Walk allows you to hike through the entire solar system by shrinking it more than 2,360,000,000 times. To get an idea of the mind-boggling distances we are talking about, get your kids to try these two experiments: First, with every step, imagine crossing close to a million miles of empty space; second, to walk at the speed of light, take one step every five seconds. How many parks turn you into an astronaut hiker?

Return to the Hillside Trail and continue to the right. Your road will now turn 180 degrees, first passing the junction with the Gray Pine Trail, then becoming the Meadow Trail at 1.9 miles. Admire the old-man's beard (usnea lichen) hanging from the branches of oak trees. Cross the wooden bridge over the creek, and if snack time is near, take a break at the picnic tables under big-leaf maples and white alders. Getting to the Saturn marker is all level, and the Jupiter marker stands in front of wide-open meadows with views of the horse stables. Look up the mountain and spot a reddish rock outcropping, made of andesite, a volcanic rock related to basalt. Sugarloaf Ridge was created by volcanic forces, and these rocks, seven to ten million years old, are hard evidence of the cooled-down and broken lava flows jutting out of the mountain sides.

The Mars marker is close to the observatory. At 2.5 miles, reach the observatory and peek in the courtyard to find the beach ball-sized sun marker. Return to the Meadow Trail and turn right on the unsigned dirt

Following a trail to the planets of our solar system

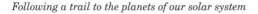

trail that crosses the meadow to Sonoma Creek. At 2.7 miles, turn right on the Creekside Nature Trail and retrace your steps to the parking lot.

THE ROBERT FERGUSON OBSERVATORY

The Robert Ferguson Observatory (www.rfo.org) was named for Bob Ferguson, a Petaluma astronomer dedicated to involving young people in astronomy. The facility houses a 40-inch and a 20-inch telescope and is operated by the Valley of the Moon Observatory Association.

 BARTHOLOMEW PARK WINERY

BEFORE YOU GO
Map: USGS Sonoma. Trail map posted at the trailhead and parking lot.
Information: Bartholomew Park (707) 935-9511. www.bartpark.com. This private park is open seasonally. Call ahead to check trail restrictions.

ABOUT THE HIKE
Day hike; Easy/Moderate; Year round
2.5 miles, loop
Hiking time: 2 hours
High point/elevation gain: 625 feet/400 feet

GETTING THERE
■ From Sonoma Town Plaza on CA-12, turn east on Napa Street and drive 1 mile.
■ At 7th Street East, turn left.
■ After 0.4 mile, turn right on Castle Road and follow the signs for Bartholomew Park Winery. Park in the trails parking lot, left after the entrance.
■ Sonoma County Transit operates buses to Sonoma Town Plaza, roughly 2.3 miles from the winery.

ON THE TRAIL
Close to the heart of Sonoma, this hike will satisfy a nature craving with a local finish on landscaped picnic grounds at a winery next to the

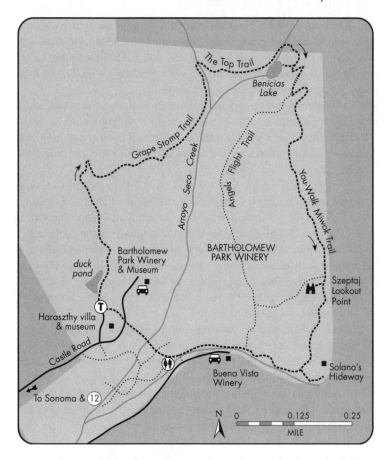

replica of a Palladian villa. These wooded hills and this wine-growing estate were the property of Baron Agoston Haraszthy, a Hungarian aristocrat who was in at the origin of the wine industry in Sonoma Valley. He christened and operated the property as Buena Vista but faced financial difficulties, and the property was sold. After several changes of hands in the early 1940s, pioneer journalist Frank Bartholomew bought the estate and resurrected Buena Vista Winery. His family sold the 15-acre site that included the original winery (it is still operated today and you will see it on this hike) and retained 400 acres. In 1994, the current Bartholomew Park Winery was founded on these 400 acres and the historic buildings were renovated. Before or after the hike, visit the Bartholomew Park Museum inside the winery (www.bartpark.com) where kids can learn how wine is made and see old winery tools. The Palladian villa, a replica of Agoston Haraszthy's Palladian villa, which was destroyed by fire around the turn of the century, is open Saturdays and Sundays for visits from noon to 3:00 PM.

As trail markers show symbols for each trail name, kids can easily lead the way on this hike. They will find a cluster of grapes for the Grape Stomp Trail, a pair of wings for the Angels Flight Trail, a red-and-black circle with two feathers for the You-Walk Miwok Trail, spectacles for Szeptaj Lookout Point, and a black-and-red top for The Top.

From the parking lot, find the sign HIKING TRAIL/NORTH GATE and proceed west through the vineyards to the windmill. At the duck pond, turn right and follow the pond's fence, keeping an eye out for waterfowl. Continue left and go through a wooden gate. At 0.2 mile, turn left onto the Grape Stomp Trail, a single-track dirt trail that rises rather steeply initially but levels out under a mixed oak forest where the bare red-purple bark of madrone trees stand out. Walk up a series of steps to reach a narrow gulch. On roots and rocks the ascent continues on the other side.

At 0.6 mile a map shows your location next to the Grape Stomp bench. A paved road comes into sight at 0.8 mile. Cross Arroyo Seco Creek on a rock bridge and continue on the Grape Stomp Trail after the sign TO THE TOP across the paved road and a flight of steps.

Steadily, you keep climbing through a mixed forest of Douglas fir, redwood, and black oak. Right after the 1-mile mark, Benicias Lake appears through the trees, a reservoir named after Francisca Benicia Carillo, the beautiful wife of General Vallejo, a rancher and military commander. California hazel and honeysuckle grow on the side of the trail.

At 1.1 miles, the East Fork of seasonal Arroyo Seco Creek feeds into the lake. During dry months, you can reach the lake by following the creek bed. Otherwise, simply go up through the redwoods and find a small offshoot on the right to a bench overlooking the lake.

In early summer, the lake is a hot spot for bullfrog-spotting. Here, your kids will be able to see dozens of plump tadpoles and delicate young frogs gliding and jumping under the surface. Stay still! Some "leaves" on the shallow muddy bottom are frogs ready to move.

Back on the trail, you climb several sets of steps, some pretty high for small legs. At 1.3 miles, turn left onto the You-Walk Miwok Trail. Sticky monkey flowers, green tufts of grass, and madrones accompany your

Always offer a hand to small children at creek crossings.

walk. After a bench, you finally get out in the open at 1.4 miles among shrub-size manzanita. On clear days, views extend all the way down to San Pablo Bay.

The trail now descends steadily on a mixed terrain of packed dirt and steps. At 1.7 miles, take a left and left again past the turnoff to the Szeptaj Lookout Point. At the 2-mile marker, turn left to find Solano's Hideaway, a spot reachable by climbing a few rocks and following a narrow path to hidden kid-sized caves. Chief Solano did live in Sonoma from 1823 to 1846, but there is (sadly) no historical evidence he used these caves. Just let your mind wander at this nice secluded spot.

Retrace your steps to the You-Walk Miwok Trail and keep straight to reach a creek shaded by tall redwood trees at 2.1 miles. Turn right and follow the creek.

A fence leads you to a gate north of an old stone cellar belonging to Buena Vista Winery. A second gate opens into Bartholomew Park and a lovely landscaped garden with restrooms and a pavilion. To return to the parking lot, follow the PARK/WINERY signs past a bamboo grove and bear left after the winery.

NAPA
COUNTY

ROBERT LOUIS STEVENSON STATE PARK

BEFORE YOU GO

Maps: USGS Detert Reservoir. Map included in the Bothe–Napa Valley and Robert Louis Stevenson State Parks map sold at Bothe–Napa Valley State Park.
Information: Bothe–Napa Valley State Park (707) 942-4575. www.parks.ca.gov

ABOUT THE HIKE

Day hike; Moderate; Spring, Fall, Winter
1.6 miles, round-trip
Hiking time: 1 hour
High point/elevation gain: 2650 feet/400 feet

GETTING THERE

- From CA-29 in Calistoga, drive 8 miles north toward Clear Lake.
- After signs indicating the entrance of the park, watch for a small dirt parking lot at the summit on the left, or if this one is full, park across the road at the bigger lot (trailhead for Table Rock). The hike starts at the smaller lot on the west side. (If you park on the other side, cross the road with caution.)
- There is no public transit.

ON THE TRAIL

Miles away from tropical islands, the flanks of Mount St. Helena inspired mountain and cave scenes to Robert Louis Stevenson for his famous pirate book *Treasure Island*. In 1880, the Scottish writer was just a newlywed when he honeymooned in Calistoga with his wife, Fanny. He later incorporated some of their experiences into *The Silverado Squatters*. They traveled up the forests of Mount St. Helena and stayed at an abandoned miners' house in front of a derelict silver mine. This is the site where this hike leads you in Robert Louis Stevenson State Park.

Note that this park is undeveloped, which means no restrooms, no water, and no entrance fee. This park gets very hot during the summer,

Opposite: *Discovering the wild side of Napa with a young one at Bothe–Napa Valley State Park*

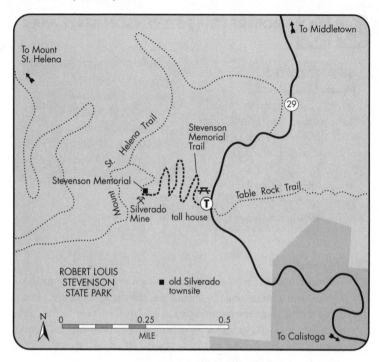

To Middletown

To Mount
St. Helena

29

St. Helena Trail

Stevenson
Memorial
Trail

Mount

Stevenson Memorial

Silverado
Mine

toll house

Table Rock Trail

T

ROBERT LOUIS
STEVENSON
STATE PARK

■ old Silverado
townsite

N

0   0.25   0.5
MILE

To Calistoga

very cold during the winter, and trails can get slippery after rains so in the wet season, wait until it has been sunny a few days to get on the trail.

From the parking lot, look for wooden steps on an unmarked trail leading up to an open meadow with picnic tables. They are scattered on a former croquet ground, also used for bocce ball before World War II. A raised platform on the left flanked by two sets of steps is all that remains from the ancient toll house where stagecoaches stopped on their way to and from Calistoga. Imagine stables attached to the house, which also served as a boarding hotel for the teacher of the local school down the hill. The school served children of the miners.

Continue straight to the sign STEVENSON MEMORIAL TRAIL and start your ascent of the mountain's low hills. A series of gentle switchbacks leads you up the next 0.5 mile. Fragrant bay laurels, tall Douglas firs, and gracious madrones line the path of this evergreen forest. On your right, big boulders announce a different recreational use of this park, a mountain known for its rock-climbing routes both on boulders and steep faces.

This rocky jumble leads to the Silverado Mine.

As you progress, roots and rocks crisscross the trail, signs of one of the park's main problems, soil erosion. You will reach an open area with partial views of the valley before entering deep forest again. Adventurous kids will enjoy climbing rocks along the trail. After you bend around the hill to leave CA-29 behind, you get to the Robert Louis Stevenson Memorial. Standing on top of a crystal-spangled mined-rock pedestal, the book-shaped marble monument bears part of a Stevenson poem. Though nothing indicates the traces of buildings anymore, the flat area around the monument is where his honeymoon cabin stood.

At the end of the clearing, opposite the steps continuing up the mountain, a large rockslide tumbles from the upper shaft of the Silverado Mine. Do not attempt to climb the rockslide, as it is dangerous. Imagine instead that miners roamed these hillsides to dig silver out of a quartz vein flecked with silver and gold. On this mountain the mining town of Silverado boomed and disappeared in only eight years. For a safe rock adventure, the big climbing boulder next to the marble monument has a small child-size cave at its base.

Retrace your steps on the same trail to the parking lot.

BOTHE–NAPA VALLEY STATE PARK

BEFORE YOU GO
Maps: USGS Calistoga. Map of this park and Robert Louis Stevenson State Park available for purchase at the park or online at www.napa net.net/~bothe. Map of hiking trails posted at the trailhead.
Information: Bothe–Napa Valley State Park (707) 942-4575. www.parks.ca.gov

ABOUT THE HIKE
Day hike; Moderate/Difficult; Year round
4.4 miles, round-trip
Hiking time: 2–3 hours
High point/elevation gain: 1050 feet/750 feet

GETTING THERE
- From CA-29/128 in St. Helena northbound, drive 5 miles to Bothe–Napa Valley State Park on your left.
- From CA-29/128 in Calistoga southbound, drive 4 miles to Bothe–Napa Valley State Park on your right.
- Drive past the visitor center and park at the trailhead parking lot.
- There is no public transit.

ON THE TRAIL
Surrounded by vineyards and hot springs, Bothe–Napa Valley State Park is a forested hill rich with redwoods, riparian habitats, and an underground spring that feeds the summer-only public swimming pool. Standing as a reminder to the valley's flora and fauna before the wine age, Bothe–Napa Valley State Park offers 10 miles of hiking trails and a nice shaded campground to visitors. Green in the spring, yellow and red in the fall, the park makes a day excursion coupled with the Bale Grist Mill State Historic Park (Hike 71) down the road. As unusual as a swimming pool may be for a state park, it is a legacy to the park's past as Paradise Resort, a full-flown family resort with swimming pool, cabins, lodge, and airstrip.

In the summer, bring your own drinking water to avoid water restrictions at the drinking fountains. As poison oak is prevalent in the park, wear long sleeves and pants and remember the mantra: Leaves of three,

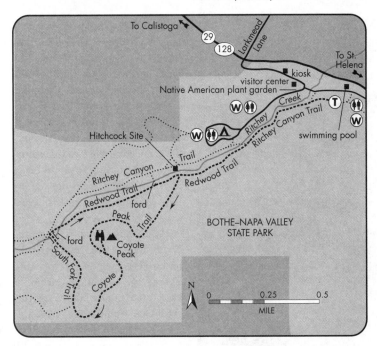

let them be. Before starting the hike, visit the Native American plant garden next to the visitor center for a good introduction to the local flora for kids, and to learn about important plants used by the Wappo people.

From the parking lot, head west following the sign RITCHEY CREEK TRAILS on a dirt track that crosses a paved road and continues straight. The trail parallels the main road for the first 500 feet before widening on the left into a pleasant dirt path by Ritchey Creek, lined with hazel-nut, bay laurel, and big-leaf maple trees. Did you know that the young shoots of hazelnut trees (broad serrated leaves, pale green color) were so pliable that they could be used as weaving material for baskets and animal traps?

At 0.5 mile, keep left to leave the Ritchey Canyon Trail and get on the Redwood Trail. Even on hot summer days, the tree canopy is so dense that this trail is much cooler than anywhere else under the sun. The trail rises slowly to a junction with the Coyote Peak Trail at 0.9 mile. Make a left and start a moderately strenuous ascent over the next mile.

Cutting through steep slopes of laurel and oak trees, the Coyote Peak Trail finally leads you to aerial sections where low chaparral and rocky

Enjoy valley views from the top of the hike.

volcanic soil open up views on the opposite ridges covered in pine forests. At 2 miles, a side trail departs on the left for Coyote Peak. This 0.1-mile optional excursion leads you to scenic views from higher up. Continue on the Coyote Peak Trail until you cross the saddle connecting the two ridges and reenter the forest. The path drops to a creek and picks up among redwoods and Douglas firs, sometimes slightly overgrown.

At 2.5 miles, turn right on the South Fork Trail. Suddenly the path slides down the hill smoothly. There's an explanation for this. Look around and find moss-covered tree stumps. The trail was used by loggers to haul redwoods out of the canyon, and you can still see the scars today.

After the path crosses a stream, it follows its course and reaches Ritchey Creek on another bridge at 2.9 miles. Turn right on the Ritchey Canyon Trail, a wide service road. Immediately after the concrete bridge, look for a narrow entrance to the Redwood Trail on the right. Turn right to follow this nature trail. Note that at the fallen log by the creek, you need to ford the creek and continue on the other side.

If the creek is impassable, instead of the Redwood Trail, continue east on the Ritchey Canyon Trail and after 0.5 mile ford Ritchey Creek (0.1 mile before the Hitchcock Site) to find the Redwood Trail across the creek and turn left to retrace your steps to the parking lot.

If you successfully crossed Ritchey Creek, follow the creekside Redwood Trail as it meanders between redwoods and eventually meets the Ritchey Canyon Trail. Keep straight to stay on the Redwood Trail and turn left at the next junction at 3.4 miles.

Retrace your steps to the parking lot.

THE STORY OF THE DOUGLAS FIR AND COYOTE

Stop under a Douglas fir and pick up a relatively intact cone to tell the following story to your kids: "A long time ago there lived only animals and plants. Coyote loved to play tricks on his friends and after a while, the other animals decided to take their revenge. They left a big pile of food in the woods and hoped Coyote would stuff himself sick and fall asleep. He did find the food and ate it all, then closed his eyes and fell backward. To make sure Coyote was asleep, the animals sent mice to poke Coyote. Coyote jumped and yelled! The mice ran and took cover in the pine cones. To this day, you can still see the tails and rear ends of mice underneath the scales of the Douglas fir pine cones."

 BALE GRIST MILL STATE HISTORIC PARK

BEFORE YOU GO
Maps: USGS Calistoga. Map of this park and Robert Louis Stevenson State Park available for purchase at the park or online at www.napa net.net/~bothe.
Information: Bale Grist Mill State Historic Park (707) 942-4575. www.parks.ca.gov

ABOUT THE HIKE
Day hike; Easy/Moderate; Spring, Fall
2 miles, round-trip
Hiking time: 1 hour
High point/elevation gain: 50 feet/50 feet

GETTING THERE
■ From CA-29/128 in Calistoga southbound, drive 5.5 miles to the entrance of Bale Grist Mill State Historic Park on your right.
■ From CA-29/128 in St. Helena northbound, drive 3 miles to the entrance of Bale Grist Mill State Historic Park on your left.
■ There is no public transit.

ON THE TRAIL
Before the Napa Valley was known for wine, it was a valley planted in wheat fields and fruit orchards. The Bale Grist Mill was one of the

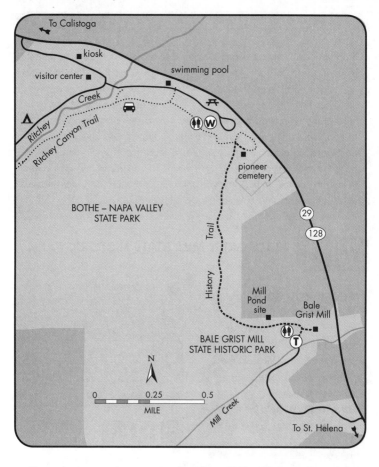

earliest pioneer settlements in the Napa Valley. Built in 1846 by Edward Bale, this water-powered grist mill was used to grind wheat and corn from the valley. However, the resulting flour was initially of poor quality, and Bale accrued debts. The mill became the center of the valley's social activity after his widowed wife, Maria Sobrantes, niece of General Vallejo, studied the mechanisms of mills and altered the design to make it a profitable operation.

Today the mill still runs with the original grinding stone, shipped by boat from France, and docents offer remarkable tours of the mill with hands-on milling activities for children. It is a fantastic day trip, but be warned that your children will probably end up dusted in flour! As

The mill's live demonstration is a lesson in mechanics, grain milling, and helping!

a tasty souvenir of your hike, you can bring some flour back home and bake cookies with the kids.

The hike starts by the imposing water mill. As you walk by, point to the aerial flume that carries water pumped from the ground onto the waterwheel. Your children will get the concept quickly if you compare it to a waterslide.

The History Trail goes over the hill to the oldest cemetery and the site of the first Anglican church in the Napa Valley. It starts as a paved trail right behind the mill, passes a water tank, and follows a fence. Nearby are the remains of the pond (Mill Pond) and ditches that provided a constant supply of water to make the wheel turn. Cross the wooden bridge over a small tributary of Mill Creek and keep left to the trail.

While the bottom of the hill is covered in oaks and grasses, your route will soon be shaded only by oaks as it crosses the rocky bottom of a seasonal creek. Take a deep breath, because the climb is in front of you, short and steep. Twisting now through claret-colored trunks of madrone, the trail keeps ascending until you hit the ridge. Fortunately once you reach the top, the path is wider and meanders lazily between tanoaks, Douglas fir, madrone, and black oak, before dipping again to go down the other side of the hill. Since the hill is the shape of a bell, the top descends gradually and drops abruptly before hitting the valley floor again, in Bothe–Napa Valley State Park (see Hike 70).

Once out in the open, you will see a square white picket enclosure on your right. Leave the main trail to walk over to the pioneer cemetery, the last resting place of the Tucker family as well as other pioneer settlers of the Napa Valley. Look for the marker of the White Church, a church named after Reverend Asa White and built in 1853 as the first church in Napa County. If you are visiting in the summer, you can pay a quick visit to the spring-fed swimming pool of Bothe–Napa Valley State Park.

Retrace your steps to the parking lot.

 ALSTON PARK

BEFORE YOU GO
Map: USGS Napa.
Information: Napa Parks & Recreation (707) 257-9529.
www.cityofnapa.org

ABOUT THE HIKE
Day hike; Easy/Moderate;
Spring, Fall, Winter
2.5 miles, loop
Hiking time: 1.5– 2 hours
**High point/elevation
gain:** 200 feet/200 feet

GETTING THERE

■ From CA-29 in Napa, exit at Trower Avenue and go west for 1 mile until it dead-ends at Dry Creek Road.

■ Alston Park's entrance and parking lot are straight across Dry Creek Road.

■ In Napa, the VINE transit system stops at Trower Avenue and Linda Vista Avenue two blocks from the entrance of the park on Dry Creek Road.

ON THE TRAIL

Known as a dog-walking wonderland for locals, Alston Park offers several miles of hiking trails on former orchards at the edge of Napa. Alternating between grassy meadows and the edges of a redwood canyon, Alston Park has eight well-maintained trails from which you always have open views of the rest of the park.

From the parking lot, walk on the Valley View Trail, which starts to the right of the signboard. At 0.1 mile at the trail junction, turn left on the Prune Picker Trail. Up until the 1950s, Napa was not a monoculture county whose only crop was grapes. The valley had a reputation for its orchards: pears, peaches, and particularly, plums (sold dried as prunes).

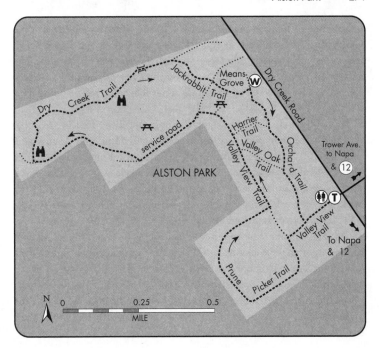

While the Prune Picker Trail is just a vast meadow with a squarish trail encircling it, you can imagine neat rows of trees where Napa Valley plums were grown and hand-picked to be dried and shipped by boat down the river to San Francisco. Today's landscape has erased most traces of this past, but the trail is still a pleasant, level, wide road, bordered to the south and west by vineyards and with a few plum trees around the edges.

As you circle clockwise, the path rises gently, curving right. Turn left at 0.3 mile to go through the opening in the wooden fence separating the off-leash from on-leash dog areas. This portion of the Valley View Trail ambles very close to vineyards and water tanks, along another wide, grassy expanse. The trail connects with a paved service road.

Turn left uphill and then right on the Dry Creek Trail, a gravel trail that veers off at a 20-degree angle. Get ready for a display of 3-D perspective. While the terrain so far has been uniformly flat, the Dry Creek Trail explores foothills, redwood and oak forests, while always keeping an eye on the city.

At 1.3 miles, the trail bends right. You will have 360-degree vistas of the area: vineyards on one side, city streets on the other, a former orchard where you are; the contrast is striking. Skirting the edges of the oak foothills, the trail curves right. If the sun is too strong, find a bench under the tree cover right before a wooden fence starts on your left. The trail keeps going up. Keep to the left by the fence as you progress, now overlooking Redwood Canyon and its venerable oak trees dripping with old-man's beard.

The trail bends right again, now facing east. Leaving the forest behind and reentering vineyard country, you will go up and down a succession of hills offering beautiful views of the park. Finally on the valley floor, the trail gets closer to a seasonal creek. So close, in fact, that if you take a side trail under a big oak tree at 1.8 miles, you might find the creek bed with a knotted rope hanging from a branch across from you, ready for a Tarzan swing creek crossing.

Get back on the trail and in 100 feet cross the creek in a more civilized manner on a wooden bridge. At the next junction, turn right on the Jackrabbit Trail. This narrow path goes over the hill, crosses a paved service road, and continues straight up the opposite hill. At the top, take a break at a picnic table before continuing straight to connect with the Orchard Trail. Continue straight to the junction with the Valley View Trail and turn left to get back to the parking lot.

Two families enjoy a walk around Prune Picker Trail.

WESTWOOD HILLS REGIONAL PARK

BEFORE YOU GO
Map: USGS Napa.
Information: Napa Parks &
Recreation (707) 257-9529.
www.cityofnapa.org

ABOUT THE HIKE
Day hike; Moderate/Difficult;
Spring, Fall, Winter
1.5 miles, round-trip
Hiking time: 2 hours
**High point/elevation
gain:** 400 feet/400 feet

GETTING THERE

- From CA-29 in Napa, exit at First Street and go west for 0.8 mile until it becomes Browns Valley Road.
- The park's entrance and parking lot are 0.3 mile farther on the left.
- In Napa, the VINE transit system 1A and 1B stop next to the entrance of the park on Browns Valley Road.

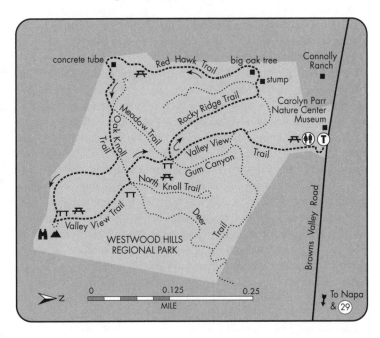

ON THE TRAIL

A park with hills, valleys, and views a mile from downtown Napa is something of a wonderful treat. An added bonus for young animal lovers is the presence of cows freely grazing around the park to reduce the fire risk. Also, both a nature center and an educational farm are located next to the park: The Carolyn Parr Nature Center Museum, on the northern edge of the park (707-255-6465; http://creec.edgateway.net/cs/creecp/view /creec_org/889), is open on Saturdays and Sundays from 1:00 to 4:00 PM (free). The Connolly Ranch Education Center, on the western edge of the park (www.connollyranch.org), is an educational farm reserved for school field trips but open to the public for two yearly events in June and October.

From the parking lot, walk up the Valley View Trail to a metal gate guarding the park entrance, past a farmhouse and water tower that used to be part of the original cattle farm. Go through a second gate 100 feet beyond and continue up to a bench at the junction with the Rocky Ridge Trail. Make a hard right on the Rocky Ridge Trail (none of the trails are marked in the park, so follow the accompanying map) at 0.2 mile, which takes you up the hill to another gate. Go past that gate and make your way between a corridor of low bushes, some of which offer nesting branches to the local birds. If you are lucky, you might see a nest at eye level, so look closely.

At the next junction at 0.3 mile, turn left, still on the Rocky Ridge Trail, where a madrone tree spreads a lazy branch across the trail. A soft green moss has taken over the trunks of surrounding live oak trees and rocks. At the next trail junction at 0.4 mile, turn left and pass another gate. Right after a stump covered with white fungus 30 feet later, make a hard right on the Red Hawk Trail, a rocky dirt trail that goes over the ridge. Keep to the right at the signed junction. This trail goes down the hillside around a beautiful big oak tree. You might even find a scruffy rope swing hanging from a branch for swing enthusiasts.

Wooden steps go down a steep section before you enter a meadow at 0.5 mile. Views of surrounding vineyards and forests give a rural character to this part of the park. Stay on your path as another one shoots up the hill, and continue your downward journey until you get to a seasonal creek, at which point the trail goes up again. Skirting the edges of the park, you will go over a concrete tube that channels rainfall into the creek during the wet season. Keep going up until a densely connected network of oak branches forms a ceiling over the trail.

Out in the open, scan the grassy slopes to find your bearings. The Red Hawk Trail descends to a junction with the Meadow Trail and the Oak Knoll Trail at 0.7 mile. Bear right onto the Oak Knoll Trail to explore an ancient oak woodland. Some of these trees are several centuries old.

At 1 mile, bear right on an unnamed trail to ascend the steepest portion of the trail, fortunately shaded by tree cover. Walking

Reaching the hilltop was a piece of cake for this junior explorer.

along a fence, you reach a flat hilltop with breathtaking views over downtown Napa and the mountain ranges from north to south. Take a moment to rest on the bench, and if cows are munching nearby, admire their grazing skills!

Turn left on the Valley View Trail to continue down the hill, past a long picnic table and under arching oak trees, to a four-way junction at 1.2 miles in front of a bench. Here the Valley View Trail intersects with the Oak Knoll, North Knoll, and Deer trails. Bear left to continue on the Valley View Trail, between eucalyptus trees. This service road takes you back to the entrance gate and parking lot.

 JOHN F. KENNEDY MEMORIAL PARK

BEFORE YOU GO
Map: USGS Napa.
Information: Napa Parks & Recreation (707) 257-9529.
www.cityofnapa.org

ABOUT THE HIKE
Day hike; Easy; Year round
0.8 mile, loop
Hiking time: 1 hour or less
High point/elevation gain: 0 feet/0 feet

GETTING THERE

■ From CA-29 southbound in Napa, exit at CA-121 north onto Lake Berryessa/Imola Avenue and drive east to Soscol Avenue/Napa–Vallejo Highway after the bridge. Turn right and after 0.7 mile, turn right onto Streblow Drive.

■ From CA-29 northbound from Vallejo before Napa, turn right onto Soscol Avenue/Napa–Vallejo Highway toward downtown Napa/Lake Berryessa and continue for 2 miles. Turn left onto Streblow Drive.

■ Follow Streblow Drive to John F. Kennedy Memorial Park at the end of the road. Turn left and park at the boat launch parking lot.

■ Napa Valley County Transit System bus line 10 stops at Streblow and CA-121.

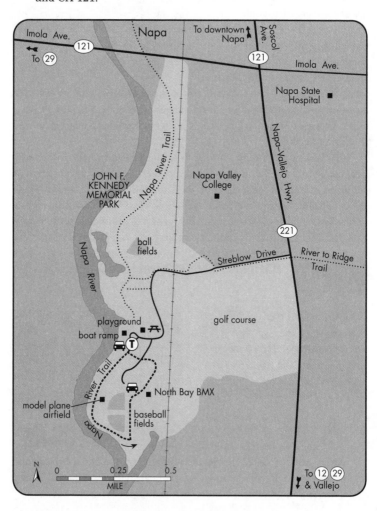

ON THE TRAIL

Napa Valley visitors tend to forget that the town of Napa was originally founded because of the river—and that the river was the commercial and touristic pulse of the valley until the 1920s. It is only fitting that a hike should celebrate the Napa River, a 55-mile waterway flowing from the flanks of Mount St. Helena to the north end of San Pablo Bay. Downstream from Napa the river forms a tidal estuary and becomes a marsh on the edge of San Pablo Bay.

Prior to European settlement, the Wappo and Patwin peoples navigated the river on boats made out of tule reeds. When in 1847, Nathan Coombs laid out the plan of the city of Napa on the banks of the Napa River, the site was chosen for its navigability. Upstream, the river was too shallow to allow big boats to go through. The riverside location made Napa a successful nineteenth-century hub for passenger, industrial, and agricultural transport to and from San Francisco.

In 1875, Napa Valley State Hospital opened its doors on the current Napa–Vallejo Highway and purchased land to make the hospital more food-self-reliant through farming. The initial 192 acres of land were bought from the Mexican land grant known as Rancho Tulucay, but as the hospital population grew, so did its food needs. Additional land purchases increased the hospital lands to over 2000 acres, from a wharf on the Napa River to the eastern edge of Skyline Park. After the hospital's farming operations ceased in the late 1960s, the land was sold to become Napa Valley College, Skyline Wilderness Park, and, in 1967, John F. Kennedy Memorial Park. Kennedy Memorial Park now covers 362 acres of prime riverside land, one of the few places where visitors can enjoy trails directly along the Napa River.

This part of the park encompasses an airfield where members of the Napa Valley Radio Control Club fly model airplanes on Saturday mornings, so watch out for flying machines zooming above your head—although your little ones will probably love that.

This level loop hike is paved and multi-use, and appropriate for stroller hikes, energetic

Families come to the park to fish as well as to watch the model planes, bike, or hike.

preschoolers, and bicycles. Along the river, families enjoy fishing or watching boats. At the end of the hike, swing by the playground and meadows.

From the boat launch parking lot, go left (south) on the Napa River Trail. This part of the Bay Trail follows the Napa River from 8 feet above, past several shore access points for a closer look to the river. On your left is the model airplane airfield. The trail follows the course of the river and after 0.2 mile gently curves left (east), offering views of marshes and industrial plants. Some of these marshes are former salt ponds and are now part of the Napa–Sonoma Marshes Wildlife Area, best explored by boat with a map and tidal charts. For more information, contact the Napa–Sonoma Marshes Wildlife Area in Napa at (707) 944-5567.

The Napa River Trail rounds the peninsula and at 0.3 mile leaves the river behind to return north on the east-side baseball fields, west of the railroad tracks and the Napa Golf Course at Kennedy Park. Up in the hills, the big wooded area is Skyline Wilderness, behind Napa State Hospital. At the end of the baseball fields at 0.5 mile, the trail turns right toward the North Bay BMX (bike racetrack). Follow the path, and shortly after turn left to return to the parking lot.

75 LAKE BERRYESSA RECREATION AREA/ SMITTLE CREEK

BEFORE YOU GO
Maps: USGS Chiles Valley. Free map at visitor center.
Information: Bureau of Reclamation (707) 966-2111. www.usbr.gov/mp/ccao/ berryessa/index.html

ABOUT THE HIKE
Day hike; Easy; Spring, Fall, Winter
1.5 miles, loop; 5.2 miles round-trip to Coyote Knolls
Hiking time: 1 hour
High point/elevation gain: 200 feet/30 feet

GETTING THERE

- From I-80 northbound in Fairfield, exit at Suisun Valley Road (which turns into Wooden Valley Road) and go west/north.
- Turn right on CA-121 toward Lake Berryessa.
- At Moskowite Corners, turn left on CA-128.

- Turn right on Knoxville Road and after roughly 10 miles, turn right into Lake Berryessa Recreation Area's parking lot for Smittle Creek.
- There is no public transit.

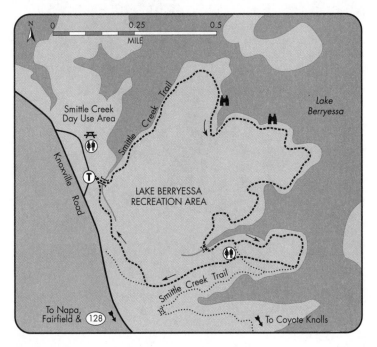

ON THE TRAIL

Under the waters of Lake Berryessa almost 300 feet down is a deep canyon traversed by ranch roads leading to a submerged ghost town with an arched stone bridge, and a swimming pool telling tales of the sunken city of Monticello. Sound like a Scooby-Doo scenario? Lake Berryessa, an artificial lake, was created in 1957 when the farming city of Monticello was flooded and the Putah Creek Valley was dammed to supply water to nearby cities and industries. At capacity, the lake boasts 165 miles of shoreline and is a favorite recreation destination for local families who come to camp at Oak Knoll or Pleasure Cove, or simply picnic for the day before a splash at the Oak Shores, Acorn, or Coyote swim beaches. Though boating, fishing, swimming, and waterskiing are

Depending on the time of the year, you'll see the reservoir's edges high and clear or low and cloudy.

popular activities at Lake Berryessa Recreation Area, lakeside trails attract hikers, too.

If your children are between five and twelve years of age, stop at the visitor center and ask for a Junior Ranger activity book. Your kids might earn a Junior Ranger badge today! This 1.5-mile loop only explores a section of the entire Smittle Creek Trail, so feel free to continue if your children's stamina begs for more trails. Indeed, the Smittle Creek Trail follows the contour of the lake 2.6 miles down to Coyote Knolls at the Oak Shores Day Use Area and makes a nice 5.2-mile out-and-back hike.

From the Smittle Creek Day Use Area parking lot, find the trail at the southern end next to a big signboard. If you didn't pick up one at the visitor center, grab a laminated guide to the nature trail, the first 0.7 mile of the Smittle Creek Trail. You cross a wooden bridge before heading off toward the lake among blue oaks, interior live oaks and grassy slopes. The vegetation here is at its best in the spring when dominated by vibrant greens and wildflowers.

The views open up on the narrow fjords that surround the lake with a background of layered mountain ridges. The trail is perched high above the water surface (and even higher during dry months, as the lake level fluctuates 10 to 20 feet across the seasons). If you look across the lake, you'll notice several islands, the tops of sunken hills. In the summer as the water level goes down, both Small Island and Big Island become reachable by land again—until the next rains.

At 0.2 mile the level path crosses over to the next cove and new views open up on the jagged edges of the lake. At 0.3 mile the trail turns away from the lake for a short foray in the hills where some tree trunks seem to defy gravity. In front of trail marker 10, a wooden birdhouse awaits potential nesters (ducks, bluebirds).

Look up in the trees to see if you can spot a raptor's nest. The easiest to spot are osprey nests, big piles of interwoven sticks perched at the tippy top of trees or snags. These nests are prominently positioned on the tops of telephone poles, electric powerline towers, and dead or sickly trees around the lake. The succession of small coves is such a pretty sight, you may want to stop at the bench next to the trail marker 15 to enjoy the landscape.

Continue beyond the end of the nature trail, crossing a second bridge and getting to the second big arm of the Smittle Creek Trail. At 1 mile, veer left to stay on the trail. On top of the hill are restrooms. The shaded path turns around the point to face the distant buildings of Oak Shores to the south. Right after the steps, turn right and make your way up the hill. Past the restrooms, the path is paved and heads toward Knoxville Road. At 1.3 miles, turn right at the arrow to get a connector trail back to the parking lot. Though this trail is not maintained, it is easy to follow and parallels the road. The parking lot is at 1.5 miles.

UVAS CANYON COUNTY PARK

BEFORE YOU GO
Maps: USGS Loma Prieta.
Free map at entrance kiosk.
Information: Santa Clara
County Parks (408) 355-
2200. www.parkhere.org

ABOUT THE HIKE
Day hike; Moderate/Difficult;
Year round
3 miles, loop
Hiking time: 2–3 hours
High point/elevation
loss: 1800 feet/600 feet

GETTING THERE

■ From I-280 west of San
Jose, take CA-85 south toward Gilroy. After 13 miles, exit at Almaden
Expressway, stay in the ramp's middle lane, make the first left, then
take the next right onto Almaden Expressway. Drive about 4 miles
to the end of Almaden Expressway, and turn right onto Harry Road.
Almost immediately, turn left onto McKean Road, which becomes
Uvas Road after about 6 miles. Continue on Uvas for about 3.5
miles, and turn right onto Croy Road.

■ From US 101 northbound in Morgan Hill, exit at Bailey Avenue
and go west for 3.2 miles on Bailey Avenue. Turn left at McKean
Road, which becomes Uvas Road after 2.4 miles. Continue another
3.7 miles and turn right at Croy Road.

■ Drive 4.4 miles on Croy Road, through Sveadal, a private
Swedish community (drive slowly, there are kids), to reach the park
entrance. Park at the Black Oak Group Area or, if this is full, at the
parking lot right below.

■ There is no public transit.

ON THE TRAIL

With a high ratio of waterfalls per mile walked, Uvas Canyon County
Park offers a remote nature escape tucked at the back of narrow Uvas
Canyon. Named after Uvas Creek, the canyon is actually where Uvas
Creek and Swanson Creek merge in a series of waterfalls that draw

Opposite: *Some trees are perfect for treehouse play fun.*

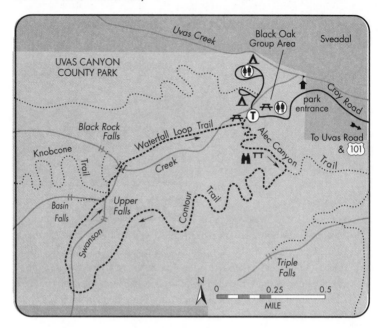

waterfall lovers in the winter and spring. Thanks to the cooling effect of the dense forest that grows on all sides, Uvas Canyon County Park remains a great outdoors option even during toasty summer days. It's also a good pick for an autumn walk as big-leaf maples turn to bright yellows before their leaves cover the trails with an orange crunchy blanket.

With little children, you may prefer to stick to the 1-mile trail called the Waterfall Loop Trail. It takes you to Upper Falls, and kids can skip stones and look for wildlife around the boulders. The loop described here is more demanding and adapted for kids who are not afraid of heights, as the Contour Trail features steep drops on one side of the trail. It is, however, a classic loop of this park and very pretty.

From the parking lot, walk up to the Black Oak Group Area and follow a sign for the Alec Canyon Trail to find the trailhead at a metal gate. Past the gate, walk along the wide service road, and at 0.1 mile, veer left at the junction to get on the Alec Canyon Trail. From the service road, you can hear the waters of Swanson Creek down below. Steadily the trail goes up through switchbacks until it reaches a lookout at a bench. This is your chance to recharge before the Contour Trail.

Uvas Canyon is famous for its waterfalls.

At 0.6 mile after a bend, make a sharp right on the Contour Trail. This narrow dirt path skirts the edges of successive canyons whose north-facing slopes are covered in pure stands of bay laurel trees and east–west-facing slopes host oak and madrone habitats. The pattern will become obvious after the second canyon or so, but watch your footing and don't get distracted. The path is really narrow and the drop on the right side intimidating at best, becoming increasingly steep as you climb the canyon side. You will want to hold children's hands.

At 1.8 miles the noise of a creek gets louder, a sweet reward after the long Contour Trail. At 2 miles you reach the creek, jumping on rocks, and a hairpin turns you around to follow the creek downstream. Skip stones to cross the creek after the TRAIL sign. At 2.2 miles the trail for

Basin Falls comes from the left. If you want to check it out, it's just a 0.3-mile addition to your route (out and back). Kids can even wade in the pool if the fall is past its powerful prime.

Otherwise just keep going down as the trail turns to wooden steps. Upper Falls is right above the next trail junction at 2.3 miles. If the weather has been wet, it is gorgeous and flows way into the summer, but by early fall it'll most likely be close to a trickle. Look for ladybugs from November through February as they hibernate along the creek.

Cross the wooden bridge and bear right on the Waterfall Loop Trail. To see a third waterfall, follow the signs for Black Rock Falls, 0.1 mile from the main trail. The Waterfall Loop Trail is a wide service road that returns to the parking lot following Swanson Creek. Just head straight, and enjoy some easy walking all the way down.

 HENRY W. COE STATE PARK

BEFORE YOU GO
Maps: USGS Mount Sizer. Henry W. Coe State Park Trail and Camping Map sold at the store. Free brochure with map and hike descriptions at the ranger station.
Information: Park office (408) 779-2728. www .coepark.org California State Parks, www.parks.ca.gov

ABOUT THE HIKE
Day hike; Moderate/Difficult; Spring, Fall, Winter
3.7 miles, round-trip
Hiking time: 3–4 hours
High point/elevation gain: 2550 feet/320 feet

GETTING THERE
- From US 101 southbound in Morgan Hill (south of San Jose), take the East Dunne Avenue exit.
- Drive east on East Dunne Avenue 13 miles, past Anderson Lake, to the end of the county road and the Henry W. Coe State Park headquarters, Coe Ranch. The road is winding, and the trip between US 101 and the Coe Ranch headquarters takes about 30 minutes.
- For public transit information, see www.transitandtrails.org /trailheads/444.

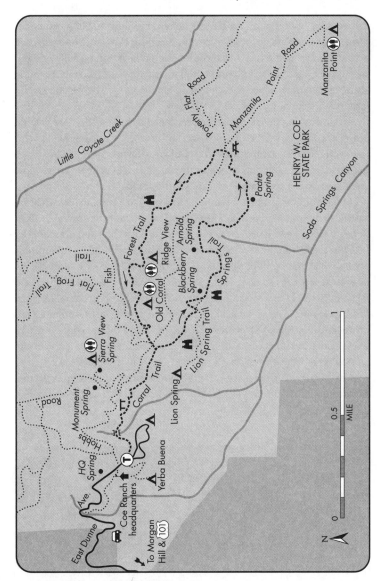

ON THE TRAIL

A former cattle ranch, Henry W. Coe State Park is the largest state park in Northern California with 87,000 acres of wild open spaces. Yet despite its proximity to large urban centers, it receives only 40,000 visitors per year. For a complete nature escape minutes from the San Jose area, pack a picnic lunch and expect grand vistas on endless rolling hills without the crowds. This trail combination follows the easiest trails in the park, starting on sunny slopes and ending on shady paths. The vegetation differences are simply stunning.

From the headquarters parking lot, head south on the Corral Trail, a dirt trail lined with coyote brush that crosses a wooden bridge and passes the old ranch buildings. The trail goes down slightly before leveling up on a ledge above a wooded canyon. After a bench you cross wide-open meadows interrupted by stately valley oaks.

At 0.6 mile you get to a three-way junction. Turn right to head to Manzanita Point via the Springs Trail. At 0.7 mile the trail enters a mixed forest with oak and laurel trees but soon reemerges in open grassland.

Wildlife sightings are common on the Springs Trail, so you might come across wild turkeys, California quails (always traveling as a family), deer, or even coyotes. If you don't see the actual animals, this trail is still great for animal tracking, especially if it's muddy or very dry (the soil is really fine). Ask your kids to walk ahead of you and to scout for animal footprints and scat (poop). Overturned soil mounds are typical of areas where wild pigs search for worms, acorns, or roots, making a royal mess at the base of trees. That's what happens when you play with your food.

At 0.9 mile keep straight at the junction with the Lion Spring Trail. Before and after a bridge you will see troughs and other cattle equipment,

Gnarled oak trees grace the Springs Trail.

reminders of the park's ranching days. After a switchback the trail goes up, leading to a wooden bench under tall black oak trees around 1.1 miles by Blackberry Spring. Enjoy the views of rolling hills unfolding one after the other.

After a long level stretch, the trail meets Manzanita Point Road at 1.9 miles. This three-way junction on a ridge is the perfect opportunity for a snack or picnic lunch at the picnic table under the tall oak tree. At this point, you are halfway through the hike.

Cross Manzanita Point Road and go north and west on the Forest Trail, grabbing a laminated self-guided tour of this nature trail; just return it in the box at the other end. The Forest Trail is dramatically different from the Springs Trail in that you leave open oak grassland behind for forested slopes with a wide plant variety (hence the nature trail). The contrast is fascinating. Around the trail marker 14, look for a boulder area. Kids can walk inside—it's like a rocky hallway—and return to the trail a few yards beyond. Leaving wooded slopes, the trail enters a pine forest and comes back on the ridgeline.

At 3.2 miles the trail intersects again with Manzanita Point Road. Cross the road to get on the Corral Trail toward the park's headquarters.

 SANBORN SKYLINE COUNTY PARK

BEFORE YOU GO
Maps: USGS Castle Rock Ridge. Free map of the park at entrance kiosk.
Information: Park office (408) 867-9959. www .parkhere.org

ABOUT THE HIKE
Day hike; Easy/Moderate; Year round
1.2 miles, loop
Hiking time: 1 hour
High point/elevation gain: 1440 feet/120 feet

GETTING THERE

- From Saratoga, drive 2 miles west on CA-9 to Sanborn Road; turn left.
- The park entrance is 1 mile down Sanborn Road, on the right.
- Inside the park, turn right and drive to the parking lot below the meadows with picnic areas (including the Sequoia Group Area).
- There is no public transit.

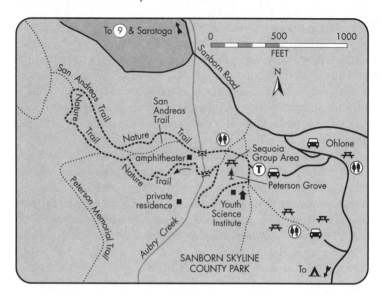

ON THE TRAIL

On the eastern slopes of the Santa Cruz Mountains, Sanborn Skyline County Park is a family magnet. While the top of the park includes climbing routes for rock lovers (it's across from Castle Rock State Park; see Hike 89), the bottom part features Lake Ranch Reservoir. The middle part, where the ranger station is, is a perfect mix of green meadows and group picnic areas with a nature trail and the Youth Science Institute. If your kids love space to run around, this park is an easy day trip.

Formerly a ranch with produce and cattle activities, Sanborn Park was badly shaken during both the 1906 and the 1989 earthquakes. In 1906, some streams changed their course. You might not realize it at the parking lot, but you are standing on the San Andreas Fault Zone. Thanks to this incredible location, the park is a paradise for geologists and earthquake enthusiasts of all ages.

Though this trail is short, trail junctions can be confusing, but since you're never far from the trailhead, chances of getting lost are pretty low. To get the full biology extent of the Nature Trail, grab a hike description at the kiosk.

From the parking lot, head west toward Peterson Grove and look up on the meadows to find old ranching tractors. Continue to an elevated boardwalk leading to Peterson Grove, a lovely redwood fairy ring whose center is now a platform surrounded by benches facing a raised stage, making it an ideal wedding spot.

Exit the grove to find the sign NATURE TRAIL at 0.1 mile. Turn right on the paved path, passing the Youth Science Institute (www.ysi-ca.org), an arts and crafts–style building housing live animals that populate the Santa Cruz Mountain Range, earthquake and geology displays, an arthropod zoo, and a garden. To visit you need to call ahead and book an appointment.

The trail curves down to a pond fed by Aubry Creek and loops around it. Turn right to follow the trail in the direction of the Sequoia group picnic area, but don't go all the way there. At 0.2 mile, the Nature Trail continues left on a dirt path south of the amphitheater. If you come during the summer months, plan to stay into the evening for family-friendly performances of Shakespeare in the park with Shady Shakes (www.shadyshakes.org) in this amphitheater. After you cross a bridge, the rustic trail goes up a few steps to a large clearing before curving left under bay trees. The trail is so shaded that kids like to pretend it's spooky.

At 0.4 mile, turn right on a wide alley and left, still on the Nature Trail. You will see a wooden PETERSON TRAIL sign with a directional arrow. At roughly 0.5 mile the road forks. While the left fork climbs a steep hill heading west, the right fork is a gentle forest stroll heading northwest. Turn right on this connector with the San Andreas Trail, a flat alley that meanders through the redwood forest. The grove on your right is a perfect place to stop and build forts or fairy houses.

At 0.6 mile, make a sharp right on the San Andreas Trail, now a gentle grade down under maple and fir trees. At the next junction, turn left to hop on the Nature Trail, following signs for the visitor center and Youth Science Institute (YSI), going downhill. After a double redwood tree, turn left to

Spice up the kids' hike with walkie talkies!

stay on the Nature Trail that you follow until you reach the north side of the amphitheater. Enter the amphitheater and cross the wooden bridge over Aubry Creek to retrace your steps to the parking lot.

HAKONE GARDENS

You can combine a visit to Sanborn Park with the nearby Japanese-inspired Hakone Gardens (www.hakone.com) featuring an elaborate pond garden with stepping stones and waterfalls, a teahouse, wisteria-covered alleys, maple trees, and a bamboo grove. Come in the spring for wisteria and cherry blossoms, in the summer for blooming water plants, in the fall for blushing maple trees, and in the winter for blooming camellias.

 ALMADEN QUICKSILVER COUNTY PARK

BEFORE YOU GO
Maps: USGS Santa Teresa Hills. Free trail map and historic trail map at trailhead.
Information: Park office (408) 268-3883. www .parkhere.org

ABOUT THE HIKE
Day hike; Moderate/Difficult; Spring, Fall, Winter
3.6 miles, loop
Hiking time: 2–3 hours
High point/elevation gain: 1400 feet/1000 feet

GETTING THERE

▪ From I-280 southbound in San Jose, take CA-17 south to CA-85 south and drive 12 miles on CA-85 south.

▪ Exit at Almaden Expressway and head southeast for 4.2 miles.

▪ Turn right on Old Almaden Road (which becomes Almaden Road) and drive 3 miles through the village of New Almaden, to find the Hacienda park entrance 0.2 mile after the village on the right.

▪ There is no public transit.

ON THE TRAIL
Almaden was the name of the most famous cinnabar mine in the world, located in Spain and used since Roman times. In the sixteenth and seventeenth centuries, the extracted cinnabar was shipped from Spain

to the Americas to be used in the amalgamation process of silver and gold. When a Mexican officer named Andres Castillero visited the Santa Clara Mission in 1845, he experimented on silver with the mineral coming from the area, and discovered quicksilver. The Santa Clara mine was quickly named after the famous Spanish mine.

The former home of nearly two thousand miners, this county park was operated as a mine until 1976. It is still a honeycomb of mine tunnels, some going below sea level. Discovering English Camp at the summit of this hike, think about this mine when it was behind the scenes of the Gold Rush. Before heading out, grab a map of the Historic Trail, a trail whose markers were created as an Eagle Scout project by the Boy Scouts of Sunnyvale's troop 466.

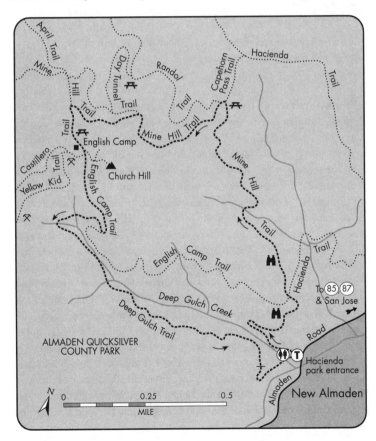

The park's historic markers were part of an Eagle Scout project of Sunnyvale's troop 466.

From the Hacienda trailhead, head west on the Mine Hill Trail, a dirt road that curves up the hill next to trail marker 15. The climb is steady and soon rewards you with a bird's-eye view of the valley. At 0.4 mile, keep straight at the three-way junction to stay on the Mine Hill Trail. Enjoying some shade under oak trees, you reach a lone picnic table at 1.1 miles. Turn left to stay on the Mine Hill Trail, a wide road that keeps going up. On top of the hill, the California bear flag flaps in the wind.

At the fork with the Day Tunnel Trail at 1.5 miles, continue left on the Mine Hill Trail and at 1.8 miles, bear left on the Castillero Trail to a small pyramid marker about English Camp, a mining town established here in the 1860s by Cornish miners. A few crumbling buildings are still standing, notably an old garage and barn next to picnic tables, and up the hill are the walls of the map house, which was used as the mine's office and housed maps, surveyors' books, core samples, and records of the mines. A small dirt trail up Church Hill takes you to the remains of the mine manager's house.

To continue your loop, find the hiking-only dirt English Camp Trail left of the picnic table and start your descent. At 2.3 miles, the road forks with the English Camp Trail on the left and the Deep Gulch Trail on the right. Turn right and get ready for a steep (and quick) descent. Initially lined with sycamore trees, the narrow trail enters an oak forest and follows the steep course of Deep Gulch Creek. The Ohlone people climbed this trail to Capitancillos Ridge to the sacred cave where they retrieved the red-colored cinnabar. Traded up the Pacific Coast to Oregon, it was used for religious ceremonies and to paint their bodies.

Steep all the way down, the Deep Gulch Trail leads you to a gate at 3.5 miles that takes you to a meadow where a collection of equipment from the New Almaden Mine and the Guadalupe Mine wait out the passage of time. Circle the meadow and continue left to reach the parking lot at 3.6 miles.

ALUM ROCK PARK

BEFORE YOU GO
Maps: USGS Calaveras Reservoir. Free map at entrance kiosk.
Information: Park office (408) 259-5477. San Jose Parks Department, www.sjparks.org

ABOUT THE HIKE
Day hike; Moderate/Difficult; Spring, Fall, Winter
4 miles, loop
Hiking time: 2–3 hours
High point/elevation gain: 1175 feet/600 feet

GETTING THERE
■ From I-680 in San Jose, exit at McKee Road and drive west 1 mile.
■ Turn left (north) on North White Road and after 1.2 miles, right onto Penitencia Creek Road.
■ The park's entrance kiosk is 0.7 mile up Penitencia Creek Road. Park by the visitor center, almost at the end of the road.
■ Santa Clara Valley Transportation Authority buses and light rail go to Alum Rock Park.

ON THE TRAIL
Tucked at the back of Alum Rock Canyon in eastern San Jose, this park has a colorful history linked to its geothermal resources. From 1890 to 1932, the park was a health spa with twenty-seven mineral springs coming out of the canyon. In the late Victorian era, San Jose's middle class traveled to Alum Rock by horse-drawn car to enjoy the properties of the canyon's natural hot springs. A railroad was built, as well as bath pavilions, naturally heated swimming pools, an aviary, and a mineral water pagoda.

The park is back to a more natural state, boasting some unique geological features. Its family appeal comes from a unique combination of playgrounds, a Youth Science Institute, miles of hiking trails, and picturesque remains of the Victorian spa.

From the parking lot, get to the visitor center and head left (east) on the paved trail. Past the Youth Science Institute (www.ysi-ca.org) a domed pavilion houses a mineral spring-fed drinking fountain. At 0.1 mile, make a sharp right on an unmarked paved trail, the Woodland

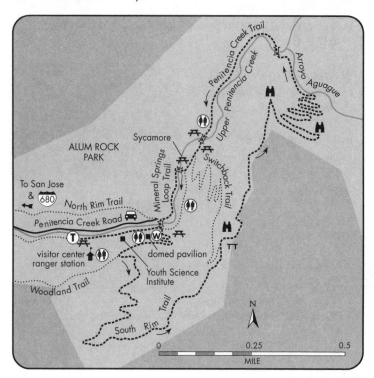

Trail. This gentle grade heads for Inspiration Point and takes you to a junction (look for a low, wooden square pile to the left of the trail) with the South Rim Trail at 0.4 mile. Make a hard left on the South Rim Trail, a wide path that goes up the canyon through gentle switchbacks, offering occasional views of the back of the canyon. Though you still hear swings squeaking at the playground at the beginning, little by little the South Rim Trail trades the sounds of civilization for the chirp of local birds.

At 0.7 mile after a bench, the switchbacks ease up and you reach the summit at 1175 feet. Walking 600 feet above the valley floor, you head northeast toward the convergence of Penitencia Creek and Arroyo Aguague. On a narrow ledge with steep drops below, the trail sometimes hugs the hill so close that you could have vertigo. Fortunately, vegetation barriers will prevent the youngest from getting too close to the edge. Admire the contour of the opposite hills crisscrossed by dirt trails.

Pass a junction with the Switchback Trail at 1.4 miles and continue down until a series of steps announce the ten switchbacks leading down

Find remnants of Victorian spa baths along Penitencia Creek.

to the valley floor; a rock jumble stands on your right. Much tighter and shorter than the switchbacks on the way up, these tread on slippery terrain that's occasionally reinforced to prevent erosions. Do not attempt to take shortcuts on this portion. Halfway through your descent, the bed of Arroyo Aguague will show through the oak foliage. This creek has its headwaters in Joseph D. Grant County Park (see Hike 84) and flows at the junction of two major earthquake faults: Hayward and Calaveras. On the way down, you pass a junction to the Upper Meadow Rest Area as well as two viewing platforms.

At 2.8 miles, follow the creekside path to a bridge with a fancy circular stone foundation that marks the convergence of the two creeks. Across the bridge, get on the Penitencia Creek Trail. This scenic leisurely trail shadows the creek under sycamores, maples, and alders.

After the Sycamore picnic area at 3.3 miles, turn right on an arched bridge for a turn-of-the-century scavenger hunt. Here, grottos and mineral pools with Palladian designs echo days when the sulfur hot springs were the main draw of this park. Kids will delight (and go "eeew"!) in the rotten-egg smell of the sulfur springs and love to get their hands close to the springs to feel if they're hot. Retrace your steps to the parking lot.

PALO ALTO BAYLANDS NATURE PRESERVE

BEFORE YOU GO
Maps: USGS Palo Alto. Free map at the ranger station.
Information: Baylands Nature Preserve (650) 329-2506. City of Palo Alto, www.cityofpaloalto.org /depts/csd/parks_and _openspaces/

ABOUT THE HIKE
Day hike; Easy/Moderate; Year round
0.9 mile, round-trip; 1.9 mile for Byxbee Park Hills loop
Hiking time: 1 hour
High point/elevation loss: 50 feet/50 feet

GETTING THERE

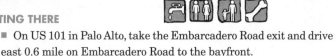

- On US 101 in Palo Alto, take the Embarcadero Road exit and drive east 0.6 mile on Embarcadero Road to the bayfront.
- Turn left toward the Sailing Station, and park by the duck pond.
- There is no public transit.

ON THE TRAIL

In the days of the Ohlone native people, San Francisco Bay was a vast expanse of wetlands and marshes, with large lakes even, where non-natives got lost navigating on labyrinthine canals. The variety of wildlife was astonishing. Then Europeans arrived. In 1761, the Spanish Portola Expedition, on its way north to the Golden Gate and the future site of San Francisco, camped by Francisquito Creek under a tall redwood tree, El Palo Alto—literally, "the tall stick." The tree still stands tall, and a thriving city was founded, now symbolic of the Silicon Valley, Palo Alto. Most wetlands have been dried out, but Palo Alto Baylands Nature Preserve remains as an unexpected refuge amid the tech industry landmarks.

This preserve provides miles of protected salt marshes and wetlands that you can discover on solid ground, on man-made levees, and on boardwalks that stretch out onto the bay. An ideal introduction to the Palo Alto Baylands starts with a visit to the duck pond, followed by a bayside stroll, and finishes at the Lucy Evans Baylands Nature Interpretive Center. Go for an extended hike to Byxbee Park, a 1-mile loop with views of the bay and the sloughs (see sidebar), and you will

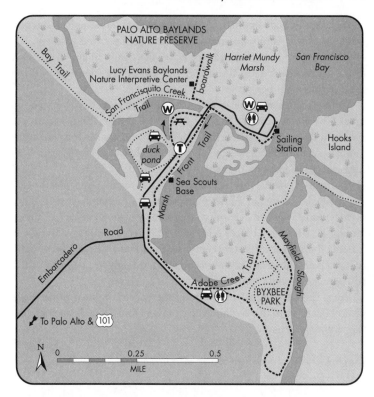

discover salt marshes surrounded by newly covered and landscaped landfills. If you have binoculars at home, bring them along.

Start the hike at the duck pond. Though it's hard to believe, the concrete-lined round basin was a saltwater swimming pool when built in the 1930s. Converted into a bird refuge in 1947, it now hosts a colony of ducks that locals like to feed. However, rangers are trying to break that habit of waterfowl-feeding, as it makes the birds sick (no bird diet should include chips and crackers) and spreads diseases. Look for a sign on this topic by the pond, and please refrain from feeding the ducks or the geese; watch them frolic instead.

From the duck pond, find the Marsh Front Trail, a dirt path that heads north from the parking lot. It runs along a saltwater marsh heading northeast toward the bay, and already you will catch a glimpse of the local bird life. Soon you see the strikingly geometrical Lucy Evans Baylands Nature Interpretive Center, suspended over the salt marsh on top of fifty wooden pilings. The nature center serves as the starting point of outdoor family programs. Turn left at the paved road and left after the bridge to go through the gate, then walk along on the San Francisquito Creek Trail toward the nature center. The boardwalk to the bay runs right behind it.

Walk around the center to the boardwalk, an elevated deck that extends 850 feet out toward the bay. It is great fun walking several feet over water level and getting to see marshes and canals from up close. Can you spot any birds nearby? Remember what they look like; the nature center has exhibits that will help you identify them.

The salt-resistant vegetation is mostly cordgrass and pickleweed. The latter is a common marsh plant that gets its name from its salty taste because it grows in a salty environment. Directly east is Harriet Mundy Marsh, named after environmental activist Harriet Mundy. It extends from the interpretive center to Sand Point. On your way to the bay, you'll encounter an off-limits catwalk used only by engineers of the powerlines running through the marsh.

From the observation platform at the end of the boardwalk, have your children scan the bay and the canals to find animals such as turtles, crabs, or birds.

The park's elevated boardwalk offers close up views of the marsh.

Retrace your steps to the San Francisquito Creek Trail, turn left, and go east along the Marsh Front Trail, a paved road, to the Sailing Station. This floating boat launch is right across from Hooks Island. Come back on the Marsh Front Trail and follow it around the slough. The 1940s streamlined modern Sea Scouts base was designed to resemble an actual ship. The Sea Scouts were an offshoot of the local Boy Scouts that taught boys and girls the essentials of seafaring: knot tying, compass reading, sailing, and sea customs, among other marine skills. The base is currently being remodeled.

BYXBEE PARK

For a different type of adventure, drive to the southeast end of Embarcadero Road to Byxbee Park, a combination of nature and art. Though retired landfills are many, this one is peppered with site-specific landscape sculptures, including a hill covered with telephone poles of varying heights, emulating pier pilings in the bay—and hillside paths covered with crushed oyster shells, reminiscent of the native Olympian oysters, once abundant in San Francisco Bay. For a 1-mile loop around Byxbee Park from the parking lot adjacent to the recycling center, go east on the Adobe Creek Trail and circle the hill via the trail along Mayfield Slough. After the *Wind Wave Piece*, a giant metal mobile that sways with the wind, return over the hill. You can also access Byxbee Park from the duck pond by following the Marsh Front Trail for 0.55 mile (1.1 miles out-and-back).

PICKLEWEED AND THE SALT MARSH HARVEST MOUSE

Sold at farmers markets as an edible succulent, pickleweed was used by the Ohlone to season and flavor their food. It also serves as food and habitat for a tiny mouse that can swim and is an endangered species in San Francisco Bay. The salt marsh harvest mouse is essentially a nocturnal animal preyed upon by owls, hawks, and domestic cats in urban areas. The dark brown rodent loves to feast on glasswort and pickleweed, and can climb marsh plants to munch on their seeds. If you see one on your exploration, consider yourself lucky.

LOS TRANCOS OPEN SPACE PRESERVE/ SAN ANDREAS FAULT

BEFORE YOU GO
Maps: USGS Cupertino. Free brochure with map at trail-head or printable at www .openspace.org.
Information: Midpeninsula Regional Open Space District (650) 691-1404. www.open space.org

ABOUT THE HIKE
Day hike; Moderate; Year round
3.6 miles, loop
Hiking time: 2–3 hours
High point/elevation loss: 2300 feet/500 feet

GETTING THERE

■ From I-280 in Palo Alto, exit at Page Mill Road and drive 7 miles west to Los Trancos Open Space Preserve's main vehicle parking lot (after the roadside parking lot) on Page Mill Road.

■ From Skyline Boulevard/CA-35 south of Skylonda, drive 1.5 miles east on Page Mill Road to the park's main entrance.

■ There is no public transit.

ON THE TRAIL

Los Trancos Open Space Preserve hosts a beautiful oak forest, yet from the parking lot on top of the mountain you wouldn't know it. The wind-swept hills around you are mostly covered with low bushes and grasses; otherwise the area is bare. Known for its interpretive trail on the San Andreas Fault, the park offers a peaceful walk along creeks and cente-nary oak groves.

From the west end of the parking lot, find a narrow dirt trail that leads to a platform. Look south, and 23 miles away lies Loma Prieta Mountain, epicenter of the 1989 earthquake. Looking north, try to trace the route of the fault with its fractures passing through the re-markably straight valley of Crystal Springs Reservoir. This is geogra-phy from above.

Continue down the hill, heading north on a dirt path peppered with the tiny skunk weed and its blue flower. At 0.1 mile at the wooden fence, bear left and turn left again at the three-way junction onto the Francis-can Loop Trail. Descending among bracken fern and coyote brush, the trail enters a thick oak forest.

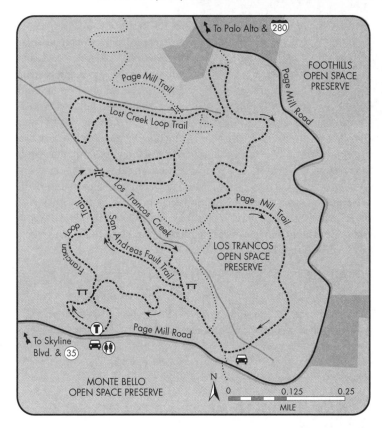

Green mats of aromatic yerba buena—the mint-family herb that gave its prior name to San Francisco—spread underneath elderberry bushes.

Along the trail, you'll pass several bay laurel trees felled by the 1989 earthquake with new trees sprouting from the branches of their "nurse tree." The path crosses Los Trancos Creek over a bridge and meets the Lost Creek Loop Trail at 0.7 mile. Turn left and continue your descent, getting close to Los Trancos Creek, only to follow its course in a canyon. After leveling out, the path rises again and connects with the Page Mill Trail at 1.3 miles after a bridge. From this bridge, the Page Mill Trail heads to Foothills Open Space Preserve. Continue straight (east) on the Page Mill Trail, which soon breaks into the open and meanders through grassland.

At 1.5 miles, turn right to keep to the Page Mill Trail, now a wide dirt road entering the woods. At 1.8 miles, turn sharp left to remain

Starting on a bare ridgetop, Los Trancos hides a dense forest and lost creeks.

on the trail, which takes you on an elevated path over a seasonal wetland. At 2.2 miles, a bench allows you to rest before exploring the San Andreas Fault Trail. Turn right and follow the trail clockwise, turning left at the next junction. If you have the park brochure handy, look up the explanations related to the markers. Numbered markers refer to the interpretive stops described in the brochure while posts with yellow bands mark the main fault break from the 1906 earthquake. Back at the previous junction, head west to retrace your steps to the parking lot on the Franciscan Loop Trail.

EARTHQUAKE WALKS

To experience the San Andreas Fault Trail with lively explanations and discuss plate tectonics and earthquake preparedness, families can join an "Earthquake Walk" docent-led tour on the first Sunday of each month from 2:00 to 4:30 PM. Check www.openspace.org for dates and times.

83 MOUNT MADONNA COUNTY PARK

BEFORE YOU GO
Maps: USGS Mount Madonna. Free map at entrance kiosk.
Information: Santa Clara County Parks (408) 355-2200. www.parkhere.org

ABOUT THE HIKE
Day hike; Moderate/Difficult; Year round
3.4 miles, loop
Hiking time: 1 hour
High point/elevation loss: 1850 feet/1000 feet

GETTING THERE

- From US 101 in Morgan Hill, exit at CA-152 west.
- From CA-1 on the coast, exit at CA-152 east.

▪ Drive 6.3 miles to the Mount Madonna County Park Pole Line Road entrance at the pass, 10 miles west of Gilroy. Park at Hilltop, by the ranger station.

▪ There is no public transit.

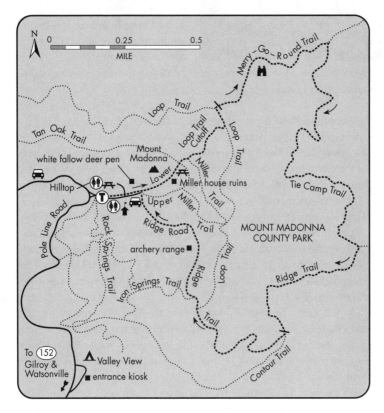

ON THE TRAIL

Mount Madonna County Park is heaven for families, and there's more to it than the yurts at the campground or the white fallow deer in their hilltop pens. This redwood forest on top of a mountain offers some incredible hiking opportunities with panoramic views on the spine of the Santa Cruz Mountains and the Santa Clara Valley.

From the ruins of the elegant mansion of cattle baron Henry Miller to the cool archery ranges scattered in the woods, everything invites you to stay longer. If you have time, you can even extend your adventure

Henry Miller's estate still stands as ruins under the redwoods.

by going another 2.3 miles west of the park to visit the Kim Son Vietnamese Buddhist Monastery. There, a spiritual walk of another sort awaits visitors on the landscaped temple grounds. Kids are welcome and vegetarian food is available at lunchtime.

Before starting this hike, pick up a self-guided brochure for the Miller ruins at the ranger station, as the multitude of tiny trails in that area can be confusing.

From the Hilltop parking lot, head east toward the Miller ruins on the Lower Miller Trail. This paved path feels like a timeless alley with its stately redwood forest and filtering sunlight. At 0.1 mile you reach a clearing with a trail fork. Look for an interpretive sign about the Miller estate and nature trail marker 1. The moss-covered sanctuary of Henry Miller's estate is spread on these hills. Explore at leisure before continuing to marker 5, behind standing walls whose windows look in and out onto the redwoods. Go down some steps and turn left immediately on a wide alley. At 0.3 mile, turn right on the Loop Trail Cutoff. As the name suggests, this trail cuts pretty well into the mountain and descends steadily in the cool forest.

At 0.5 mile, the trail dead-ends onto the Loop Trail; turn left. Go north on the Loop Trail until you reach a gate at 0.6 mile, then go right on the Merry-Go-Round Trail. This former service road offers some of the best views of the park as it steps out of the forest and remains in the open.

At 1 mile, turn right onto the Tie Camp Trail, a level trail that skirts the flanks of Mount Madonna for 1 mile. Oaks and madrones are common on these lower reaches, as well as manzanita varieties that are specific to this type of soil. Snaking down the mountain, you will be surprised by tall redwood trees shooting out of the slopes. After an incursion through moisture-loving redwoods, the trail enters a chaparral habitat with sun-loving coyote brush and poison oak. The trail gets narrow before finally arriving at a dirt-and-gravel road by a metal gate.

At 2.1 miles, turn onto the Ridge Trail and pace yourself to go up the 800 feet you've enjoyed on the way down. Fortunately, the grade of the road is moderate and redwood and maple trees provide a much-welcomed shade when the sun is high. At 2.6 miles, stay right to remain on the Ridge Trail and walk past a fenced-in power station.

Around 3 miles, you start seeing secluded archery practice grounds with paper animal targets on straw stands. Robin Hood or Narnia enthusiasts will find this stretch exciting.

Past the actual archery range, keep going up the Ridge Trail, now a road. At 3.4 miles, the trail meets Lower Miller Trail, a few feet from the parking lot.

 ## JOSEPH D. GRANT COUNTY PARK/THREE LAKES LOOP

BEFORE YOU GO
Maps: USGS Lick Observatory. Free map at entrance kiosk with park admission.
Information: Ranger office (408) 274-6121. www.parkhere.org

ABOUT THE HIKE
Day hike; Moderate/Difficult; Spring, Fall, Winter
3.5 miles, loop
Hiking time: 2–3 hours
High point/elevation gain: 1800 feet/320 feet

GETTING THERE
- From I-680 in San Jose, take the Alum Rock exit and turn right on Alum Rock Avenue.
- After 2.2 miles, turn right on Mount Hamilton Road (CA-130) and continue 7.7 miles to the Joseph D. Grant County Park entrance.
- Park by the ranger station.
- There is no public transit.

ON THE TRAIL
At 9500 acres, Joseph D. Grant County Park (formerly known as Grant Ranch Park) is the largest park in Santa Clara County and a hidden gem with grasslands, lakes, and oak trees. At the foot of Mount Hamilton, the park's scenic Halls Valley is suspended at 1400 feet between two ridges in the Diablo Range. Along the hike you will find elements of the ranch's legacy. If time allows, visit the historic rose garden west of the white farmhouse whose extensive porch overlooks a neat lawn.

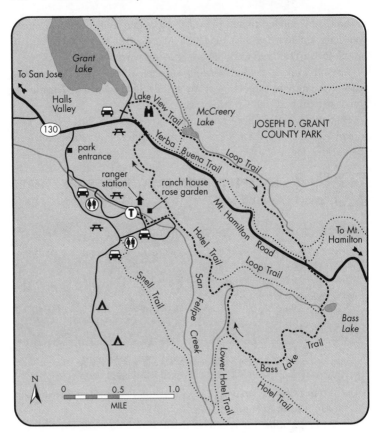

Notoriously haunted, the ranch house attracts lovers of the supernatural with its resident ghosts.

From the parking lot, find a paved path that follows San Felipe Creek. Heading southeast, it leads you past a shed housing a horse-drawn freight wagon. Turn left at the metal gate onto a wide path that leads you to the Hotel Trail, a wide ranch road. Turn left and gently walk up the hill until you cross Mount Hamilton Road (CA-130) at 0.3 mile.

Continue left across the road on the Yerba Buena Trail until you reach a parking lot; turn right. You are at the southern end of Grant Lake, a pretty lake fed by a spring and a good spot for picnicking. Walk along the shores to admire the views and at 0.5 mile, veer right on a steep dirt road called the Lake View Trail. From the ridge, a panorama

Families start at the Joseph D. Grant house to explore the surrounding lakes and hills.

of rolling hills unfolds both left and right. However, the trail doesn't stay on the ridge for long and descends toward McCreery Lake, reaching the lake at 0.8 mile. This is a good spot to observe waterfowl such as coot or cormorant.

Bear left along the south bank to get on the Loop Trail. At the edge of the lake, the trail enters an oak canyon and emerges into the open at the base of a hill. Head straight and walk over a cattle gate to continue along the bed of a seasonal creek. The Loop Trail swerves right and follows the contour of a hill.

At 1.1 miles, the trail meets the Yerba Buena Trail at a junction beside CA-130. Turn left on the Loop Trail, at this point a narrow dirt path that rises steadily until it again reaches CA-130. Cross the road and continue left on the Loop Trail, now in open grassland and still going uphill. At the ridge, the narrow trail stays level while curving right until you overlook the Halls Valley and Bass Lake at the bottom.

Getting down to Bass Lake is a steep affair, so be careful where you step. At 1.7 miles, you reach the western shore of the pond. Follow it on the left to turn right onto the Bass Lake Trail, a wide dirt road that takes you west down the hill, curving across open hillsides.

At 2.1 miles, the Bass Lake Trail bends right to merge with the Hotel Trail. Turn right and follow this wide road, going straight after it merges with the Lower Hotel Trail at 2.7 miles. Keep following the road, now closer to the course of San Felipe Creek, until the junction for the parking lot at 3.4 miles.

HISTORY OF JOSEPH D. GRANT PARK

Once the home of the Ohlone people, the land now known as Joseph D. Grant Park was part of a 15,000-acre Mexican land grant dated 1839 to Jose de Jesus Bernal, son of Jose Cornelio Bernal who owned the land on which San Francisco's Mission Dolores was built—and whose last name was bestowed on one of San Francisco's seven hill names (Bernal Heights). This rancho was called Rancho Cañada de Pala.

After the Mexican land grants and the validity of Rancho Cañada de Pala were contested with the cession of California to the United States, the "Halls Valley" area, which encompasses most of the present-day Joseph D. Grant Park, was deeded to Bernal's attorney, Frederick Hall, to pay for processing his claim. Adam Grant, founder of a dry goods store that supplied miners of the Gold Rush, bought his initial holding of Cañada de Pala in 1880. After his death, the land became property of his son Joseph D. Grant, who changed the name of Bernal Lagoon to Grant Lake, built dams, and diverted streams. He remodeled the original house (built in 1882) and added a cookhouse, servants' quarters, other houses and buildings, a rose garden, and a large aviary to the property. After his daughter's death in 1972, the property was purchased by Santa Clara County for park use.

 PICCHETTI RANCH OPEN SPACE PRESERVE

BEFORE YOU GO
Maps: USGS Cupertino. Map of the preserve at trailhead.
Information: Midpeninsula Regional Open Space District (650) 691-1404. www.open space.org

ABOUT THE HIKE
Day hike; Easy/Moderate; Year round
1.3 miles, round-trip
Hiking time: 1 hour
High point/elevation loss: 950 feet/200 feet

GETTING THERE

■ From I-280 north of Cupertino, exit at Foothill Expressway and travel 3.5 miles southwest (toward the mountains) on Foothill Boulevard/Stevens Canyon Road.

- Turn right on Montebello Road. The Picchetti Ranch Open Space Preserve is 0.5 mile up Montebello Road on the left.
- There is no public transit.

ON THE TRAIL

This preserve overlooks the calm waters of Stevens Creek Reservoir and features 3.7 miles of trails starting at a historic winery. Whether or not you include a zinfandel tasting in your hiking plans, the rustic buildings at the trailhead are worth a quick tour with the kids, if only to look for the resident peacock. The homestead behind the winery was built in 1882 as a temporary home by the Picchetti brothers. A large lawn surrounded by picnic tables and barrel trash cans by the creek makes a safe place for younger ones to run around and practice their front and back rolls.

Note that the upper parts of this trail are very close to dense poison oak, so dress your family in long sleeves and pants. Good walking shoes will be useful to get down and up the steep portions of the Orchard Loop Trail.

From the parking area, pick up a map of the trails at the signboard and walk over to the winery buildings, admiring the brickwork on the outside walls of the winery tasting room. After you walk through the winery complex, find the Zinfandel Trail, which starts at the little bridge

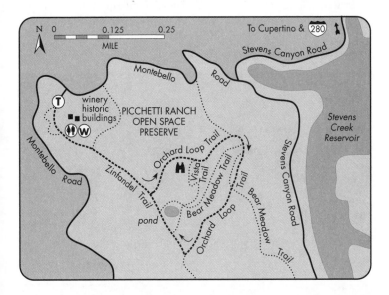

on the creek. On your left after the bridge are the classiest restrooms you will ever see on a hike. Continue on the Zinfandel Trail, a wide service road with good downhill views giving you the lay of the land. In front of you are the rural and not-so-wild remainders of Picchetti Ranch's days as a grower of wine grapes, fruit, and nut trees. This hike loops around what remains of the orchards and has a bucolic feel.

At 0.2 mile, turn left on the Orchard Loop Trail and see if you can identify some of the fruit trees that still stand. Plums, apricots, walnuts, and peaches thrived in this climate and are historic reminders of the orchards that used to line the length of Stevens Creek downstream from the dam. They have long since been replaced by residential housing.

Heading toward the reservoir, the path crests a small ridge at 0.4 mile before dropping rather steeply through open grassland. If the path is slippery, grassy edges provide much better footing. The view of the reservoir would be perfect if you didn't hear the sand and gravel quarry being carved away by loud trucks on weekdays.

At the bottom of the hill at 0.5 mile, turn right on a road now shaded by oak trees. You will notice a particularly majestic coast live oak with branches arching over the path like a stooped green giant. The trail dips left and curves toward oak hills before rising again until it butts into the Zinfandel Trail.

At 0.8 mile, turn right on the Zinfandel Trail and walk over to the pond area. The No swimming sign can be surprising in the summer when

Orchards grace the trails next to the winery.

the pond has dried up into a meadow, but during the rainy season, this pond provides critical habitat for newts, tree frogs, and toads. Watch where you step, because lots of tiny frogs jump around the edges of the pond in the early summer, especially late June and early July.

Keep going straight until you see the winery. Retrace your steps to the parking lot.

 ## MONTE BELLO OPEN SPACE PRESERVE/ BLACK MOUNTAIN

BEFORE YOU GO
Maps: USGS Mindego Hill. Map at trailhead.
Information: MidPeninsula Regional Open Space District (650) 691-1200. www.open space.org

ABOUT THE HIKE
Day hike or overnight; Difficult; Year round
5.9 miles, loop
Hiking time: 3–4 hours
High point/elevation gain: 2800 feet/1000 feet

GETTING THERE

■ From I-280 in Los Altos Hills, take the Page Mill Road exit and drive west 7 miles to the Monte Bello Open Space Preserve entrance and main parking lot.

■ From CA-35/Skyline Boulevard south of Skylonda, drive 1.5 miles east on Page Mill Road to the preserve's main entrance.

■ There is no public transit.

ON THE TRAIL

From lush canyons to a summit that overlooks the whole Santa Clara Valley and the Mount Hamilton Range, Monte Bello offers beautiful trails and visual rewards to match the effort it takes to reach them. This hike is not for everyone and should only be attempted with children who are seasoned hikers, as the climb on the Indian Creek Trail is a grueling and steep one. However, once you're on top of the world it's all downhill, and if you backpacked in for an overnight stay at the Black Mountain Campground (by permit only) roughly halfway through, you can take a breather here and enjoy the sunset on the mountains.

Pack plenty of water and sun protection, as the climb to Black Mountain is in full sun once you're out of the woods by Stevens Creek. Remember long pants and sleeves, too—poison oak is abundant here.

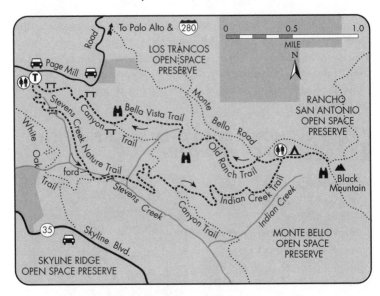

For a gentler 3-mile option, hike only the Stevens Creek Nature Trail and loop back on the Canyon Trail.

From the parking lot, go straight on the Stevens Creek Nature Trail. From the trail, you are treated to tall grasses swaying in the wind and open views of the eastern Santa Cruz Mountains. At 0.15 mile, make a hard right and go down steps to stay on the Stevens Creek Nature Trail. This dirt trail zigzags down the hill to reach Stevens Creek, shaded by a forest of oaks and bay laurels. The bright light from the hill gives way to a filtered green light, and only the twittering of birds disturbs the quiet underbrush. The trail continues at the bottom of a mossy canyon where fallen trees and intertwined branches create an intricate pattern of lines. You cross the creek twice, first on a wooden bridge at 0.3 mile and then on rocks at 0.4 mile. Right before the rock crossing, look for an unmarked path leading to large pools where you can sit and relax with the kids. Then cross the creek and continue. At 1.1 miles, go left toward the Canyon Trail and start your ascent up the canyon to reach the open meadows surrounded by fir trees.

At 1.7 miles, turn right on the Canyon Trail, which rises steeply before getting to a more moderate grade. At 1.9 miles, bear left onto the Indian Creek Trail, heading toward the Black Mountain backcountry campground. This is where the climbing is going to get serious. Stop

Rocks make a great climbing spot for kids on Black Mountain.

for water regularly. Steadily the trail rises above the valley, with superb views all around. When you see electric towers, you are almost there. At 2.9 miles, you reach a junction for the campground; for now, continue right toward the Black Mountain summit. At the junction with Monte Bello Road at 3.1 miles, turn right toward the broadcasting towers.

At 3.3 miles, you finally reach the summit. Time to break out the picnic lunch! Culminating at 2800 feet, this mountaintop enjoys 360-views of the Silicon Valley and the Santa Cruz Mountains. If the kids feel like a change of pace, they can climb on rock outcroppings. Have them look for the bronze disc of the U.S. Geological Survey marker embedded in a boulder. These markers are prized findings for geocachers looking for landmarks. The triangle in the middle denotes it as a triangulation station whose position was determined by measuring distances and angles from other stations.

Get back on the trail to head for the backcountry campground via the Indian Creek Trail, and turn right to walk through the camp—unless you have planned an overnight backpacking trip. At 4 miles, turn left on the Old Ranch Trail, skirting the edges of the mountain, and left to continue down on the Bella Vista Trail. Compared to the ascent, these two trails are a breeze and offer exceptional views. At 5.3 miles you reach the Canyon Trail and turn right to go past the sag pond surrounded by cattail. At 5.5 miles veer left toward the Stevens Creek Nature Trail, and turn right at the next junction to retrace your steps to the parking lot.

RANCHO SAN ANTONIO COUNTY PARK/DEER HOLLOW FARM

BEFORE YOU GO
Maps: USGS Cupertino. Free map at the trailhead.
Information: Deer Hollow Farm (650) 903-6430. Midpeninsula Regional Open Space District (650) 691-1200. www.openspace.org

ABOUT THE HIKE
Day hike; Easy; Year round
2 miles, round-trip
Hiking time: 1–2 hours
High point/elevation gain: 400 feet/minimal

GETTING THERE

- From I-280 in Mountain View, take the Foothill Boulevard exit. Drive south and turn right almost immediately on Cristo Rey Drive.
- At 1 mile, take the second right at the roundabout and turn left into the Ranch San Antonio County Park entrance. Proceed to the main (northernmost) parking lot, where bathrooms are.
- There is no public transit.

ON THE TRAIL

Traditional home of the Ohlone people, Rancho San Antonio was deeded to Juan Prado Mesa in 1839 as part of a Mexican land grant by Governor Alvarado. Mesa distinguished himself by serving as an officer at the San Francisco Presidio but didn't enjoy his rancho long, as he died in 1845. After the cession of California to the United States, the rancho title was contested in court and in 1861, John and Martha Snyder purchased 850 acres on Permanente Creek for a farm, orchard, and winery. This land later became Rancho San Antonio Open Space Preserve.

Deer Hollow Farm was created by a homesteader called Theodore Grant. With his wife, he operated the farm from 1861 to 1937, after which the farm was sold to George Perham, who in turn sold it to the Midpeninsula Open Space District in 1975. This is the farm you will see today. In the tradition of a working homestead, Deer Hollow Farm produces food (though only eggs are sold on-site) and maintains farm animals, with a nature center and long picnic tables under a historic open-air hay barn. Bring a picnic to enjoy this fun family outing at the farm. An easy 1-mile walk from the trailhead, this level hike is extremely

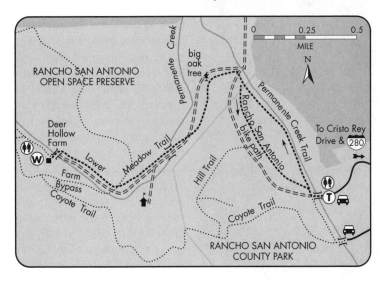

popular with families, whether with stroller or not, as the distance can be covered on either paved or dirt paths. The farm site is open to the public Tuesday through Sunday from 8:00 AM to 4:00 PM, with the exception of Wednesday afternoon when it is closed from 1:00 to 4:00 PM.

Spring is the season of baby farm animals and spring farm tours. Autumn is when Ohlone Day takes place, a living-history event to celebrate the Ohlone way of life. Indeed, the farm includes the replica of an Ohlone village that's usually reserved for school groups but is open to the public one day in October. For events, check the website of the Friends of Deer Hollow Farm at www.fodhf.org.

Allowing you to fully appreciate the diversity of Rancho San Antonio's 3800 acres of open space, 23 miles of hiking trails are available to explore the hillsides, meadows, and remains of farming days.

From the parking lot, go north to find a trail that crosses a wooden bridge over Permanente Creek. Past the bridge, you have two choices to reach Deer Hollow Farm. You can decide to continue straight on a paved path (the Rancho San Antonio bike path) or right on the Permanente Creek Trail. Turn right on the Permanente Creek Trail to walk at the edge of grassy meadows along the creek lined with stands of willows. At 0.3 mile after tennis courts, the trail comes to a multiple junction. Turn left (west) on a dirt trail that goes between two wooden fences before crossing the paved bicycle trail (the Lower Meadow Trail). After

River crossing— the wilderness way

crossing the Lower Meadow Trail, keep straight on the dirt path that closely hugs the paved road. Look for an oak tree on your right with a hole big enough for a child to stand in. The path continues on through meadows dotted by tall trees, perfect sun shelters during the warm summer months.

At 0.5 mile, the Lower Meadow Trail merges with the bike path and both separate quickly, each running next to the other. Keep to the hiking trail lined with bay laurel and buckeye trees, following the creek bed where several spots offer easy access for wading time. Cross the wooden bridge at 0.7 mile and continue on the other side of the creek. Watch for a giant stump, and have the kids climb it for impromptu photo ops.

Two wooden posts at 0.8 mile mark a fenced-in area. The farm is just 0.2 mile ahead after another bridge. Once at the farm, kids will want to visit the farm animals, but if you visit on the third Saturday of a month, you might be able to explore the nature center, open from 10:00 AM to 1:00 PM. Of course, if kids are hungry, the picnic area is under the hay barn at the end of the farm. Have fun!

When you are ready, retrace your steps to the parking lot.

Opposite: *The Roaring Camp Railroads steam train winds through the redwoods next to Henry Cowell Redwoods State Park.*

SANTA CRUZ COUNTY

BIG BASIN REDWOODS STATE PARK/ SEMPERVIRENS FALLS

BEFORE YOU GO
Maps: USGS Big Basin. Trail map posted at trailhead.
Information: Park office (831) 338-8860. www.parks .ca.gov

ABOUT THE HIKE
Day hike or overnight; Moderate/Difficult; Year round
4.5 miles, loop
Hiking time: 2–3 hours
High point/elevation gain: 1150 feet/400 feet

GETTING THERE

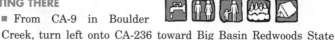

■ From CA-9 in Boulder Creek, turn left onto CA-236 toward Big Basin Redwoods State Park.

■ Drive 9 miles north and west along this curvy road to the park entrance. Park by the park headquarters.

■ CA-9 can be reached via CA-17 from Santa Cruz or San Jose, via CA-1 from Santa Cruz or Half Moon Bay, or via CA-85 from I-280 or US 101.

■ There is no public transit.

ON THE TRAIL

Big Basin Redwoods State Park is the granddaddy of all California state parks, established over a hundred years ago as the first of a long series. The founders of the park camped here in 1902, passed around a hat on Slippery Rock, and collected $32 to bring to fruition a novel idea: protect ancient redwood forests from being logged.

Because of dynamic living-history and nature-related programs, the park is a fantastic family outing. People apply months in advance to snatch one of the prized campsites or to reserve a yurt. Children love to explore the visitor center (where a warm gas stove awaits you in the winter), the nature museum, or the spectacular 0.5-mile Redwood Trail, a self-guided nature trail among towering coast redwoods. Check www.bigbasin.org for details on current activities.

From the park headquarters, walk south (across from the Redwood Trail) to find the Sequoia Trail leading toward Sempervirens Falls. This dirt trail lined with pine needles follows the road closely during the first mile, passing a few group campsites along the way. Some trees arch

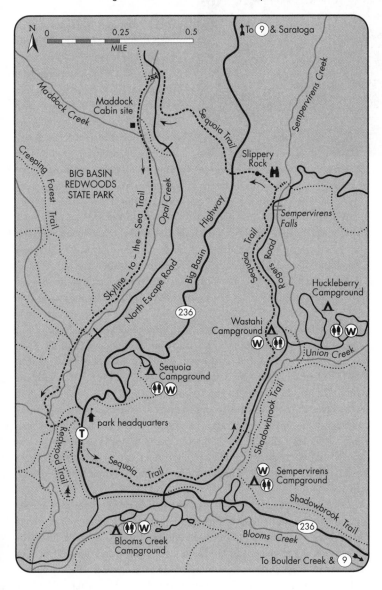

gracefully over the trail, others hide child-size alcoves at their base, and most are vibrant green with moss. The trail follows the course of Sempervirens Creek; though separated from the water by Rogers Road, you

Climbing on redwoods gives children an idea of how tall the trees really are.

can still see and hear the stream along the way. After the Wastahi Campground, look for the Chimney Tree at 1.5 miles, a tree that burned in 1904, blew its top, but kept on living as a hollow tree. Redwood trees are extremely resilient trees that can resist forest fires, well deserving their Latin name of *Sequoia sempervirens*— *sempervirens* meaning "always alive" in Latin.

At 1.7 miles, make a sharp right down a flight of stairs to the road. Cross with caution and find the ramp that leads to a viewing platform above Sempervirens Falls, dropping 20 feet in the redwoods. Dozens of ferns hang down from the cave-like rocks around the waterfall.

Come back to the Sequoia Trail and turn right, heading northwest. Before you is Slippery Rock, the giant rockslide where the founders' concept of the park germinated. This exposed sandstone formation offers just the setting for a picnic lunch, with great views of the Santa Cruz Mountains. Turn left up the rock to stay on the Sequoia Trail. It might be challenging to find, but at the top left of the rock there is a narrow dirt trail leading under cover to a wooden trail marker at CA-236 (Big Basin Highway). Cross with caution and continue on the Sequoia Trail on the other side of the road, where a signpost indicates you are heading to the Skyline-to-the-Sea Trail. This 29.5-mile hiking trail is a classic ridge-to-sea trail that starts at the top of the Santa Cruz Mountains in Castle Rock State Park (see Hike 89), crosses Big Basin Redwoods State Park down the coast, and finishes at the Pacific Ocean at Waddell Beach (see Hike 90).

Skirting the edges of a ravine, the Sequoia Trail plunges into a thick oak, redwood, and fir forest. At North Escape Road, cross a bridge over Opal Creek and turn left onto the Skyline-to-the-Sea Trail at 3.3 miles. Shortly after, you reach the Maddock Cabin site where an interpretive signboard tells you about the homesteader who came in 1883 to build a 24-by-26-foot cabin with his eleven-year-old son. The other side of the sign explains the use of tanoak in the leather industry.

Continue on the Skyline-to-the-Sea Trail, following Opal Creek, until you reach park headquarters at 4.5 miles.

CASTLE ROCK STATE PARK

BEFORE YOU GO
Maps: USGS Castle Rock
Ridge. Trail map posted at
trailhead.
Information: Park office
(408) 867-2952. www.parks
.ca.gov

ABOUT THE HIKE
Day hike; Easy; Year round
**0.9 mile, loop; 1.9 miles
with Falls Overlook**
Hiking time: 30 minutes–
1 hour
**High point/elevation
gain:** 3200 feet/200 feet

GETTING THERE

■ From I-280 in San Mateo,
take CA-92 west toward Half Moon Bay and turn left (south) onto
Skyline Boulevard/CA-35. After 25 miles, Skyline/CA-35 intersects
with CA-9/Big Basin Way (Saratoga Gap) at a crossroads. Continue
straight (south) on Skyline Boulevard.

■ From CA-85 in Saratoga, take the Saratoga Avenue exit. Drive
west into Saratoga and continue on CA-9/Big Basin Way. At the
junction with CA-35/Skyline, turn left.

■ The Castle Rock State Park entrance is 2.5 miles south on
Skyline Boulevard on the right.

■ There is no public transit.

ON THE TRAIL
Castle Rock State Park owes its fame to the generations of Bay Area
climbers who've come here to boulder and conquer overhangs on sandstone outcroppings of massive proportions. Castle Rock is also a popular backpacking destination, either for overnights or longer trips like
the Skyline-to-the-Sea Trail (see Hike 88). Children of all ages will love
kneeling down, crawling, and climbing through the many caves that
crisscross the 50-foot-high monumental Castle Rock. Many of the boulders, when not used by climbers, create lovely picnic backdrops.

From the parking lot, turn left on the Castle Rock Trail, rising into
the oak and fir forest. Most trees are green with moss, and temperatures
are on the low side. In the winter, Castle Rock even gets snow, so prepare accordingly. Follow the eroded trail, reaching a wooden fence and
a wide service road at 0.2 mile. Turn right and keep your eyes peeled.

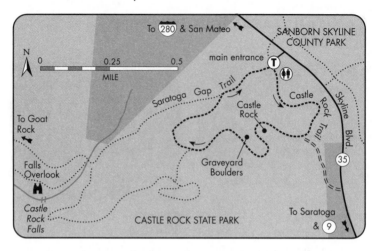

The first boulders appear shortly on your left, with exotic names like Jumbalia, Yabo, or Magoo. If your kids already want to feel the rock and tunnel in, watch them closely here, as most of the boulders are anchored on steep slopes and can result in bad falls.

At 0.3 mile, you arrive in front of Castle Rock proper. The best caves for kids are on the eastern side at eye level. Your children might need a lift to crawl in there, but once they're in, it's hours of imaginative play while you relax outside. Turn right to circumnavigate Castle Rock, pausing to examine the small pockets of tunnels and hidden chambers.

Turn right at the trail sign at 0.5 mile to go downhill, passing several bouldering "problems" (jargon for climbing routes to conquer). You will see white dust marks on the rocks from climbing chalk used by climbers to improve their grip. The oak forest gives way to burgundy madrones. At 0.8 mile, you reach the junction with

Finding secret hideouts takes climbing experimentation!

the Saratoga Gap Trail, heading west to Saratoga Gap and Goat Rock, east to the parking lot.

For a spectacular view of the San Lorenzo watershed and the Pacific Ocean, turn left on the Saratoga Gap Trail and push another 0.5 mile west to the Falls Overlook, a wooden platform at the top of a 100-foot rock. After the winter rains, Castle Rock Falls plunges 80 feet over the precipice, and most of the time you can see rock climbers tackling various routes on the same rock.

Retrace your steps to the previous junction and turn east on the Saratoga Gap Trail to return to the parking lot.

 ## BIG BASIN REDWOODS STATE PARK/ RANCHO DEL OSO

BEFORE YOU GO
Maps: USGS Año Nuevo. Park map at ranger station. Nature trails map at Rancho del Oso Nature Center.
Information: Park office (831) 338-8861. www.parks .ca.gov or www.bigbasin.org

ABOUT THE HIKE
Day hike or overnight; Moderate/Difficult; Year round
4.7 miles, loop
Hiking time: 2.5–3 hours
High point/elevation gain: 400 feet/400 feet

GETTING T HERE
■ From CA-1 in San Francisco southbound, drive 55 miles to Waddell Beach after the San Mateo–Santa Cruz county line.
■ From CA-1 in Santa Cruz northbound, drive 17 miles to Waddell Beach.
■ Park at the beach parking lot.
■ Santa Cruz Metro Transit makes two daily trips to Waddell Beach.

ON THE TRAIL
Starting at one of the best windsurfing beaches on the coast, this hike combines great coastal views with a redwoods and marsh experience, in addition to a nature center where kids can learn about the area. Literally "the ranch of the bear," Rancho del Oso at the mouth of Waddell Creek was grizzly bear country and still features perfect grizzly bear habitat.

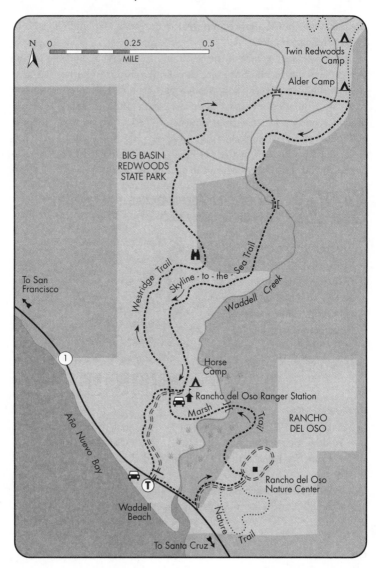

South of Waddell Creek, the nature center (www.ranchodeloso.org; open weekends from noon to 4:00 PM) hosts family programs in the former ranch house of Hulda Hoover McLean, the niece of President Hoover.

Combining two different nature trails, this hike starts at Waddell Beach. Parking at the nature center is reserved for backpackers or nature center visitors. To reduce mileage, you can park at the ranger station and hike either of the trails from there.

From the beach parking lot, walk south to find the access road signed NATURE CENTER just after the creek. This wide dirt road takes you to the Rancho del Oso Nature Center at 0.5 mile. Turn left on the Marsh Trail by a wooden fence.

The smooth path meanders through willows and blackberry bushes, a virtual grocery store for grizzly bears who were mostly vegetarian. Grizzly bears became extinct in California in 1922 when the last grizzly bear was shot, but their habitat still remains intact at Rancho del Oso. The bears' diet consisted of blackberries, nuts, roots, insects, and grasses, with the occasional salmon at the creek or young animal. Right after the fourth walkway, look for a stump with two sizes of holes. While the bigger ones were made by woodpeckers, the tiny holes hide nests of termites that grizzly bears ate by ripping apart the tree's bark and sticking an extremely long tongue into the holes.

Continue over the creek, where salmon spawn in the spring, and continue on the mostly level trail. It rises slightly to reach the ranger station at 1.2 miles. Turn right on the access road, heading east, and grab a self-guided nature trail description. Before the gate, veer left and start an uphill climb on the Westridge Trail.

This single-track dirt trail snakes through an oak forest and rises 400 feet over 0.2 mile, then hovers over the valley at roughly the same elevation for 1.1 miles. At 1.6 miles, the trail circles around the hillside and offers spectacular views of the sandy stretch of Waddell Beach and kite- and windsurfers. Once you turn the corner, green and tidy farm fields spread at the bottom of the valley.

At 2.2 miles after a short section through redwoods, the trail begins its descent, crossing Waddell Creek at 2.3 miles. Turn right on the Skyline-to-the-Sea Trail (see Hike 88) after the bridge. A wide fire road at this point, the Skyline-to-the-Sea Trail is very popular with bikers and horses, so

Rancho del Oso's moderate grades make it the perfect place for backpacking with children.

be ready to share the road. Majestic redwoods and ferns grace the first 0.5 mile of this road.

At trail marker 13 the road connects with a farm entrance. Keep straight to walk on the bridge and past farm buildings. Now in the open, the road skirts an old oak grove and rises just enough so you can see the opposite ridge before dipping down. At the next V-junction next to trail marker 15, bear right.

At 4.2 miles, you reach the gate of the ranger station. Walk straight on the Skyline-to-the-Sea Trail to reach the beach.

WILDER RANCH STATE PARK/FERN GROTTO

BEFORE YOU GO
Maps: USGS Wilder Ranch. Trail map posted at trailhead.
Information: Park office (831) 423-9703. www.parks .ca.gov

ABOUT THE HIKE
Day hike; Easy; Year round
2 miles, round-trip
Hiking time: 1–2 hours
High point/elevation gain: 50 feet/50 feet

GETTING THERE

- From CA-1, 2 miles north of Santa Cruz, turn west into the Wilder Ranch State Park entrance and proceed to the parking lot.
- There is no public transit.

ON THE TRAIL

Featuring a unique agricultural preserve with fields of brussels sprouts, Wilder Ranch State Park is a diamond in the rough just outside Santa Cruz. At the ranch itself, families find a cultural preserve with a historic farm surrounded by Victorian buildings. Here, kids can watch farm animals and take part in living-history activities. In the backcountry, hikers and bikers enjoy 34 miles of steep valleys, ridgetops, and meadows. On the coast, bluff-top trails wind along the rugged coastline and overlook Wilder Beach, a nature preserve for nesting snowy plovers. Farther along the coast, you can enjoy spectacular views of hidden sea caves with the opportunity for whale-watching.

Pack sweaters for this coastal hike even when the sun is out, as winds chill the bluffs more than you might expect.

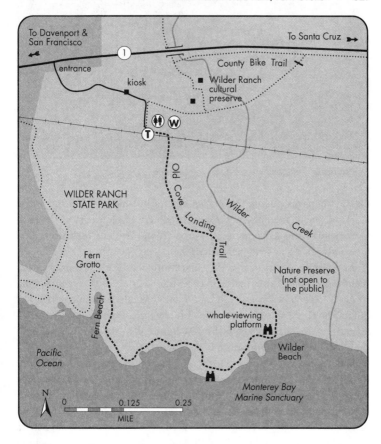

Before or after the hike, spend some time around the ranch buildings and the visitor center, where you can find a copy of the Old Cove Landing Trail self-guided tour brochure. On weekends, docents demonstrate black-smithing and other farm activities. In front of the main house, encourage your children to crawl in the aloe vera bushes crisscrossed with toddler-friendly tunnels, or to climb the low-lying branches of a bald cypress tree. Around the farm buildings, the kids will enjoy visiting the chicken coop, the old barn, and the goats, sheep, and cows. If you enjoy living-history programs, come back for the old-fashioned Independence Day celebration, the fall harvest festival, or the winter holidays.

From the parking lot, get on the Old Cove Landing Trail, heading east. Past trail marker 1, the wide service road crosses railroad tracks on a trestle dating from 1900. Red-winged blackbirds are at home in the

Wilder Ranch's rugged coastline is a great whale-watching spot.

coastal chaparral, while butterflies abound in the wild radishes, wild mustard, poison hemlock, and coyote brush. After a few curves, the path reaches an overlook over a marshy area around Wilder Creek, preceding the sandy shores of Wilder Beach at 0.4 mile.

At 0.5 mile, a platform with a bench provides a perfect observation spot for gray whales migrating in the winter. If you see two spouts going off close to each other, it could be a mother whale swimming with her calf on the shore side so as to protect it from great white shark attacks. Sometimes, the whales are just a few hundred yards off the beach and you don't even need binoculars to see them.

Follow the trail as it now starts its bluff-top exploration—make sure young ones don't roam too close to the edge. At 0.7 mile, the trail reaches a rocky cliff top covered with bird poop. The area is a popular hangout for western gulls, pelicans, terns, and cliff swallows. Notice how vertical these cliffs are. They are Santa Cruz mudstone cliffs slanting slightly to the sea, indicating that they're still "cliffs under construction." Looking down, you may spot black birds facing the cliff on narrow ledges. These are pelagic cormorants, birds that need to take off backward so as not to knock their eggs out of the nest.

Continue along the coast and see if there are any harbor seals on the rocks below. They sleep during the day and hunt at night. At 1 mile, follow a narrow trail that leads down to Fern Beach, a quiet sandy cove. On the beach at 1.1 miles, turn right (north) and have the kids find a sea cave—Fern Grotto. Listen to the sound of water dripping from the ceiling and watch the deer and chain fern hanging from the ceiling. This is as *Treasure Island* as a hike will ever get! Apart from hiking to the Robert Louis Stevenson Memorial (see Hike 69), of course.

When you are ready, retrace your steps back to the parking lot.

**NATURAL BRIDGES STATE BEACH/
MONARCH BUTTERFLY NATURE PRESERVE**

BEFORE YOU GO
Maps: USGS Santa Cruz.
Free map of the park at the
visitor center.
Current conditions: Ranger
station (831) 423-4609.
www.parks.ca.gov

ABOUT THE HIKE
Day hike; Easy; Spring, Fall,
Winter
1 mile, loop
Hiking time: 1 hour
**High point/elevation
loss:** 50 feet/50 feet

GETTING THERE

- From CA-1 in Santa Cruz, take Swift Avenue west or follow West Cliff Drive north along the in-town bluffs until it ends at Natural Bridges State Beach.
- Santa Cruz Metro Transit bus lines 3 and 20 stop at Natural Bridges State Beach.

ON THE TRAIL

This beach, along with its famed maritime arch, is a great vantage point for admiring migrating whales and seabirds, as well as a good spot to walk through coastal scrub right in the city. Before hitting Santa Cruz's iconic beach boardwalk, you have to see this butterfly boardwalk. This miniature maze with open views and almost no elevation gain will have your kids running ahead. With picnic tables perched on a sandy bluff overlooking a spectacular natural bridge, and nearby restrooms with showers and changing rooms, this beach is bound to become your family favorite.

Come between October and February to see thousands of black and orange monarch butterflies fluttering in the eucalyptus trees and blackberry bushes during their annual migration. (The park celebrates their return each year with Welcome Back Monarchs Day, held on the second Sunday of October; the Migration Festival, held the second Saturday in February, is an opportunity to learn about natural migrations.) In the winter, the fantastic tidepools right off the beach are at their best. Summers are foggy—it's the coast, remember? In 1900, this park featured three arches and sea stacks formed out of Santa Cruz mudstone. The arches were formed millions of years ago when silt, water, and clay sediment, combined with marine plants, formed blocks of soft rock that

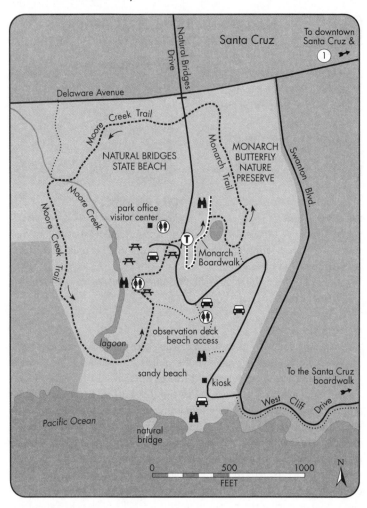

were eroded by the action of waves, resulting in tunnels and openings through the rock formations—hence the arches. Two earthquakes later, only one arch remains, but you can tell by the missing "keystone" where the most recently fallen arch used to stand. Before starting the hike, your kids may want to grab a description of the self-guided nature trail.

From the visitor center, find a sign MONARCH TRAIL and get on the stroller- and wheelchair-accessible Monarch Boardwalk. This delightful entrance into the butterflies' overwintering grove zigzags down to a small

The arching bridge at the beach makes a beautiful ending to this easy hike.

pond. At 0.15 mile, turn left to reach the observation platform just a hundred feet beyond. Surrounded by lush blackberry bushes and eucalyptus trees, this place could almost be a slice of Australia. Get out the sketchbooks and nature journals, or simply enjoy the butterflies in season.

Back on the trail, numbered trail markers announce the nature trail. Follow the path around the pond and up the bluff to a level stretch in a meadow. At 0.2 mile, turn left toward marker 4 and continue to tall Monterey pines, a Phoenix-rising-from-its-ashes kind of tree. Not only does it survive fires, but the seeds from its pods are only released during fires.

The walk continues through meadows and dips down to a bridge before rising. Adults will need to bend over to go under a low-lying willow branch. At 0.4 mile, cross a paved road and continue on the Moore Creek Trail (unmarked), a wide service road. Undulating through coastal scrub, the trail is now under full sun.

At 0.6 mile turn left to head south toward the beach. Several elevated boardwalks crisscross the seasonal wetland before going over Moore Creek, a stream that drops from the Santa Cruz Mountains to the ocean. After the trail bends, you can now see the famed natural bridge, out in the distance. Gradually dirt turns to sand under your feet, and you reach the sandy beach.

To go around the lagoon, look for a narrow ledge carved in the rocky bluff to the west. The footing can be tricky, but it is short. Get down on the beach, admire the natural bridge, and turn left to find the ramp that leads up to the parking lot. Or linger at the beach if the kids want to dip their feet in the water.

HENRY COWELL REDWOODS STATE PARK

BEFORE YOU GO
Maps: USGS Felton. Map for
sale at the ranger station.
Information: Park office
(831) 335-4598. www.parks
.ca.gov

ABOUT THE HIKE
Day hike; Easy; Year round
0.8 mile, loop
Hiking time: 30 minutes–
1 hour
**High point/elevation
gain:** 270 feet/minimal

GETTING THERE

■ From Santa Cruz, go north
on CA-17 to the Mount Hermon/Big Basin exit.

■ From San Jose, go south on CA-17 to the Mount Hermon Road exit.

■ Drive 3.5 miles northwest on Mount Hermon Road to Felton. Mount Hermon Road ends at Graham Hill Road. Turn right on Graham Hill Road and left (south) on CA-9. The park entrance is 0.5 mile down on CA-9.

■ Santa Cruz Metro Transit bus line 34 stops at Henry Cowell Redwoods State Park and Felton Covered Bridge, a short walk from the park.

ON THE TRAIL

Henry Cowell Redwoods State Park shelters a wonderful old-growth redwood grove whose level trails invite young walkers to discover the tallest trees on Earth. Pack a picnic lunch and a swimsuit in the summer, because this hike follows the San Lorenzo River and could finish with a splash.

Adjacent to Henry Cowell Redwoods (just a 2-minute walk from the ranger station) lies the hugely popular Roaring Camp Railroad (www .roaringcamp.com) whose steam trains go up the Santa Cruz Mountains and down to the Santa Cruz boardwalk. If you want to make a Santa Cruz weekend trip, stay at the park's campground, hike the trail, and board the steam train to the boardwalk. Kids will love it!

Note that a flashlight is useful for this hike, as kids can explore a secret chamber inside a tree.

From the parking lot, find the trailhead for the Redwood Grove Loop Trail on the right (south). At the trailhead, self-guiding trail

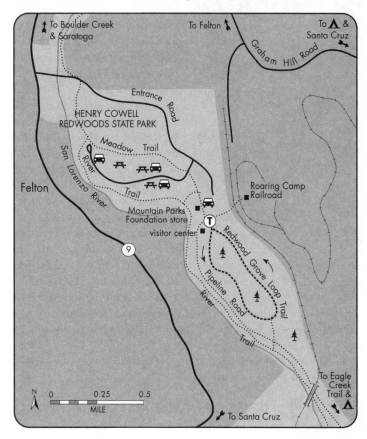

brochures wait to be picked up by eager readers. Under majestic coast redwood trees, where sunlight struggles to filter through the dense canopy, the trail feels special. Go straight on the wide path lined with rustic fences and follow the trail markers to understand the history of a redwood grove.

At trail marker 35, fairy lovers will delight in the description of circular groups of trees called fairy rings. As you keep walking, look for baby redwood trees clustered at the base of ancient trees. Children can also play games by finding shapes in the twisted patterns of some trees.

At 0.4 mile, turn right to a round clearing with picnic tables. Have the kids look for a tree with an opening at the base. Hand the children a flashlight so they can crawl inside the tree famously known as the Fremont Tree. Though Colonel Fremont didn't sleep inside, kids will

The self-guided nature trail is a treasure trove of fun facts about redwoods.

find the square frame of a window and shelves carved inside the tree. The Fremont story was invented by the owner of a hotel that was built next to the tree.

Out of the tree, imagine that all the roots of the trees around you interlock and sometimes fuse in the ground. Scientists argue whether such large fairy rings should be considered as one living organism, but for nature lovers just hugging the tree feels great. Kids may be able to identify the tree left of the Fremont Tree called the Jumbo Tree. Its bark has the shape of an elephant.

If you want to wade by the river, take the connecting trail to the River Trail and head northwest until you find a suitable "beach" area. The river may not be very warm, but kids love to splash around.

To return to the parking lot, return to the Redwood Grove Loop Trail and turn right to complete the loop.

94 FOREST OF NISENE MARKS STATE PARK/ MAPLE FALLS

BEFORE YOU GO
Maps: USGS Soquel, Loma Prieta, Laurel. Trail map posted at trailhead.
Information: Park office (831) 763-7062. www.parks .ca.gov

ABOUT THE HIKE
Day hike; Difficult; Year round
6.6 miles, round-trip
Hiking time: 3–4 hours
High point/elevation gain: 800 feet/600 feet

GETTING THERE

■ From CA-1 south of Santa Cruz, take the State Park Drive exit and drive north on State Park Drive.

■ Turn right on Soquel Drive and left on Aptos Creek Road before Aptos Station.

■ The Forest of Nisene Marks State Park entrance is 0.8 mile up the road on the left.

■ Continue 1 mile to the Porter Family picnic area, where the trail starts, and park.

■ In winter, you have to park at George's Picnic Area, 1.1 mile farther south, which increases the total hike mileage to 8.8 miles.

■ There is no public transit.

ON THE TRAIL

With its 10,000 acres of rugged wilderness on the western slopes of the Santa Cruz Mountains, the Forest of Nisene Marks is a great discovery offering quiet trails and remains of old logging camps to explore. Until the 1920s, this forest was the site of small logging towns and a narrow-gauge railroad running to the farthest reaches of the park. Almost a century later the forest is healthy once again, but you can still find scattered vestiges of the logging days along this historical trail. The additional mile to Maple Falls is an absolute must when the waters are high. It's the most fun mile of the hike and exactly at midway, providing an exciting interruption in the hiking pattern.

From the Porter Family picnic area, walk past the service gate on a wide service road. At 0.2 mile, turn left on the Loma Prieta Grade, a wide trail flanked by tall trees that feels like a stately alley leading to a secret estate. The trail narrows and follows a steep canyon uphill. After a bridge, the grade eases up. Note the logs across the trail, former tracks of the old railroad. At 0.9 mile, you reach the site of the Porter House where an interpretive sign provides photos of the logging camp and interior photos of the elegant house that once stood there. Take the trail left of the sign and continue uphill, looking for red bricks half buried in the slopes. After the ridge, the trail closely follows the edges of a ravine.

At 1 mile, veer left toward the Hoffman Site, following the remnants of the railroad. When the trail narrows, think how narrow the wagons must have been to navigate these hills. Steadily the trail goes up, passing a massive landslide area where the hill separated into an island of trees. After three bridges, you reach Hoffman's Historic Site at 2 miles. Only broken piles of beams and doorways opening onto the forest are left of this site. Continue straight and meander through the forest, passing a lot of cut stumps, reaching the Bridge Creek Historic Site at 3.2 miles.

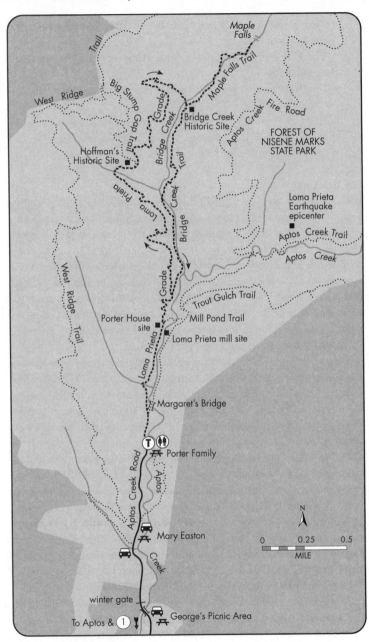

Maple Falls

Maple Falls Trail

West Ridge Trail

Big Stump Gap Trail

Bridge Creek

Grade

Bridge Creek Historic Site

Aptos Creek Fire Road

FOREST OF NISENE MARKS STATE PARK

Hoffman's Historic Site

Loma Prieta Earthquake epicenter

Loma Prieta

Bridge Creek Trail

Aptos Creek Trail

Aptos Creek

West Ridge Trail

Bridge Grade

Trout Gulch Trail

Porter House site

Mill Pond Trail

Loma Prieta

Loma Prieta mill site

Grade

Margaret's Bridge

T

Porter Family

Aptos Creek Road

Aptos

Mary Easton

Creek

winter gate

George's Picnic Area

To Aptos & 1

N

0   0.25   0.5
MILE

Getting there is as fun as splashing in the pool at the base of Maple Falls.

Right after the bridge your kids might feel the mileage, but tell them something exciting is ahead. Turn left on the Maple Falls Trail and follow a lush damp canyon for 0.5 mile along Bridge Creek. Young adventurers will love the interrupted trail, the occasional rock climbing, and going under fallen trees. Think of it as a total jungle course with a waterfall splashing from fern-covered rocks at the end.

After you've rested by the waterfall and splashed, turn back and at the junction with the old bridge at 4.2 miles, bear left (south) to return to the Loma Prieta Grade via the Bridge Creek Trail. This narrow trail passes an impressive log construction that can be used as a treehouse by the kids. After 1.4 miles, the Bridge Creek Trail merges with the Loma Prieta Grade at 5.6 miles. Continue straight on the Loma Prieta Grade and retrace your steps to the Porter Family picnic area.

SOLANO COUNTY

LYNCH CANYON OPEN SPACE PARK

BEFORE YOU GO
Maps: USGS Cordelia. Map online at www.solanolandtrust.org.
Information: Solano Land Trust (707) 432-0150, extension 200. Open seasonally. Check dates online at www.solanolandtrust.org

ABOUT THE HIKE
Day hike; Easy; Spring, Summer, Fall
1.4 miles, round-trip
Hiking time: 1–2 hours
High point/elevation gain: 350 feet/50 feet

GETTING THERE

- From I-80 between Vallejo and Fairfield, take the Hiddenbrooke/American Canyon exit south toward Hiddenbrooke Parkway.
- Just before entering the Hiddenbrooke development, turn east (left) on McGary Road and proceed to the I-80 underpass.
- Turn left at the underpass and drive through a gate into the Lynch Canyon Open Space Park entrance. The parking lot is at the end of the road.
- There is no public transit.

ON THE TRAIL

Known for a wide range of migratory birds and raptors as well as spectacular ridgetop scenery in the western hills of Solano County, the Lynch Canyon Open Space Park offers hiking trails for all abilities. While this easy stroll follows the creek to Lynch Reservoir, hikers looking to explore the backcountry can design 4- to 6-mile loops up the hills to an old homestead and Patwin grinding rocks.

Formerly a hunting and acorn gathering ground of the Patwin Suisunes, Lynch Canyon provides a welcome escape from bug-infested Suisun Marsh (see Hike 99) onto higher land. Several grinding rocks in this preserve attest to the continuous use of the land to make acorn

Opposite: *Navigating the narrow canyons of Stebbins Cold Canyon Reserve*

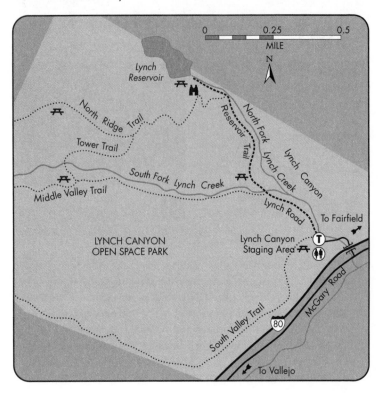

flour, the staple of Patwin meals. Between the time General Vallejo acquired the land in 1844 and the early 1980s, when it was slated to become a landfill, the hills of Lynch Canyon were mostly used as grazing land for cattle. This explains the short vegetation, which makes small mammals easy targets for hungry raptors.

Note that Lynch Canyon is open seasonally (usually spring to fall), so check opening dates with the Solano Land Trust. In the winter you can still visit this preserve by coming to one of the raptor nature walks.

From the parking lot, head northwest past the gate onto wide Lynch Road. This former ranch road is the starting point of all the trails of Lynch Canyon. Open hillsides slide down smoothly to the bottom of the valley where you are hiking. Hedges of willows on your right follow the course of Lynch Creek, a waterway that drains all the winter rains runoff into Suisun Marsh.

Look for owl boxes in big oak trees by the creek.

At 0.3 mile, the Middle Valley Trail forks off on your left. This leads you to an old homestead 1 mile away and Patwin grinding rocks 0.4 mile away if you want to extend the day's exploration. Bear right to stay on Lynch Road. At this point, Lynch Creek splits into two tributaries, the South Fork and the North Fork. Just look at the tree line to confirm this. Curving right, you pass under a graceful arch of willows and live oak trees, now following the North Fork of Lynch Creek. Kids may see ground squirrels scurrying about the hills. The open grassland makes them really easy to spot. Soaring golden eagles and red-tailed hawks know that too!

At 0.4 mile you reach a cattle gate where an old homestead used to be. The buildings have been torn down for safety reasons, but the orchard still features plum and walnut trees. Past the metal gate, the road bends left to enter the welcome shade of coast live oaks. Look on the path to find owl pellets. They look like fuzzy gray fur balls, and if you open them, you'll find bones, jaws, and anything that the owl has eaten and not chewed. Look up in the trees, and you will find two big wooden owl boxes. One of them has been colonized by a beehive.

At 0.6 mile, the road becomes the North Ridge Trail, heading west uphill. You want to stay to the right and follow the Reservoir Trail for the last 0.1 mile to the Lynch Reservoir overlook. Kids may find grebes, American coots, gadwalls, and other waterfowl gliding along the water. Retrace your steps to the parking lot.

STEBBINS COLD CANYON RESERVE

BEFORE YOU GO
Maps: USGS Fairfield North.
Map posted at trailhead.
Download topo map at
http://nrs.ucdavis.edu
/stebbins.html.
Information: UC Davis
Natural Reserve System,
http://nrs.ucdavis.edu
/stebbins.html

ABOUT THE HIKE
Day hike; Moderate; Spring,
Fall, Winter
2.5 miles, round-trip
Hiking time: 2–3 hours
**High point/elevation
gain:** 800 feet/600 feet

GETTING THERE

- From I-80 eastbound in Vaca-ville, continue north on I-505.
- In Winters, exit at CA-128/Lake Berryessa and drive 11 miles west.
- After an RV resort, cross the bridge over Putah Creek and continue 0.2 mile to the second parking area on your left on a curve by a silver metal gate. (If you turn, you've gone too far.) This gravel pullout is the trailhead. If it is full, three other gravel lots stand between this point and the bridge.
- There is no public transit.

ON THE TRAIL

Northeast of Fairfield, Stebbins Cold Canyon Reserve is a secluded oak-lined canyon that offers one of the prettiest short hikes in the Bay Area. No sign at the metal gate, no signs on the road—you just don't end up on this trail by chance. A stone's throw from the family-friendly farming town of Winters and fishing opportunities along Putah Creek, Stebbins Cold Canyon deserves a visit from late winter to early summer when the creek flows down the canyon. In the fall the creek is dry and trees lose their leaves, but mellow temperatures make this an attractive Indian summer hike.

From the gravel parking lot, go past the metal gate where two unmarked trails start. Take the right fork that dips down to a panel with

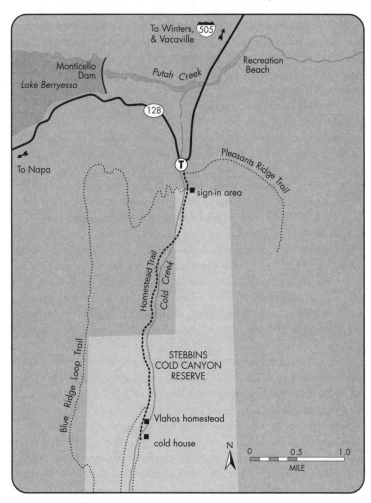

a map of the reserve. Small trail markers are numbered from here to the homestead of John Vlahos, a Greek dairy farmer who settled here in 1938 and lived here until 1968. You can find a printable self-guided tour with marker descriptions at http://nrs.ucdavis.edu/stebbins.html. This level dirt trail leads to a second gate at 0.2 mile, with an information signboard where you can sign in. Do sign in—there aren't many opportunities to do so on trails other than extreme summits these days!

The Homestead Trail follows the course of Cold Creek up the narrow canyon. At the fork, turn left to stay on the main trail. The right path, the Blue Ridge Loop Trail, goes to a creek overlook where a large boulder with a hole was used as grinding rock by the Patwin people. The main trail continues, lined with thick chaparral before entering a forest of interior live oak. If you hear knocking sounds nearby, it might be acorn woodpeckers at work.

Alternating between open space and a mixed hazelnut and willow forest, the path sticks to the middle of the canyon with impressive slopes shooting up both sides. At 0.4 mile comes the always-exciting river-crossing adventure when you encounter a river with no bridge. With boulders the size of rhinos to play hopscotch on, you may have to go Indiana Jones (roll up your pants) to reach the other side. Trail marker 23 awaits under a large gray pine tree.

For the next 0.5 mile, the trail rises steadily with the help of wooden steps to prevent soil erosion and facilitate the ascent. After 0.5 mile, walk over a small bridge and continue up on a path surrounded by a tunnel of green shrubs. Smooth rocks next to marker 26 make resting stools for kids. After 0.75 mile, the path gets narrower before surfacing on open hillsides with outstanding views of Cold Canyon where raptors soar high.

Past a fence, bear left to reach a gigantic gray pine and the Vlahos homestead at 1 mile. The remaining stone wall of the homestead is buried in the hill. Handmade by John Vlahos, this cabin faced the creek at the edge of which Vlahos had dug a well. You can still see the round opening of the well, now covered with a metal grate.

Follow the meandering course of the trail until you cross the creek to a large pleasant clearing. Here are the most impressive remains of Vlahos's goat-herding legacy, four walls that constituted a cold house for cow and goat milk cheeses made by the Greek immigrant. Cool and serene, this place invites a stop. If you go up the creek a couple hundred yards, you will find a small waterfall in the spring. Retrace your steps to the parking lot.

The old Vlahos homestead is an intriguing bit of local history in the woods.

JEPSON PRAIRIE PRESERVE/VERNAL POOL LOOP

BEFORE YOU GO
Maps: USGS Dixon. Download brochure with self-guided trail guide at www.solano landtrust.org.
Information: Solano Land Trust (707) 432-0150. www.solanolandtrust.org

ABOUT THE HIKE
Day hike; Easy; Spring, Fall, Winter
0.5 mile, loop
Hiking time: 30 minutes
High point/elevation gain: 0 feet/0 feet

GETTING THERE

- From the intersection of CA-12 and CA-113 southeast of Fairfield, go north on CA-113.
- Take the first left at a warning light, and turn left onto Cook Lane at the second warning light.
- Continue down Cook Lane across the railroad tracks to the Jepson Prairie Preserve parking area on the left, near the eucalyptus trees. The trailhead is across the road.
- There is no public transit.

ON THE TRAIL

Just an hour away from San Francisco sways a slice of Wild West prairie with a landscape like nowhere else in the Bay Area. On the edge of the Central Valley, Jepson Prairie protects an island of natural prairie in a wide alluvial floodplain. Stretching 430 miles along the Sierras, the Central Valley once supported prairies, grass savannahs, desert grasslands, riparian woodlands, freshwater marshes, and vernal pools. Virtually all habitats have been altered. This is why Jepson Prairie matters in the patchwork of the Bay Area. It features one of the last remaining vernal pool habitats as well as native bunchgrass prairie that covered a quarter of California.

The preserve displays its most flamboyant colors in the spring after winter rains have saturated the soil and fields of wildflowers bloom in unison. If you can, it is well worth going on one of the docent-led tours to learn more about the microhabitats of the preserve. In the summer and fall the lake is dried out and the wildflowers mostly gone. The

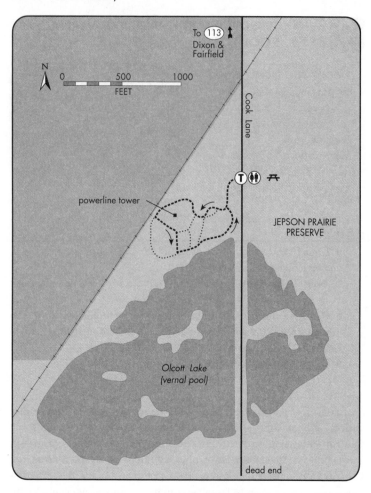

prairie then becomes golden yellow and seems dormant until the new rains bring it back to life.

Start at the parking lot and cross the road to go through the gate. The well-marked path meanders through the prairie from marker to marker (most standing, some down) and despite the absolute flatness of the area, you will learn to understand and appreciate the subtle forces at work in this fragile ecosystem. At marker 1 imagine pioneers traveling on vast prairies like this one and the various types of raptors that would have roamed free. You soon reach marker 2, a place where your

Meandering through the prairie can be a windy experience.

child can stomp the ground and tell you whether the soil is hard or soft. On a hot day, it is rock hard. It is, in fact, a dense clay zone that even water cannot infiltrate. Because of this specific soil, farmers deemed the prairie unfit for agriculture, saving it from development. Follow the lightly treaded trail to marker 3, which explains how California has a typical Mediterranean climate with cool moist winters and springs followed by dry, hot summers.

The short bumps called mima mounds seen from marker 4 are a mystery that your little nature detectives will love. The origin of these pimples in the landscape has been blamed on several factors: gophers, glaciers, earthquakes, tsunamis, wind erosion, even aliens. What do you think? One thing is sure: the prairie is covered in mima mounds. Follow the trail and bear right to marker 5. Without noticing it, you just passed a hog wallow, also called a swale. It is a waterproof depression lined by a layer of clay. When it rains, the water cannot drain through the clay; it needs to move sideways. Because the swales and vernal pools remain flooded a long time, few native plants can survive.

The vegetation around marker 6 and throughout the depressions of the prairie is mostly native. In comparison, non-native plants have succeeded into settling on higher grounds such as mounds. Under marker 7 you hear the crackling of electricity in the powerlines ahead, the railroad is in plain sight, and cattle fences are a stone's throw away. For all its wildness and agricultural unfitness, Jepson Prairie has still suffered from human interaction.

Bear right at the fork for marker 8, a place to reflect on the native Southern Patwin people who visited the prairie to hunt, harvest plants, fish, and trade goods. They too impacted the land, as marker 9 indicates that the Southern Patwin used fire-management techniques to increase the seed crop of their favorite grasses and prevent growth of trees and shrubs on the grassland. Tell your children to get down at ground level and examine the grasses around them. They should easily find purple needle grass, whose hollow stalk resembles a thin straw.

Proceed to marker 10 and look to the south. From here, Mount Diablo is less than 30 miles away. At marker 11 look at Olcott Lake. In the wet season it will be full of water, but by the summer you will be looking at cracked mudflats. As the waters of Olcott Lake recede with the seasons, they expose the bottom of the lake in successive intervals, allowing certain species to retain moisture and thrive longer than others, hence the ring pattern of plant distribution around the lake.

Marker 12, near the shore of the lake, explains how you will likely never see the rare protected plants and animals at Jepson Prairie. While tadpole shrimp, a living fossil, or fairy shrimp thrive in the vernal pool, the water obscures them. You children will love learning a very Dr. Seussical fact about these shrimps: Vernal pool tadpole shrimp swim or scoot along typically muddy or rocky bottom sediments "right side up," whereas fairy shrimp swim higher up in the water "upside down." You might be able to see them on one of the docent-led tours; otherwise, stick to the trails and let your imagination do the work.

At marker 13, upland and wetland interconnect in animal behaviors too, as the tiger salamander grows underwater the first months of its life in Olcott Lake and then emerges from the pool to live on the grassland as an adult. Move to marker 14, a place to explain this fun shrimp fact: Several species of shrimp live in Olcott Lake, but the lake dries out each summer. The cysts (eggs) the shrimp lay are drought-resistant. They can actually stay dormant until the vernal pool refills at the next rains and, once rehydrated, start a new life cycle. Marker 15, the last on this hike, indicates that this prairie is also used by migratory birds as a "rest stop" between their usual and overwintering destinations. Think ducks, geese, and shorebirds too.

Return to the parking lot.

ROCKVILLE HILLS REGIONAL PARK

BEFORE YOU GO
Maps: USGS Cordelia. Map online at www.ci.fairfield.ca.us.
Information: Rockville Hills Regional Park rangers (707) 428-7614. City of Fairfield, www.fairfield.ca.gov

ABOUT THE HIKE
Day hike; Moderate; Spring, Fall, Winter
3 miles, loop
Hiking time: 2–3 hours
High point/elevation gain: 500 feet/350 feet

GETTING THERE

■ From I-80 eastbound from Vallejo, take the Suisun Valley Road exit and head north for 1.7 miles to Rockville Road. Turn left.

■ From I-80 westbound in Fairfield, take the Rockville Road exit.

■ Drive 3 miles on Rockville Road to where it crosses Suisun Valley Road. Continue straight.

■ Drive 1 mile on Rockville Road to the entrance of Rockville Hills Regional Park on the left.

■ There is no public transit.

ON THE TRAIL

Covering 633 acres of the eastern side of the Sonoma Mountains, the landscape of the Rockville Hills was created by volcanic eruptions in the Pleistocene era, and you can still see today some peculiar rock formations and caves throughout the park. The Suisun people lived in a village east of the park called Yul Yul, the place of the setting sun. Attacks by Spanish missionaries in 1817 and a smallpox epidemic decimated the Suisun population, and the native land became part of a Mexican land grant granted by Governor Alvarado to Chief Solano under the name Rancho Suisun. After Rancho Suisun changed hands and was used for cattle grazing, woodcutting, and a quarry operation, the place-name Yul Yul was changed to Rockville. The park almost became a golf course after the city of Fairfield purchased the land in 1968, but fortunately it became this park after city residents voted against the golf course in 1982.

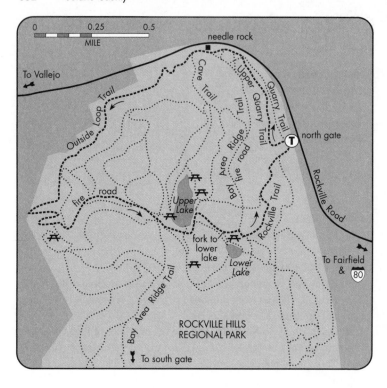

Children will love to see the park's history illustrated with kid draw-ings and explained in child-friendly terms at www.rockvilleexploration .com, a website for children dedicated to teaching them about the park's history, geology, and plants. The website also features pages you can print if you want to go out and explore with a pencil.

With two lakes and a nature trail, Rockville Hills Regional Park of-fers a pleasant nature outing, but the multitude of unmarked trails and shortcuts can sometimes be confusing. Getting sidetracked is a possibil-ity, but the park isn't very big. As long as you find a way to climb over the ridge and find the lakes, you can find your way back to the parking lot. Just think of it as an adventure!

From the parking lot at the north gate, go straight and make a sharp left on a wide path that curves and rises up the hill. The north gate also serves as the entry point to the Bay Area Ridge Trail portion of Rock-ville Hills Regional Park. At the trail junction at 0.05 mile, turn right to get on the Upper Quarry Trail, a dirt track heading north. This narrow track crosses oak chaparral with shrubby coyote brush, live oaks, manzanita, and grasses. At 0.2 mile, rock formations start to appear as exposed slab on the slopes, and you can see the Quarry Trail running below. At 0.3 mile the trail rises steeply at a left angle and zigzags up to a service road. Turn right and keep to the right in the shade of coast live oaks and bay laurel.

Unusual rock formations dot the slopes of Rockville Hills.

At 0.5 mile, the trail merges with the Quarry Trail. Keep straight to follow the park boundary northward. At the next three-way junction, the middle fork takes you to a paved road where you turn right to reach Rockville Road and a gate at 0.6 mile. Two dirt trails depart from that access. Take the right trail and at the junction, turn left to go uphill. Meandering through manzanita in open grassland, you have good views of a volcanic plateau across the valley. Out of the blue, a needle-shaped rock comes into sight. Walk past this unique rock formation and continue following the park boundary to circle the park. Slowly leaving the road, this rocky and eroded trail is bordered with barbed wire in places.

The trails and shortcuts in this area are confusing. Stick to the main trail along the fence. You will reach a stone wall with views of the valley. Look up at the next small trail to find a cave in the cliff above you. Keep going around the promontory. At 2 miles, look for a rock jumble after a canyon. Turn left on a wide rocky path and left again to ascend the hill on roots and rock. It's steep but short. At the top, veer left onto a wider road with a trail marker for the lake. You've conquered the maze of dirt trails and are entering the world of wide paths!

Veer left again at 2.1 miles to follow a paved road that leads to Upper Lake through meadows and oak woodland. At Upper Lake, curve around the lake to the right (both the paved trail and the lakeside dirt trail merge later so you can choose) and turn right before the picnic tables on another paved road at 2.4 miles down to Lower Lake. Take the right fork at 2.5 miles to check out the lake (kids might like exploring the boardwalk on the other side) and go straight at the information sign to return to the parking lot.

RUSH RANCH OPEN SPACE/SUISUN MARSH

BEFORE YOU GO
Maps: Free maps and trail guides inside the visitor center.
Information: Solano Land Trust (707) 432-0150.
www.solanolandtrust.org

ABOUT THE HIKE
Day hike; Easy; Year round
2.2 miles, loop
Hiking time: 2–3 hours
High point/elevation gain: 50 feet/50 feet

GETTING THERE

- From CA-12 in Suisun City, head south on Grizzly Island Road for about 2 miles.
- Turn right into the Rush Ranch Open Space entrance and park by the hay barn.
- There is no public transit.

ON THE TRAIL

Once a native Patwin village and the homestead of a pioneer family of Solano County, Rush Ranch is a protected area covering 2070 acres of open space along Suisun Slough, the waterway part of larger Suisun Marsh. Suisun Marsh is the largest brackish marsh in the western United States. "Brackish" refers to a swamp area where fresh water (in this case, from the Sacramento and San Joaquin rivers) mixes with salt water (from the Pacific Ocean), creating a unique ecosystem. Suisun Marsh used to spread over 68,000 acres, featuring islands inundated by tides and separated by sloughs (stagnant marshes or swamps part of a larger network). Today, the landscape has been modified for agricultural needs and recreational activities that include boating and fishing. Rush Ranch Open Space is one of the few places where you can actually get the lay of the land in the Sacramento River Delta by hiking it.

As you arrive inside the main area of the ranch, show your children the horses in the corral. Every third Saturday, free wagon rides take visitors through this reserve as part of a nature program for people with limited mobility—however, everybody is welcome. The hay barn was used for the ranch's activities and was recently restored. Inside, owls sit on the main beam below the roof. Right across, the blacksmith shop will show your kids how ranchers made the tools they needed long before

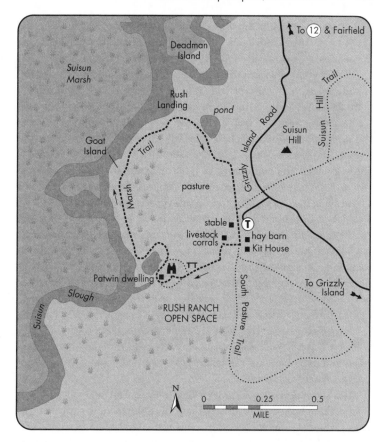

hardware stores existed. The visitor center is housed in the Kit House, a little white building that was ordered from a Sears catalog so the Rush children could live in it. Here you can pick up a self-guiding description of the Marsh Trail if you want to follow the interpretive signs.

Find the Marsh Trail just right of the Kit House and proceed along the wooden fence to a grove of eucalyptus trees. Any land beyond these trees is grassland, pastureland, and marshland as far as the eye can see.

When you get to marker 3, turn right to climb the hill and enjoy the best views of the marsh on this trail. While spring offers incredible displays of wildflowers on green backdrops, summer and fall offer the stark contrast of yellow grass with dark green reeds. Whatever the season, winds cool off a full-sun hike.

Left of the bench at the top, follow an S-curved dirt trail down the small hill to the Marsh Trail. Turn right and walk to the tule house, an authentically reconstructed dwelling of the Suisun people, a tribal unit of the Patwin people who lived in Suisun Marsh and the plains. The round structure to its right is a granary and would have been used to store food, protecting it from the elements and wildlife. To the left, look for a grinding rock and imagine Patwin people gliding on tule boats on the sloughs to hunt for fish and other wildlife.

Continue on the Marsh Trail and take a left through two old wooden gates, entering the marsh area. You are now walking on a levee. From here to Goat Island, you will pass thick tangles of blackberry bushes that thrive along the marsh. Look for two tide gates on each side of the trail. To your left is the unregulated saltwater marsh where tides submerge and expose the land. To your right is the freshwater marsh where tidal gates are adjusted throughout the year to provide habitat for ducks. Most of the remaining Suisun Marsh belongs to duck-hunting clubs.

The trail angles right after the gates to follow the straight course of Suisun Slough. On and off you will see the brackish water of the slough appear through cattails and tule reeds, when blackberry bushes haven't taken over the area. The path might be slightly overgrown, but keep walking. If you can get close enough to cattails, have your children touch them and ask them how the texture feels. For soft-looking plants, they are remarkably rough!

At trail marker 12, you have reached a natural island known as Goat Island, though the levee connects the trail throughout. Right before you pass through the metal gates that separate marsh from pastures, note the second set of tidal gates. Turn left on the trail and walk along the fence. As the path veers right uphill, take a look at the cove to your left. It may not seem like much, but this cove called Rush Landing is where the Rush family used to load hay bales onto flat-bottomed boats that could navigate these shallow waters.

You will now go uphill until you can look down on an alkaline pond fed by an underwater spring. This alkaline pond catches water

Flat trails follow an intricate network of marsh waterways.

draining from Suisun Hill up above. The dirt tumulus to your left is home to a colony of active ground squirrels that zip through the grasses like flashes. Stay still and you might observe a bushy tail scurrying away. Keep going straight, through the gates, until you reach the parking lot by the barn.

THE PATWIN PEOPLE AND SUISUN MARSH

Prior to Spanish colonization, native Suisun people maintained small seasonal villages along the edge of Suisun Marsh, including one village at what is now Rush Ranch. The Suisunes lived in harmony with the land and honored the peregrine falcons that inhabit this area as their creator spirit. Evidence of the Suisun presence remains at Rush Ranch in two places. Along the South Pasture Trail sits a sandstone rock with grinding holes where Suisun women processed seeds, fish, and dried meat. On the Marsh Trail you can see and go inside a Suisun home.

 **GRIZZLY ISLAND WILDLIFE AREA/ HOWARD SLOUGH**

BEFORE YOU GO
Maps: USGS Denverton. Map online at www.dfg.ca.gov.
Information: Grizzly Island often closes in the winter due to flooding, and in the summer for hunting. Call (707) 425-3828 to check for closures before visiting. www.dfg.ca.gov

ABOUT THE HIKE
Day hike; Easy/Moderate; Spring, Fall
3 miles, loop
Hiking time: 1–2 hours
High point/elevation gain: 0 feet/0 feet

GETTING THERE
- From I-80 in Fairfield, exit at CA-12 east toward Suisun City and Rio Vista.
- Turn right onto Grizzly Island Road and drive 9.5 miles to the wildlife area headquarters. Continue to the designated parking area (P3) under a tall eucalyptus tree.
- There is no public transit.

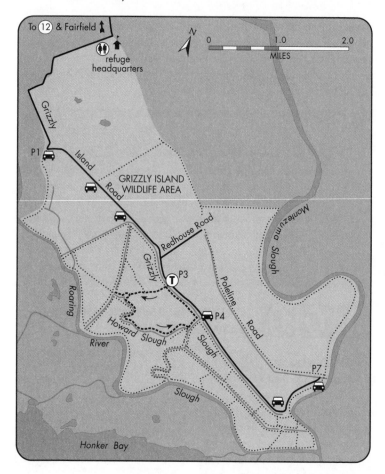

ON THE TRAIL

Part of the largest contiguous estuarine marsh in the entire United States, Grizzly Island Wildlife Area occupies over 15,000 acres south of Suisun City and provides an outdoor excursion between San Francisco and Sacramento. Wildlife enthusiasts come here to walk around on the levees and view elk, waterfowl, and marsh animals—and to fish and hunt during the open season. Because the preserve is seasonally closed, make sure you call before your visit. Usually it's open from February through July, and again at the end of September, but dates vary each year.

Tread levy tops to see waterfowl up close—and keep the camera close!

For elk viewing, February and September are the best months. In the spring you may sight bulls shedding their antlers and the first white-spotted tule elk calves on their wobbly legs. September sees the end of the rut when bulls round up their females into a harem, fight other bulls, and get ready to mate. With binoculars, kids will get all the graphic details—just be ready to answer questions on Elk Family Planning 101.

Being on the Pacific Flyway, Grizzly Island is also a fantastic spot to observe migratory songbirds as well as waterfowl. Before proceeding to the parking lot, stop by the headquarters, sign in, and check out the interpretive displays and lists of animals you may see. Note that this hike requires closed-toe good walking shoes, as the route follows mowed levee tops rather than regular hiking trails. Be prepared for tall grasses and marsh plants, as well as mud. There are no signs along the hike, but since the marshland is all flat, you can always see the horizon and find your bearings.

From parking lot P3, cross the road and walk on the footbridge over to the levee, heading toward Roaring River Slough. Keep binoculars at the ready, as entire flocks of geese, egrets, or ducks might take off from behind tule reeds at any moment. The levee cuts across the flat landscape with marshes on both sides. The lace pattern of the waterways provides great nature photo opportunities, and kids who like dragonflies and butterflies are in for a treat as both swarm the marshes and ponds.

Keep straight at the first intersection and turn left at 0.6 mile on a wide levee top to follow the north side of Howard Slough. In the distance, fields of windmills and Mount Diablo break the inexorable flatness of the Sacramento River Delta region. Alert water observers will spot river otters, beavers, striped bass, catfish, and sturgeon before they dive away from your sight.

For 1.6 miles, the levee top winds with the course of Howard Slough, a tranquil nature walk interrupted only by the sudden takeoff or landing of waterfowl. Make sure that kids stay on the levee tops, as the edges can be muddy and slippery. At 2.2 miles, the levee curves left to return to the access road. Keep your eyes peeled for colorful ring-necked pheasants or great blue herons. At 2.3 miles, make a left to follow the slough parallel to the road back to P3.

INDEX

ABOUT THE AUTHOR

Born in New Caledonia, a South Pacific island, Laure spent her childhood outdoors with her parents and two spirited brothers. Formerly a tax attorney, she moved to San Francisco in 2001 and she and her husband began thoroughly exploring Northern California, continuing after their two daughters were born. As a journalist for parenting websites such as The Red Tricycle and SFKids in San Francisco, Laure writes articles on outdoor adventures as well as art explorations, environmental education, and fun family destinations. A former climber, Laure enjoys open-water swimming in San Francisco Bay and hiking in the Sierras. She recounts her experiences in her family adventure blog, Frog Mom (www.frogmom.com) and shares hiking tips and information about public programs for families on the Facebook page "Best Hikes for Children in the Bay Area."

THE MOUNTAINEERS, founded in 1906, is a nonprofit outdoor activity and conservation organization whose mission is "to explore, study, preserve, and enjoy the natural beauty of the outdoors . . . . " Based in Seattle, Washington, it is now one of the largest such organizations in the United States, with seven branches throughout Washington State.

The Mountaineers sponsors both classes and year-round outdoor activities in the Pacific Northwest, which include hiking, mountain climbing, ski-touring, snowshoeing, bicycling, camping, canoeing and kayaking, nature study, sailing, and adventure travel. The Mountaineers' conservation division supports environmental causes through educational activities, sponsoring legislation, and presenting informational programs.

All activities are led by skilled, experienced volunteers, who are dedicated to promoting safe and responsible enjoyment and preservation of the outdoors.

If you would like to participate in these organized outdoor activities or programs, consider a membership in The Mountaineers. For information and an application, write or call The Mountaineers Program Center, 7700 Sand Point Way NE, Seattle, WA 98115-3996; phone 206-521-6001; visit www .mountaineers.org; or email clubmail@mountaineers.org.

The Mountaineers Books, an active, nonprofit publishing program of The Mountaineers, produces guidebooks, instructional texts, historical works, natural history guides, and works on environmental conservation. All books produced by The Mountaineers Books fulfill the mission of The Mountaineers. Visit www.mountaineersbooks.org to find details about all our titles and the latest author events, as well as videos, web clips, links, and more!

The Mountaineers Books
1001 SW Klickitat Way, Suite 201
Seattle, WA 98134
800-553-4453
mbooks@mountaineersbooks.org

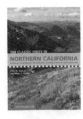
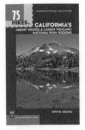